The Primitive
Methodist Connexion

Julia Stewart Werner has produced the first study of the birth and
early years of English Primitive Methodism written from the
perspective of social history. Explaining the rise of Primitive
Methodism in relation to its Wesleyan Methodist background and to
the social circumstances of its time and locales, Werner's work is
sensitive not only to the historical issues but also to religion itself. The
book focuses on Primitive Methodism as an alternative to Wesleyan
Methodism, an option which appealed primarily to working people in
rural districts, in manufacturing and colliery villages, and in
developing factory towns. Scholars of English or American history,
social history, religion, and sociology will welcome this new work.

The Primitive
Methodist Connexion
Its Background
and Early History

Julia Stewart Werner

The University of Wisconsin Press

Published 1984

The University of Wisconsin Press
114 North Murray Street
Madison, Wisconsin 53715

The University of Wisconsin Press, Ltd.
1 Gower Street
London WC1E 6HA, England

First printing

Printed in the United States of America

For LC CIP information see the colophon

ISBN 0-299-09910-5

Publication of this book was
made possible in part by a grant
from the Andrew W. Mellon Foundation.

To Steven

Contents

Contents

Preface

Like many studies in social history, this account of the origin and early years of Primitive Methodism could not be based primarily on written sources left by rank-and-file members of the connexion. Many of the first converts were illiterate, but, perhaps more important, even those who could write did not often enjoy the leisure in which to maintain diaries or to develop the habit of corresponding. The great majority certainly could not afford to pay the cost of postage, a fact which may partially explain why the excellent manuscript collection in the Methodist Archives is virtually devoid of letters written by the Ranter generation of Primitive Methodists. Both Hugh Bourne and William Clowes kept journals, the manuscript versions of which are held by the John Rylands University Library of Manchester. Apart from such publications as the *Primitive Methodist Magazine* and the minutes of Primitive Methodist conferences, the most useful printed material in the Methodist Archives was to be found in its extensive collection of local histories. Most of these were not specifically about the Primitive Methodists, but numerous Wesleyan authors did make passing mention of the Ranters. My research was done while the Methodist Archives and Research Centre was located at 25–35 City Road, London. In 1977 the Archives were permanently deposited in the John Rylands University Library of Manchester.

There are many persons to whom I owe thanks but to no one more than John C. Bowmer, former Methodist Church Archivist and now President Emeritus of the Wesley Historical Society. Kindly, erudite, and perennially helpful, Dr. Bowmer both aided me in my research and, together with his wife, did much to make my stay in London a happy experience. I am grateful to James Donnelly, Jr., of the University of Wisconsin-Madison, for encouragement as well as for constructive and incisive criticism. Steven Werner deserves special thanks for much more than his contributions as a historian, helpful as these have been. Finally, I am indebted to the American Association of University Women, whose General American Fellowship made possible ten months of research in England.

Introduction

The lay movement that took the name Society of the People Called Primitive Methodists became a distinct sect chiefly because of trends that developed in the Old Connexion between 1800 and 1820. Only by examining what was taking place within Wesleyan Methodism can the beginnings of Primitive Methodism be understood. At a time when war on the Continent and the spread of radical ideas at home were causing grave anxiety among England's governing classes, Methodism was breaking its ties with the established church. To counter charges of Methodist disloyalty, the Wesleyan conference adopted policies that stifled both lay initiative and revivalism. It did so just when democratic impulses were stirring the lower classes, and economic, social, and political tensions were breeding an optimum climate for religious awakenings. Its new status as a separate denomination laid financial burdens on Wesleyan Methodism which required monetary support from the members. The poor could ill afford to add to the connexional coffers, especially during the years of distress after Waterloo.

The immediate cause of the rupture that brought Primitive Methodism into being was Wesleyan refusal to countenance camp meetings. This American innovation was carried to England by Lorenzo Dow, a not very decorous figure who championed republicanism along with revivalism. The narrowed road that the Wesleyan conference elected to travel alienated many lay members, and this as much as camp meetings and revivalism contributed to the swift advance made by Primitive Methodism after 1816. In addition, the conversion tactics of the new sect, its fostering of lay enterprise, and the sense of community that characterized its societies fulfilled needs increasingly felt among the lower classes as they moved from a dependent and traditional pattern of life into the new ways of a rapidly evolving urban, industrial nation. Primitive Methodism preempted a significant role that Wesleyan Methodism failed to play, and it undertook this mission precisely at the time when opportunities were greatest. In consequence, the Primitive

Methodist Connexion ultimately became the preferred affiliation for many working-class Methodists.

Except for works by Primitive Methodist preachers, no history of the sect has heretofore been published. The earliest account was produced by Hugh Bourne at the request of delegates to a meeting called in 1819 to plan the connexion's first conference. Bourne's pamphlet-length history was brought up to date and reprinted in 1823. Another itinerant, John Petty, traced the development of Primitive Methodism from its birth to the conference of 1860.[1] Most often consulted by modern writers of social history is H. B. Kendall's *Origin and History of the Primitive Methodist Church*.[2] Carefully researched and laden with details, this two-volume work celebrated almost a century of Primitive Methodist achievement accomplished since the first camp meeting was held on Mow Cop in 1807.

The subject matter of this study raises once again the issue of the Halévy thesis. The debate rooted in Elie Halévy's interpretation of the role played by English Methodism was ably summarized by Elissa S. Itzkin[3] and also by Bernard Semmel in the introduction to his translation of *The Birth of Methodism in England*. Elsewhere, Semmel contributed to the pro-Halévy side of the controversy by asserting that a "Methodist revolution" in England was the counterpart of democratic revolutions elsewhere. Semmel further suggested that the way in which this change was effected within Wesleyan Methodism and the nature of that reorientation may have had a "decisive impact" in shaping the balance between liberty and order in nineteenth-century England.[4] Although his treatment of the tensions inherent in Methodist theology is admirable, Semmel's argument is somewhat flawed because he ignored the evident concern for home missions manifested by the Wesleyan conference of 1820 and the salutary policies which resulted from its deliberations on pastoral work. Halévy himself committed the same oversight when he attributed Wesleyan recovery in 1821 simply to improved trade abetted by the timely death of Queen Caroline. "Popular enthusiasm," Halévy commented, "had returned to its traditional form, religious, not revolutionary."[5]

Primitive Methodism was portrayed by Eric Hobsbawm as a nonaggressive sect partially transformed into a labor sect "under the pressure of the social agitations of its members." Such cults, he noted, are generated by those conditions typical of early industrialism which tend to disappear when the modern pattern of urbanization and factory production emerges more fully.[6] The Ranter experience in colliery and manufacturing villages and among mill workers in new factory towns confirms this characterization of Primitive Methodism. But Ranterism was also a product of the countryside, where it was both an upshot of radical change and the vehicle by which its converts made the transition to a different mode of rural life.

In this study I consider several themes that until now have been ignored by modern historians or have been treated as secondary concerns. Such topics include the quandaries and policies of the Wesleyan Connexion that bred schisms during the quarter-century following the emergence of Methodism as an independent denomination, the breakaway groups themselves, and the part each played in relation to Primitive Methodism. Likewise, the early history of the Primitive Methodist movement is interpreted in the context of contemporary secular phenomena rather than told from a sectarian point of view. In addition, I explore through particular circumstances and at a local level a disputed question: what was the nature of the relationship between political agitation and government repression on the one hand and Methodist revivalism on the other? Lastly, I also investigate those features of Primitive Methodism which enabled the sect to function as a bridge between eighteenth-century and nineteenth-century patterns of living. Because the Wesleyan milieu out of which Primitive Methodism arose was so important, the two opening chapters of the book are devoted to the problems faced by the Old Connexion and the means adopted to cope with them. Chapters 3 through 5 are an account of the birth of Primitive Methodism and its expansion into those parts of the kingdom that had been evangelized by the close of 1819—the Midlands, the East and West Ridings of Yorkshire, and a corner of Lancashire. The final chapter discusses what being a Primitive Methodist signified for the first generation of members.

England: the Midlands and the North

Chronology

Part 1

The Context of Primitive Methodism

One

The Anxious Years, 1791–1820

Despite his intentions, John Wesley bequeathed to England a new species of Nonconformity. An Anglican priest, Wesley had hoped to revitalize the Church of England from within; he had died loyal to establishment doctrine and, in principle at least, to establishment discipline.[1] By 1820, however, Wesley's "connexion" had not only evolved into a distinct denomination, but it had also bred a variety of Methodist sects. First to emerge was the Methodist New Connexion, founded in 1797 under the leadership of Alexander Kilham, a traveling preacher whose efforts to win for laymen a greater voice in Methodist government had led to his expulsion from the Wesleyan body. During the first decade of the nineteenth century a series of local schisms resulted in the forming of several Independent Methodist congregations, mostly in Lancashire and Cheshire. In the Staffordshire Potteries followers of Hugh Bourne and William Clowes established a separate connexion which in 1812 adopted the name Primitive Methodist. Thrust out of the Old Connexion on account of his irregular methods, a local preacher in Cornwall, William O'Bryan, founded the Bible Christians in 1815. Five years later a rupture in the Bristol Wesleyan circuit produced Tent Methodism.

All of these schisms took place against a background of change and stress. Throughout most of the period, England was at war, first with republican France, then against Napoleon. At home the eighteenth-century political and social order was under assault. Economic ills which troubled the nation during the wars intensified after Waterloo. Within this broader setting Methodism struggled to define itself outside the boundaries of the Anglican church and without the accustomed authoritarian guidance of John Wesley.

Methodism and the Government

> "Placid": "Do you then suspect Methodists of dis-
> loyalty?" "Gruff": "No, I can't say that I do. I believe
> they are loyal enough in all conscience—but they are
> devilish cunning, and there is no getting at their
> political sentiments."
>
> —An Anti-Methodist Pamphlet, 1811[2]

Two years before Louis XVI's head rolled beneath a Paris guillotine, John Wesley died in his house alongside London's City Road Chapel. In the biennium between these two events Tom Paine published that bible of English radicalism, *The Rights of Man.* The French regicide was a prelude to more than two decades of war with England; Paine's writings helped to catalyze profound changes in British society; and the death of Wesley inaugurated a new era in Methodist history. For Methodism the war years and their aftermath were a period of administrative reorganization, of exodus from the established church, and of serious internal schisms. The fissiparousness that plagued the connexion between 1797 and 1820 cannot be fully explained outside the wider context of political and social ferment. This is most obvious in the case of the New Connexion. Alexander Kilham's revolt was the product of a thwarted attempt to leaven Methodism with a measure of democracy. The schisms of the early nineteenth century were equally, if less patently, an outcome of wartime and postwar tensions. The frenetic determination of Wesleyan officialdom to prove their loyalty to king and country made the Old Connexion unable either to absorb contemporary revivalist impulses or to respond constructively to lay opinion.

From the beginning Wesley's societies had been resented because they stood as a rebuke to the church, but, so long as he lived, it was possible to maintain that Methodists would practice their earnest spirituality within the boundaries of Anglicanism. After 1791 even those among Wesley's heirs who opposed a breach could not overcome the mounting popular demand for denominational independence. Some laymen—mostly persons of substance and social position—shared Thomas Coke's fear that autonomy would tempt Methodists to "imbibe the political spirit of the Dissenters." In 1791 Coke confided that he would not be surprised if "in a few years some of our people, warmest in politics and coolest in religion, would toast . . . *a bloody summer and a headless king.*"[3] Fearing that separation would drain Methodism of its vitality, the lay elite at Hull hoped that William Wilberforce would intercede with the bishop of London and the archbishop of Canterbury and beg them to sponsor ecclesiastical concessions that might keep Methodists from forsaking the church of their baptism.[4]

The growing desire among society members for celebration of the Lord's Supper in their own chapels and by their own preachers reflected the spread of Methodist disaffection from the established church. In 1792 conference prohibited celebration of the rite everywhere except London, but the interdict was soon a dead letter. Only a year later it bowed to local pressures and let itinerants administer the sacrament in those societies whose members unanimously preferred separate communion. In 1794 conference yielded again and extended the privilege to societies in ninety-three places. A Yorkshire layman afterwards recalled that 1794 had marked a parting of the ways between church and chapel in Leeds.[5] Relations were deteriorating elsewhere, too; the will of the Methodist people was increasingly bent on separation from the Church of England. The means to this end were furnished by the Plan of Pacification adopted by conference in 1795. Although couched in negative terms, the plan opened a way for Methodist administration of the sacrament throughout the connexion.[6]

By the end of the decade the trend toward Nonconformity was irreversible. Still, as late as 1802 Coke was advocating a return to the "old plan"—"no sacraments, no preaching in church hours; all go to church as usual, which will preserve us from ruin." Another preacher, William Bramwell, correctly read the signs of the times when he predicted that conference would never sanction Coke's scheme and asserted that, even if it did, most lay people would resist it.[7] In a period when crises of public order were threatening the authority of government, prudence suggested that Methodism should seek refuge behind the skirts of the established church. A majority of Methodist laymen, however, valued connexional independence above safety, even if schism entailed the risk of repression.[8] Consequently, Methodist leaders faced an inescapable quandary—how to sever ties with an institution widely regarded as the main bulwark of national stability, while at the same time conveying an image of patriotic ardor. Their task was made more difficult by the animosity which influential elements in contemporary British society displayed toward Methodism.

The double menace of domestic republicanism and invasion from abroad gave rise to a spate of anti-Methodist tracts, many of which assumed that dissatisfaction with the Church of England implied criticism of the established political and social order as well. Alluding to Methodists and other malcontents, the bishop of Gloucester observed that "those who wish not well to the civil and religious polity of this nation" were clever in the ways of "concerting measures to undermine our

. . . Constitution."[9] Champions of the status quo also scented danger
from the Methodist habit of teaching that the fruits of the earth are God's
gift to rich and poor alike. "They then subjoin the inference," complained one clergyman, " 'that the rich *therefore* are usurpers of the poor
man's rights'."[10] Persecution in the style of the Birmingham riots was not
unknown. In some communities Methodist tradesmen were punished by
loss of business; laborers and servants were thrust out of work; and the
poor were denied parish relief.[11]

Just as eager as its enemies to exploit the power of the press, the
Wesleyan conference used it both to mold public opinion and to influence its own members. Control over publication was strict. Beginning
in 1796 no itinerant might print anything without the sanction of a book
committee designated by the conference. Typical of the apologias put
forward whenever the connexion found itself on the defensive was a
resolution issued in 1811. Methodism, it averred, had increased national
prosperity by promoting "subordination and industry in the lower orders
of society."[12] In times of political agitation or economic distress the
Methodist Magazine officially affirmed Wesleyan loyalty and admonished its readers to be grateful to the sovereign, patient in affliction, and
wary of reformers. Sermons circulated in printed form echoed these and
similar counsels.[13] Taking their cue from the radical press, whose cheap
pamphlets were insinuating the "pernicious principles of infidelity" into
the minds of the poor, the Methodists diligently disseminated twopenny
tracts like *The Patriot*, a tale of the woes that visited "Thomas Maxwell"
once he had been seduced into a backroom political discussion at the
Crown and Anchor.[14]

Although harassment and hostile publicity caused annoyance and
even hardship for Methodists, it was the possibility of restrictive legislation that most alarmed conference. Late in the crisis-ridden year 1795,
sources close to Pitt let it be known that some in the government wondered about the extent of disaffection among the Methodists. Antic-
ipating repressive measures from a Parliament which had already suspended habeas corpus and passed both the Sedition and Treason Acts,
Coke urged a loyal address denouncing Alexander Kilham, whose just-
published pamphlet *The Progress of Liberty among the People Called
Methodists* was a focus of suspicion. Coke emphatically rejected a suggestion that each district meeting discuss the matter; such proceedings,
he was convinced, would only foster democracy, the chief "cause of
anarchy and terrorism."[15] The idea of a loyal address was later abandoned. Instead, the Methodist conference purchased a reprieve by ejecting Kilham from the connexion. In fact, it was not until 1799 that an attempt was made to fetter Methodism through legal restraints. The attack

was launched not by the ministry itself, but by George Pretyman-Tomline, Pitt's tutor at Cambridge, his private secretary, and then, as bishop of Lincoln, his chief advisor on ecclesiastical patronage. To smooth the way for legislation, the bishop circulated a report from his diocesan clergy which charged itinerant preachers with estranging people from the church. Unless Parliament suppressed this "wandering tribe of fanatical teachers," the report warned, religious unrest was likely to become political alienation.[16] In the spring of 1800 a member of Parliament for Durham agreed to introduce legislation aimed at limiting dissenters' freedom of worship and at curtailing the activities of Nonconformist itinerants. An influential Durham Methodist managed to convince the bill's sponsor that he had been "misled by misinformation,"[17] and the project was dropped, perhaps because Pitt was reluctant to antagonize Protestant and especially evangelical opinion while courting Irish Catholic support for the mooted Act of Union. The danger of crippling laws hovered over Methodism throughout the next decade, but the government took no action until May 1811, when Lord Sidmouth proposed severe restrictions on the licensing of preachers. In the meantime conference had formed a Committee of Privileges to defend Wesleyan interests in the courts and to promote its cause in Parliament. If enacted, Sidmouth's regulations would have undercut the system on which Methodist preaching was organized. Together with the older Committee of the Three Denominations, the Wesleyan Committee of Privileges mounted a massive petition campaign. Confronted with thousands of signatures, the Lords decided that "it would be both unwise and impolitic" to press the issue. Without a division, they determined to postpone the second reading for six months.[18] In the interim—a period of acute economic crisis and of a new regency—the cabinet elected to drop the bill. This most serious threat to the Methodist organization proved to be the last. In 1812 a New Toleration Act liberalized the Clarendon Code and in effect granted legal recognition to the itinerancy.

The price of Methodist safety was a policy of discipline which sacrificed connexional solidarity. A Wesleyan leadership mortally afraid of offending the political establishment could hardly afford to smile on freewheeling revivalism or to relax its control to the point of allowing wide scope for lay initiative. A resolution passed in 1800 was calculated to quench revivalist fires by enjoining strict observance of "order and regularity" at all meetings. In 1803 preachers were reminded that love feasts and band meetings ought not be held without express permission, a memorandum probably framed less from motives of pure religion than from a desire to assert ministerial authority, to guard against untoward activities, and to avoid possible infringement of the Conventicle Act.

The 1805 conference banned the use of any hymnal not issued by the Book Room and called for more stringent enforcement of the rule prohibiting the unauthorized printing or publishing of books. Two minutes of 1807 impinged directly on the future of the camp-meeting movement in the Potteries. The first condemned open-air revival meetings as "highly improper" and "likely to be productive of considerable mischief." The other, directed at Lorenzo Dow, the eccentric American evangelist who had ties with both the embryonic Primitive Methodist community and the schismatic Independent Methodists, prescribed that no unaccredited "stranger" be allowed access to a Wesleyan pulpit.[19]

Despite its success at Westminster in 1812, the Wesleyan conference spent the remainder of the decade frozen in a posture of rigid conservatism, its outlook still conditioned by fear of governmental interference. When, after Pentridge, a London newspaper reported that one of the men about to be hanged for treason was a Wesleyan preacher, the superintendent at Derby hastened to squelch the canard and urged the Committee of Privileges to forestall trouble by proclaiming the truth of the matter.[20] In North Shields circuit, where many society members had radical sympathies, traveling preachers and "respectable friends" clashed with a local preacher who "went upon the hustings" at a reform rally and denounced the Manchester magistrates for their behavior at Peterloo. The itinerants realized that, if the offender were expelled, many would leave the society. If, however, he were not cast out and the London press got wind of the affair, the North Shields preachers might "bring down the vengeance of government upon the whole connexion."[21] In Manchester itself the Wesleyan superintendent was so violently progovernment that a local critic declared, "your vociferation has given a deadly blow to the interests of religion."[22] Guided by Jabez Bunting, the connexional solicitor drew up a post-Peterloo address forbidding Methodist involvement in radical politics. Issued by the Committee of Privileges, this letter was so strongly worded that at least one preacher was afraid to read it to his congregations. Though mistaken about the facts, Yorkshire radicals interpreted the sentiments of the Wesleyan authorities accurately enough: according to a rumor current in 1819, the Old Connexion had "lent government half a million of money to buy cannon to shoot them with."[23]

The general easing of political and economic pressures during the early 1820s coaxed conference into a less defensive attitude. Increasingly, Wesleyans were being accepted as responsible citizens. Other goals had already been secured. Recognized as an independent Nonconformist denomination, Wesleyan Methodism enjoyed the benefits embodied in the Toleration Act of 1812; the threat of repressive legislation had been per-

manently dispelled; and, for better or for worse, a connexional image of
Tory patriotism had been fixed in the public mind. Several factors had
contributed to the attainment of these ends. The legal victory in 1812 had
owed something to the Methodist alliance with Old Dissent, a united
front symbolized by the Protestant Society for the Protection of Religious Liberty. A significant asset to the Wesleyan cause had been the
growing number of locally prominent laymen whose prosperity had
lifted them into the respectable middle class. Their predilections had also
helped to determine the political stance of the entire connexion—a Methodist mill owner, after all, had as much to lose from Luddism or leveling
as did his Anglican counterpart. The rank and file in the breakaway
groups were not necessarily more radical than working-class Wesleyans,
but, initially at least, the sects to which they belonged were more per-
missive. Had conference been more tolerant, Methodism might have
been preserved intact; unfortunately for its integrity, Wesley's successors
dared not risk the consequences of freedom. Their inflexibility provoked
a series of schisms that were not healed until the twentieth century.

The Problems of the Wesleyan Purse

One man and his wife has lately left society, because
my predecessor told them, they must give more than
6d. each quarterly . . . ; many of our Leaders are
quite averse to it; whether to save their own pockets
or screen the people I cannot tell.
—A Wesleyan Itinerant, 1803[24]

Reckoned in pounds and shillings the price of rupture
with the Church of England was high, and the burden of paying it fell
directly on society members. Increasingly, chapel building became a
necessity as well as a symbol of independence. As ties with the established church were severed, and as the ranks of "Church" Methodists
thinned, the call for a larger professional ministry grew insistent. The demand for preachers was intensified by a boom in Wesleyan membership,
and conference met it by sending out more and more married itinerants,
many of whom had children to support. Unfortunately for the budget,
the enhanced social status of some Methodists was matched by heightened pretensions. Especially in the towns, the laymen who shaped policy
wanted grander chapels and more "respectable" ministers, an outlook
that coincided with the official desire for a public image of order and patriotism. Expenses were further swollen by the cost of maintaining

schools, pension funds, and, particularly after 1815, foreign missions. For ministers and stewards, putting their circuits on a "sound methodistical basis" came to mean ensuring that class and ticket money were systematically collected and that worthy causes were generously supported.

Economic pressures on Wesleyan Methodism and the means taken to deal with them made the connexion vulnerable to schism. The most obvious symptom of this was a "free gospel" reaction. The founder of the Bible Christians was accused of "trying to tear up Methodism by the roots" when he suggested that preachers ought to be supported entirely by donations. The Independent Methodists also advocated an unpaid ministry and freewill offerings; those at Warrington agreed to send their unsalaried preachers to another Lancashire community, where Wesleyan authorities had informed local leaders, "You do not deserve any preaching; you send us no money."[25] Although by 1811 the Primitive Methodists had formally abandoned free gospelism, much of their initial success depended on self-financed missionaries who refused to enforce the ruling. Even after discipline was tightened, the Primitives offered a far cheaper ministry than the parent connexion. In conjunction with other factors, financial issues also widened rifts between clergy and laity, town and country, and rich and poor, all of which contributed to the rise of Primitive Methodism.

Money matters often corroded relations between itinerants and laymen. Defenders of the people charged circuit preachers with being the hired agents of conference tyranny. Kilham, for example, once labeled yearly collections "secret service money." A closely allied but more sophisticated criticism was that which attacked the professional ministry as a needless and parasitic institution. One version of this hoary argument declared that Wesleyan itinerants fed off the laity by craftily employing class leaders to extract money from society members.[26] More disturbing to the lay majority, however, was the rising cost of the ministry. Wesley's itinerants, many of them unmarried, had traveled almost continuously through large circuits, accepting hospitality from each society in its turn. Most of the next generation were encumbered with families who had to be housed, clothed, schooled, and provided with servants. Instead of riding his circuit in the old way, the modern preacher visited country societies by day and spent his nights at home in the town, an expensive retracing of miles. The trappings of respectability, encouraged by some in his flock, irritated others.[27] Although conference eventually imposed limits on allowances, there were no fixed salaries, and wealthy circuits vied with each other to attract the best preachers. In 1815 a popular man with two children could command about £100, a house, and a horse.[28] Moreover, during the distress of the postwar years, a minister enjoyed job security and a stable income, advantages not shared by numbers of the Methodists who were supposed to provide for him. Preachers, on the other hand, felt threatened by lay power of the purse. If stewards elected to withhold their allowances, they had no legal redress. When trustees at Bradford tried to obtain the exclusive right of nominating their own preachers, James Wood urged his fellow itinerants to stand firm: "Should this be granted, the trustees of other places will claim the same privilege—then farewell to Methodism in its present form!"[29] In 1818 and 1819 Hull district collections fell short of the conference assessment, but preachers, "fearful of giving offence," would not press for more money. Already some proprietary trustees in the district were threatening to bring in the Ranters or the New Connexion, "if their will is opposed."[30] Laymen who paid for places of worship often resented interference from ministers trying to enforce conference discipline. At Manchester, for example, John Broadhurst outfitted a room for revival meetings, then clashed with the preachers over its management. What superintendent William Jenkins called a *"regnum in regno"* in 1803 emerged in 1806 as the Band Room Methodists.[31]

Especially in the countryside, Methodists were slow to accept the idea of paying class and ticket money on a regular basis. Thomas Jackson believed that resistance to weekly and quarterly dues was greater in societies which had been founded by evangelical parsons. As superintendent at Sowerby Bridge from 1812 to 1814, Jackson encountered the notion that contributing a penny each week was a needless innovation, a prejudice which he traced to William Grimshaw's labors in the district.[32] Henry Venn had fostered Methodism in Halifax circuit, and until Jabez Bunting arrived in 1811, the payment of class money had never been scrupulously required. Bunting's attempt to do so stirred "vexatious opposition," most of which he ultimately subdued. But even Bunting could not force some rural enclaves to capitulate.[33] Edward Brooke, a country squire and local preacher in Huddersfield circuit, so disliked the obligatory coupling of worship and money that he once denounced the superintendent to his congregation. "I willn't have it; there shall be no collection today," proclaimed Brooke, and after a head count he paid for the entire assembly himself.[34] For the reluctance of country Wesleyans to contribute there are several explanations—the tithe already exacted from some, distance from the center of circuit authority, the force of custom, perhaps greater solidarity of opinion. In areas where a strong town society had traditionally paid the bulk of circuit expenses, village members were in no hurry to alter the pattern. In 1819 William Myles predicted that the country places around Hull would not soon be "brought into a

methodistical form" on account of the "great kindness of the *Hull* society."[35] Finally, as salaried preachers concentrated their energies more
and more exclusively on the towns, rural Methodists often complained of
pastoral neglect. Because they were served mostly by an unpaid local
ministry, they were not so well motivated to add to the connexional coffers.

Besides alienating the countryside, the system worked to estrange
poor Wesleyans from their richer brethren. "You complain the preachers
never call to see you unless you are great folks," a pamphleteer told poor
Methodists in 1814. "Well, you may see the reason; you can do nothing
for them; money they want, and money they must and will have."[36] The
postwar collapse of prices intensified the itinerants' penchant toward
courting affluent society members. About the time of Peterloo, Thomas
Jackson was pleased to report that "many families of wealth and intelligence" were regularly attending Manchester's Oldham Street Chapel.
His senior colleague, John Stephens, had no sympathy for poor men's
radicalism, and, like Jackson, he was quick to identify the interests of
Manchester Methodism with the interests of its more prosperous
adherents. In a letter which also detailed his scheme for purging the
society of disaffection Stephens assured Bunting that, "Methodism
stands high among the respectable people. . . . Nearly every seat is let in
the New Chapel."[37] Seat rents, deemed a necessary source of chapel income, dramatized social and economic differences. A Methodist writing
in 1821 observed that poor people, who once had mingled with the rich
in common worship, were now being relegated to free benches "at a re-
spectful distance, in some *airy* situation." At Macclesfield they hid themselves in a screened-off free section of the chapel known as "Nicodemus
corner" because it was so dark.[38]

Because the Wesleyan financial system depended on members' contributions, circuit preachers were sensitive to economic conditions in
general. Particularly when collections fell off during the disturbed years
after Waterloo, they worried about such problems as the "great *commercial distress . . . increasingly* felt" at Sheffield, the shutting down of factories in Derbyshire, straitened circumstances among the farming folk in
York circuit, the failure of the only ironworks in a Black Country village,
and reverses in the whale fishing and shipping trades at Whitby. Noting
the "smallness of . . . wages" and "dearness of provisions," one itinerant
concluded that "times are now against us."[39] Shrinking collections in the
face of heavy mortgages, allowances for an army of young itinerants,
and the expenses of schools and foreign missions meant that Wesleyan
Methodism was threatened with financial ruin. To cope with this
emergency conference adopted a series of resolutions, three of which

provoked the ire of lay leaders. The first, passed in 1817, established a committee to prevent societies from building chapels unless they had adequate resources. Wise though the measure may have been, provincial Wesleyans resented the interference of London in their affairs. In 1818 a conference minute directed that the connexional debt be divided among the circuits according to their membership, and in 1819 another memorandum required that allowances for preachers' children be allotted on a similar basis.[40] The proportional-assessment scheme aroused opposition from the men responsible for making up circuit deficiencies—stewards and the wealthier members from whom additional funds were solicited. William Myles expostulated with Bunting about payment by numbers: "We had some warm words when the stewards were admitted" to the Hull district meeting. "The district does not increase in numbers or the circuits, it is not their interest so to do. . . . The trustees of the chapels are stiff; and the preachers . . . say they cannot force the people to give their money."[41] The crisis of the Wesleyan purse coincided with a decline in membership, and the two phenomena were related. From 1810 to 1816 Wesleyan Methodism had recruited an average of 8,829 people each year. Beginning in 1817 growth slowed markedly, and in 1820 there was an unprecedented decrease of nearly 5,100 members.[42] Although external factors such as emigration in search of employment may have accounted for diminishing numbers locally, connexional totals were affected by the financial crunch and the means taken to deal with it. As Myles's letter hinted, the losses were to some degree only apparent, not real. Before 1819 ministers had customarily tried to prove their pastoral effectiveness by submitting inflated reports; in 1820, however, there were circuits that claimed "as *few* as they could consistent with truth," thereby saving themselves "additional burthen." But there was also a real decline in membership, and many of the backsliders withdrew because of money. Some wearied of the perennial demands for contributions and so dropped out of society. Some balked at supporting preachers who "encourage and pray for . . . tyrants." Some left simply because they could not afford to pay class and ticket money, while others were struck off class lists for the same reason.[43]

The anxious five years after 1815 were the same ones during which Primitive Methodism pushed across the Midlands and into Yorkshire. It is unrealistic to assume that Old Connexion losses were automatic gains for the Primitives; nevertheless, they did win over many erstwhile Wesleyans. The Ranter machinery of salvation was attractively cheap. If a society wanted a chapel, its members were likely to clear the site themselves, dig the foundations, beg construction materials, and erect a tiny boxlike building. More often, these early Primitive Methodists gathered in cottages, barns, abandoned warehouses, and fields. Requests for funds were negligible, partly because unpaid local preachers were widely used and their responsibilities increased. Itinerants either paid their own expenses or received barely enough to cover their needs.[44] To at least one Wesleyan minister it grew evident that the Primitive Methodists had benefited from the financial exigencies of his own connexion; in 1830 he wondered if "we have erred in not . . . sending out more young preachers who can beg their way, but reach more places. We go to a place once a fortnight; the ranters once a week."[45] Primitive Methodist success was especially evident in villages irregularly visited by the Old Connexion's town-dwelling itinerants and in thinly populated agricultural districts that were unable to bear the weight of its financial structure. Though they exaggerated Wesleyan pleas for money, some satirical verses written about 1815 pointed to a crucial difference between the two connexions. The author, a frustrated Yorkshireman, had tried repeatedly to find spiritual nourishment in the sermons of Jabez Bunting. But Bunting never preached; obsessed with fundraising for schools and foreign missions, he only cried; "'Come forward wi' your prayers and . . . purses'." Even on the single occasion when the famous preacher spoke at an ordinary Sunday evening service, he concluded, picked up a hymnbook, and then, instead of lining out a stanza in the usual way, said: "'My friends, / You, and the members of this vast connexion, / Will recollect the quarterly collection!'"[46]

The Snares of Change: Primitive vs. Modern

> I never approve of powers exercised by Black Coats that are not clearly laid down in God's word—and methinks very little distinction is there to be found under its dispensation except between Believers and the contrary.
>
> —James Williams, 1808[47]

When people in Regency England talked about members of the Primitive Methodist Connexion, they usually called them "Ranters" or "Camp-Meeting Methodists," tags that evoke an image of open-air revival meetings. Although revivalism was certainly a key feature of the movement, no less characteristic was its emphasis on the lay apostolate and its use of pastoral techniques which Wesleyan preachers were beginning to ignore. There were other contrasts as well. To some critics the simplicity and spiritual fervor of the Primitives seemed like the renaissance of a Methodist golden age that had apparently died with John Wesley. Unless all these differences are acknowledged it is impossible to understand fully the popular appeal of early Ranterism.

Wesley had foreseen that Methodist industry and frugality would lead to prosperity. He had warned against its probable fruits—the form of religion would remain, but the spirit would wither. The founder's predictions were fulfilled. "Property brings Methodists into a different situation; and many who take pews miss of conversion," admitted a traveling preacher in 1810. Another wondered if *"primitive* Methodism" had not had "more of sanctity—holiness of Christian perfection in it than *modern* Methodism?"[48] The doubts of these preachers were shared by a section of the laity. A Methodist merchant had to concede that the "increasing opulence and respectability" of Wesleyans were inducing "worldly-minded men" to join their ranks. A layman who identified himself as one of the "old school" wished there were not so many sleek, well-fed, lax people among the chapelgoers of 1821, and a York member noted that "old and uniform professors" feared "lest the present generation . . . sink into a state of formality."[49] There were of course many poor Methodists still on society rolls, but it was the richer brethren who determined policy. The trend was recorded in bricks and mortar. These latter-day Methodists built galleried chapels in which those who could pay pew rents were quite literally stationed above the free seats of the poor. One elderly Londoner enumerated a series of complaints that climaxed: "and when I go to Liverpool there I hear one another lamenting that a chapel contrary to ancient Methodism, yea more like a cathedrall, has been fited up [*sic*]. . . . If this is Methodism, I do not like it." Bradford's *"steeple house"* troubled a circuit preacher in Yorkshire: "Are not Gothic buildings, painted windows, gorgeous chapels the outward symptoms of declining spiritual glory?"[50]

At the heart of the contrast between "primitive" and "new" Methodism were divergent views of the ministry. The old guard reasoned that, if eighteenth-century conditions could be restored, the society might recover some of its original purity. A necessary first step in this direction, they believed, was a return to the idea that, even though circuit preachers were specially called to full-time evangelism, they were essentially lay workers in a lay community. The preacher-dominated modernist school was moving toward the claim that itinerancy was the Methodist equivalent of Anglican holy orders. Their desire to vest ministers with sacerdotal authority was motivated less by egoism than by expediency. As soon as the break with the church was seen to be irreparable, Wesley's successors were anxious to weld Methodism into an integrated and self-sufficient denomination. Uniform discipline and effi-

cient government would be most readily achieved if power could be consolidated in the ministry. Society members, however, were not likely to
tolerate a black-coated regime unless they had reason to defer to the
pastoral office itself. And, until the Clarendon Code was modified in
1812, the legal status of unordained itinerants could be called into question by the government. The obvious answer was ordination, but without bishops there could be no laying on of episcopal hands. Instead,
conference eventually embraced the theory that a circuit preacher was
"virtually ordained" once he had been received into full connexion.

The tendency toward professionalism was stimulated by the
political climate of the war years. Despite their protestations of loyalty
Methodist ministers were a favorite target of anti-Jacobin alarmists. Was
not the itinerant system admirably equipped to spread a gospel of sedition? Who knew what transpired in class meetings open only to initiates
whom preachers had entrusted with tickets? Citing the "regular *correspondence* that is carried on between societies of Methodists," a Suffolk
clergyman confided, "I cannot help suspecting the preacher of the most
obscure village to be a designed link in the chain, and intended for further use perhaps than either himself or his followers are aware of. Allow
me to . . . suppose that the principal leaders of this sect are looking forward to a revolution, and of course of the *democratic* kind; they could
not concert a better plan than to have such a force in the country."[51]
Methodist preachers had long been accused of exciting disaffection
toward the church, the guardian of stability. Now crisis added urgency
to the charge. Anglicans also resented the ease with which "illiterate en-
thusiast[s]" could gain admission to the ministry. Such persons "assume
the office of teachers before they have learnt," grumbled a defender of
the established church, and then "go forth in a state of the profoundest
ignorance to preach before they are lawfully ordained."[52] As long as personal religious experience and a divine call to evangelize were the chief
prerequisites for the Methodist ministry, uneducated men could presume
equality with Oxbridge-trained gentlemen. A tract of 1805 identified the
real menace to the social order: "by denying superiority in religious
knowledge to be the result of superior education, they indirectly deny
superiority in all other cases."[53]

Partly to shield the ministerial image, partly out of fear that "improper persons" might travel under their aegis, conference ruled in 1802
that candidates must undergo public examination before both the quarterly and the district meetings. To counter the notion that itinerants were
unlettered boors they encouraged probationers to read theology and to
study Greek and Hebrew, a policy favored by the scholarly Adam
Clarke, who, a few months after Trafalgar, averred that "it must be

fairly doubted whether God would use [extensively] even such men as *our* immortal Nelson . . . in the present day." Simple fervor had fitted John Nelson to convert eighteenth-century sinners; their grandchildren, it seemed, must hear learned men whose sermons were "free from barbarisms" and embellished with "the soothing ornaments of style."[54] Old-fashioned Wesleyans, however, feared that education would make the new breed of circuit preachers powerless to save souls. As early as 1798 John Pawson had warned that "erecting schools and endowing colleges" for the training of itinerants meant "taking the matter out of the hands of Christ, and endeavouring to make ministers for him," a course likely to ruin religion "root and branch." In 1800 the revivalist William Bramwell edited a manual intended to help liberate ministers from that bookishness "which prevents immediate influence of the Holy Spirit in the act of preaching." But refinement eventually triumphed. Commenting in 1823 on the elegant manners and speech of his fellow itinerants, William Hatton wondered how much longer they could win any hearing at all from the lower classes. The lingo of professionalism also aroused criticism. When conference sanctioned the title "Reverend" in 1821, David Stoner exclaimed, "such mummery. . . . Oh! that the spirit of William Bramwell had been alive to lift up his voice . . . and show you that *Rev* was the very mark of the beast!"[55]

Local preachers were disgruntled with the subordinate role allotted to them in the modern Methodist polity. The "high hand" of Sunderland's superintendent stirred such ire that lay preachers in the circuit combined against him. Local preachers in Melksham circuit were "prejudiced against the *Connection*" because it apparently had secret laws which condoned their superintendent's arrogant "assumsion [*sic*] of power." One of the most articulate statements of the local preachers' grievances emerged from a conflict between London itinerants and the "Community Preachers." Lay preachers, asserted its author, are the sinews of Wesleyanism and the "genuine successors of the apostles," yet they are made subservient to "hirelings" who "term themselves clergymen." These "fine gentlemen" are greedy for "power, authority, and property," he warned, and if "primitive simplicity" is not soon restored, Methodism will sink under their "priesthood and tyranny."[56]

The corollary of the new clericalism was connexionalism, a strengthening of central power at the expense of local autonomy. Many Methodists, irked by itinerants who set themselves up as "reverends," were likewise vexed when, with increasing frequency, the hand of conference was visible in their affairs. John Wesley had been highly authoritarian, but he at least had been entitled to the deference customarily paid a clergyman of the established church. Moreover, with the whole of England as his parish, Wesley had necessarily left the day-to-day teaching of the gospel and the details of administration to lay helpers. The rationalizing of connexional government, the smaller circuits of the nineteenth century, and the immediacy of superintendents who resided in the circuit towns all diminished the influence of local laymen. At the same time, confronted with the task of keeping a rapidly expanding membership intact and free from the evils of political disaffection, conference temporarily stifled lay enterprises. The upshot was a hiatus in lay involvement and a frustrating of rank-and-file initiative that ran counter to the mounting tide of English democratic feeling.

The tradition of the Wesleyan lay apostolate remained vigorous well into the first decade of the nineteenth century, and, especially in the countryside, it never disappeared altogether. Many of rural Yorkshire's most popular evangelists were laymen—Sammy Hick, the "village blacksmith"; Billy Dawson; "Praying Johnny" Oxtoby; and the "praying colliers," William and George Mosely. During the late eighteenth century lay people were used extensively in Wesleyan efforts to serve England's growing urban population. Liverpool, London, Bristol, and Manchester all had Strangers' Friend Societies whose Methodist members gave a penny each week for relief of the non-Methodist poor. A layman inaugurated the house-visiting campaign that gave Methodism its first real foothold in Preston, and Manchester was "pervaded by a system of prayer meetings" led by members of the Society for Religious Improvement, an association of young laymen whose secretary was Jabez Bunting. Their simple cottage services attracted many "who longed for the privileges of the Sabbath, but busy, persecuted or ashamed of ragged poverty," would not come to church or chapel. Bunting's subsequent experiences with Broadhurst and the Band Room seem to have awakened him to the disruptive potential of lay undertakings, and his new point of view was soon shared by a majority of the conference. In 1803 the members tried to halt the centrifugal tendencies of lay evangelism by forbidding unsupervised meetings and restricting entry to legitimate ones. Some amenable superintendents sponsored lay-conducted cottage meetings in their circuits, but, on the whole, Wesleyan worship grew more staid, chapel centered, and preacher dominated. As a result, the Old Connexion forfeited a measure of lay support, some of which was channeled into Primitive Methodism.[57]

Before 1811, when the Primitive Methodist Connexion was formed, lay sabotage of the official machinery was rife, but because the antimodernists were ecclesiastical reactionaries without party unity or a coherent program, they were unable to reverse conference policy. It was the Metternich of Methodism, Hugh Bourne, who successfully harnessed

some of this latent energy and reoriented it toward the nineteenth century. Ranterism began as a lay movement, and it long bore traces of its
origin. So much local self-government was allowed that during its first
fifteen years the connexion often threatened to dissolve into anarchy.
Lay delegates at its annual meetings outnumbered itinerants by two to
one. The preachers themselves were commonly regarded as lay missionaries, and most traveled only a few years before seeking more
remunerative employment. Partly because it gave structure to tradi-
tionalist forces, Primitive Methodism flourished where the grip of the
past was most tenacious—in rural areas and among uprooted newcomers
who had yet to find a place in the grimy factory towns of industrial
England. Paradoxically, however, the same emphasis on lay participation that initially attracted the nostalgic eventually enabled Primitive
Methodism to become a favorite sect of the modern English work-
ingman. Once "Niagra" was "shot," the Primitive Methodist Connexion
served as a prime recruiting ground for trade union leaders and labor
politicians.[58]

Especially before 1821 the Ranters benefited from the pastoral lapses
of Old Connexion itinerants. More and more preoccupied with study,
administrative duties, and family matters, the new generation of
preachers found little time for counseling society members. This apparent indifference to the inner spiritual lives of those in their charge was
seen by some laymen as evidence of a decline from eighteenth-century
standards. By contrast, Ranter missionaries seemed truly "primitive" in
their concern for individual religious experience. Hugh Bourne and his
early associates stressed what they called the "conversation ministry," a
technique that was particularly welcomed by converts from the lower
classes. Overt pastoral interest in their private dramas of salvation meant
recognition by the spiritual community, and this was often crucial to
their sense of personal worth. Another source of dissatisfaction was
Wesleyan neglect of the countryside. As preachers became increasingly
wedded to the circuit towns, rural Methodists felt cheated. Despite a plea
from the 1803 conference that itinerents be more attentive to country
societies, the situation worsened. By 1819 it was obvious to at least one
Wesleyan superintendent that the "real cause" of Primitive gains was
"the present plan of the [Wesleyan] preachers living in great towns . . .
and only just preaching in the country."[59]

The sharp decrease in Wesleyan membership startled ministers at
the 1820 conference into scrutinizing their pastoral record. For six hours
they deliberated ways to "increase . . . spiritual religion among our
societies" and to extend "the work of God in our native country." Their
conclusions were published in the "Liverpool Minutes," a series of resolu-

tions on pastoral work which recommended a return to "primitive" methods and "primitive" Methodism. The procedures urged were certainly those then yielding conversions to Ranterism—open-air preaching, closer cooperation with the laity, diligence in house visiting, cottage prayer meetings, and, above all, conscientious service to rural societies. Whether or not external social and economic factors stimulated revivalism after 1820, it is significant that the preachers who sent accounts of revivals to the *Methodist Magazine* in 1821 ascribed religious renewal in their circuits to the following of the Liverpool guidelines.[60]

The Old Connexion recovered some of its momentum during the 1820s. By then, however, that insensitivity to lay opinion and those pastoral failures which marked the preceding two decades had called forth lasting alternatives. Of all the schismatic groups that had emerged during the period, it was the Ranters who profited most from the negative aspects of Wesleyan modernism. Together with revivalism and low-cost religion, Bourne's successful refurbishing of the past gave the Primitive Methodist Connexion a triple allure that consistently made its membership greater than the combined following of all its non-Wesleyan rivals.

A Legacy Fragmented

> Divisions *from* the church, though awful, are perhaps less to be dreaded than Divisions *in* the church.
> —Jabez Bunting, 1803[61]

Although he was no stranger to divisions during his lifetime, John Wesley could hardly have anticipated the speed with which English Methodism would fragment after his death. Within a generation the Wesleyan Connexion was rent by no fewer than five schisms—the Kilhamite, the Independent Methodist, the Bible Christian, the Primitive Methodist, and the Tent Methodist. In order to set Primitive Methodism in its historical context, some reference must be made to the other four breakaway groups.

The Bible Christians

In origins, outlook, and apostolate, Bible Christianity shared much with Primitive Methodism. While he was still a local preacher, William O'Bryan felt called to recover the "lost sheep" of Cornwall by preaching in lanes, fields, and barns. Expelled for irregularities, he established his own connexion in 1815. Like many of the first Primitive Methodists, most of O'Bryan's followers were rural Wesleyans disenchanted with modern clericalism and connexionalism. The Bible Christian ministry was made up of unsalaried local preachers and ill-paid itinerants— O'Bryan disliked the Wesleyan system of collections, and few members could afford lavish donations. From the beginning, revivals were a part of the Bible Christian ethos, but they did not assume significant proportions until 1818, approximately two years after the Ranter emphasis shifted from cottage meetings to large-scale revivalism. Quaker influence was evident in the Bible Christians' dress and speech as well as in their attitude toward the ministry of women. In 1820 nineteen of the connexion's forty-three itinerants were women. O'Bryan was probably familiar with Bourne's tract of 1808 defending female evangelism, and he was well aware that Primitive Methodist women were conspicuously successful as revivalists. In a letter to Bourne that stressed female preaching and other features common to both sects, O'Bryan suggested that they might "strengthen each other's hands in the work." So far, they had labored in different areas, the Primitive Methodists in the Midlands and the North, O'Bryan's people in Devonshire, Cornwall, and Kent. During 1821 he carried on a friendly correspondence with James Bourne, and the *Primitive Methodist Magazine* took favorable notice of Bible Christianity, but the hope of a joint venture was never realized.[62] In the absence of collaboration the similar appeal made by the two connexions might have led to keen rivalry. Actually, competition for members was minimal because geography continued to separate Bible Christian territory from the main strongholds of Primitive Methodism.

The Tent Methodists

Bible Christianity and Primitive Methodism were *of* the people; Tent Methodism was *for* them. Begun in 1814 as a mission to the poor, tent revivalism had an uneasy existence within the Bristol Wesleyan circuit until 1820. A split resulted when the conference of 1819 supported Bristol's traveling preachers in a struggle over authority with local laymen who, having paid for the tents, wanted to control their use. Subsequently the Tent Methodists moved into Manchester and Liverpool and made plans for bringing a free gospel to other large towns "already . . . white unto the harvest."[63] Their leadership was imbued with an "improving" spirit. The *Tent Methodists' Magazine* urged the moral and economic advantages of educating the poor and reminded potential benefactors that money spent redeeming working-class sinners was a sound social invest-ment. Like the Ranters, the Tent Methodists discovered that urban revivalism was often ephemeral, fading once the excitement of novelty wore off. Failure to create a viable sense of community among its con-verts left Tent Methodism rootless in the populous districts it aspired to save, and the movement disintegrated about 1825.

The Methodist New Connexion

For many historians the New Connexion is the classic instance of Meth-odist Jacobinism. Few neglect to remark that Huddersfield Kilhamites were called "Tom Paine Methodists" and that in 1798 nearly three-quarters of the New Connexion membership was concentrated in Leeds, Manchester, Sheffield, and Nottingham, four circuits in which political disaffection abounded. But the New Connexion story is more complex than such evidence suggests. The Huddersfield epithet gained currency not because local Kilhamites were hostile to George III's government, but because they denounced clerical tyranny. Inferences based on the statistics of secession are equally problematic; too often the figures merely reflected circumstances intrinsic to Methodism. In 1798 Leeds headed the most numerous circuit in the New Connexion, but its boun-daries were drawn to include a disproportionately large share of heavily Methodist Yorkshire. The stationing of traveling preachers was an inter-nal factor which affected connexional loyalties in some circuits.[64] Purely local disputes also prompted alliance with the New Connexion. Both at Bury and at Birmingham laymen "called in the Kilhamites" after wrangles with Wesleyan itinerants. Finally, the connexional affiliation of an entire society was sometimes decided by one or two of its members. At least two Nottinghamshire societies left the Wesleyan fold because their meeting places were owned by Kilhamite sympathizers. A third seceded when its most articulate lay preacher cast his lot with the rebels.[65]

    To some extent modern assessments of the New Connexion rest on a myth deliberately fostered by Wesleyan apologists. A reasonably unprej-udiced account written in 1823 described the early Kilhamites as men "whom the world . . . called Jacobins." Its author explained that "a great majority of the Methodists" welcomed separation "not so much" because the innovators were politically suspect as because the principle which in-spired their "attempts to revolutionize the Methodistical rules and forms" was democratic.[66] This mentality was not a Methodist idiosyncrasy. Few among Kilham's compatriots troubled to discriminate between his aims and those of Colonel Despard. Aware that their own purposes would be well served by promoting this confusion, Wesleyan leaders long represented the schism as a salutary purge. In 1810 John Stephens prefaced a sermon with a reference to those preachers who had "yielded to the fatal dereliction of Jacobinism" during the 1790s: "Their sin has found them out—they have been driven from a connection to which they were a disgrace—and our renovated body is become sound in all its members."[67] Blinded by sectarian jealousies, many in the next generation of Wesleyan writers gave uncritical assent to such propaganda, and the interpretation, though founded in polemics, soon became standard.

It is difficult to arrive at a realistic appraisal of New Connexion political attitudes between 1797 and 1820. A crucial limitation is the lack of reliable data concerning the sentiments of the rank and file. Incorporated into Wesleyan local histories and the reports of Tory magistrates is a great deal of hearsay suggesting that Kilhamite societies were heavily tainted with disaffection. Although this testimony is dubious, there are other more trustworthy indications that not all New Connexionists were content to possess their souls in patience. The "Address" of the 1820 conference, for example, castigated members who had involved themselves in the "warmth of political discussion and the general agitation" of the past year. This erring minority was "solemnly admonish[ed]" to be "quiet and peaceable" in the future. Most Kilhamites, however, seem to have found chapel loyalties incompatible with popular reform. Backsliding was a very common reaction to economic distress. "Too many" victims of the 1800 crisis "deserted their wonted stations in the societies of the saints." Others "scattered" during the "dark and cloudy day[s]" of 1812 and 1813. One preacher explicity stated that, in 1818 and 1819, want drove people in Stockport circuit out of their New Connexion classes and into radical associations.[68] It is possible to argue that Methodist Jacobins were drawn into the New Connexion because its government was fashioned along republican lines. Initially this may have been so, but the equal voice accorded to Kilhamite laymen was soon speaking in the distinctly middle-class accents of a propertied few. In any case, even where alternatives were readily available, political consciousness did not always determine sectarian allegiance. An old woman in Sheffield, after much dithering, finally elected to stay with the Wesleyans. Her dilemma was resolved, she said, when she dreamt that "a plain old oak stool" was better than a new painted one.[69]

Considerably more is known about the Methodists who assumed lay leadership in the New Connexion. Before their exodus nearly all had been influential in Wesleyan societies. At least eight had served on the sixty-seven member delegation that presented the "people's" platform at

Manchester in 1795.[70] Eager also for a share in local and national government, many had been friends of reform during the 1790s. But theirs was
the radicalism of unenfranchised merchants, millowners, and professional men, and by the end of the war few could be found who had not
grown wary of popular agitation and wholesale democracy. After the
Municipal Corporations Act was passed these New Connexion laymen
played an active role in civic affairs. Stockport's first two mayors were
Kilhamites, and Salem Chapel in Halifax provided so many councillors
that Victorian townspeople spoke of being ruled by the "House of
Salem." Prototypes of Smilesian success, the men who dominated the
New Connexion were zealous patrons of mutual improvement societies,
Sunday schools, free libraries, reading clubs, and benefit societies.[71] The
Kilhamite *Magazine* mirrored the biases of its more affluent readers. One
writer decried parish wakes because the festivities that characterized
them were "pregnant with unhappy consequences" for public order,
business, and morals. Another criticized extravagant fare in the work-
houses and averred that raising the poor rates would create a "national
danger"—increased assistance would only undermine the prudential
habits of the poor. An article on judicious almsgiving advised would-be
benefactors to limit their charity to worthy recipients. Education, a
favorite topic, was to be the panacea for social ills. Teach the destitute to
read and write, and they too can be self-made men. Meanwhile, they will
learn to "reverence the powers that be as the ordinance of God."[72]

The political and social policy of the New Connexion did not remain
static between 1797 and 1820. A decade passed before the conference
minutes hinted at any great concern about the extra-chapel pursuits of
society members. An indication that the era of tolerence was about to
end appeared in 1808 when Kilhamites in the manufacturing districts
were adjured to suffer privations passively, remembering that their fortunes were controlled by an "invisible hand." It was, however, the impact of Luddism, marching Blanketeers, Pentridge, Spa Fields, and noc-
turnal drills on the moors that fast propelled the New Connexion leadership down the path already marked out by the Wesleyan conference. In
1813 delegates disavowed all "political books which may have been published by any of our preachers" and declared that "the conference highly
disapprove of our ministers writing or disseminating works of a political
nature."[73] During the next biennium three itinerants were obliged to
withdraw from the ministry, all apparently for political reasons. Another traveling preacher, whose theological views were deemed satisfac-
tory, was required to suppress an objectionable pamphlet. In Halifax circuit a member was "charged with attending a political meeting when he
should have been at his class," and sometime after Peterloo the future

Chartist Ben Rushton relinquished his duties as a local preacher. In 1817 the New Connexion circulated an "Address to the British Public" that "repel[led]" with "honest indignation" the notion that Kilhamites might be guilty of "disaffection to the government of the land."[74] The New Connexion leadership entered the 1820s having passed through its years of decision. By 1820 popular appeal had been irrevocably sacrificed on the altar of respectability. Theirs would be the Methodism not of laboring men, but of Anti-Corn Law Leaguers.[75]

The prior existence of the New Connexion did not materially impede the spread of Primitive Methodism. The New Connexion had a number of village societies, but its real strength came to be rooted in the towns. Apart from such urban triumphs as the one at Hull, the Ranters won their lasting victories in the countryside. Geographically more diffused, Primitive Methodism also had a broader social base. The reasons for this are fairly obvious. Primitive Methodist preachers spoke and dressed like the farm laborers, miners, and stockingers who came to hear them. In contrast to the evolving middle-class oligarchy of the New Connexion, Ranter government was extraordinarily democratic. Above all, the leveling influence of revivalism so prominent in the Primitive Methodist Connexion was scarcely felt among the Kilhamites. Understandably, Primitive Methodist membership soon outstripped that of the New Connexion, and by midcentury Ranters outnumbered Kilhamites by eight to one.

The Independent Methodists

As their name indicates, the Independent Methodists rejected the connexional principle in favor of congregational autonomy. The sole purpose of their annual conferences, the first of which convened at Manchester in 1805, was for mutual assistance and the exchange of ideas. Although most Independent Methodists were ex-Wesleyans who had clashed with Old Connexion authorities, the secessions had originated at different times and in a variety of circumstances. Their common bonds were dedication to liberty, commitment to free gospelism, and disavowal of the professional ministry. Of the eight societies represented at the annual meeting in 1814, all but one were located either in Lancashire or in northern Cheshire.[76] By 1820 Independent Methodism had established outposts as far afield as Glasgow and Gateshead, but its center of influence remained unchanged.

Though, strictly speaking, it antedated Independent Methodism as such, an abortive division at Leeds illustrates the vulnerabilty of a group which was held together primarily by the magnetism of a preacher answerable to the Wesleyan conference. Rumblings of discontent began to sound at Leeds in 1801 when William Bramwell was assigned to the circuit in tandem with a pair of antirevivalists. By 1803 Bramwell and a local schoolmaster, James Sigston, were leading four classes of "Screamers" in Kirkgate's Old Assembly Rooms. During the summer Bramwell canvassed discontented Methodists in Manchester and Macclesfield to solicit support for a revivalist union. At conference, however, he capitulated to the hierarchy and was exiled to the small and lethargic Wetherby circuit. According to Lorenzo Dow, Bramwell saw the "formality and danger" into which Wesleyan Methodism was "sinking" and stood out against it until he was prevailed upon to "recant . . . and return," leaving Sigston and the Kirkgate Screamers "in a dilemma." Sigston dutifully imitated his mentor; deprived of leadership, the schism collapsed.[77]

Independent Methodism at Manchester grew out of a lengthy controversy between Wesleyan circuit preachers and the followers of John Broadhurst. A wealthy draper, Broadhurst owned a room where, from the ministers' point of view, revivalists "pursued their own course of action" with "less likelihood of official oversight and check than in the chapels." It was probably in Broadhurst's Band Room that Jabez Bunting lost his youthful zeal for cottage meetings. Sent there to deliver his trial sermon as a local preacher, the neophyte had to stand silent until a sympathetic bystander shouted down some noisy enthusiasts. Irregular worship was not the only source of contention between the itinerants and the Band Room. Hoping to bring Manchester's burgeoning population into the way of religion, Broadhurst violated Wesleyan discipline by throwing open Sunday band meetings to all comers. To the injury imposed by this "unscriptural and unmethodistical" disregard of rules, the revivalists added the insult of ignoring the circuit's preaching plan and met weekly "to appoint one another to different places." In 1803 tension ripened into schism. Temporarily mended by a "Plan of Reconciliation," the rupture became permanent in January 1806 when Broadhurst and his friends "frankly declared they could not submit" nor "suffer a travelling preacher to conduct the[ir] meeting[s]." In February more than three hundred Band Roomers proclaimed themselves Independent Methodists.[78] Their contact with the camp-meeting community was slight. Hugh Bourne preached in the Band Room in 1809,[79] but Primitive Methodist missionaries did not penetrate the area until 1819. By then the Ranters had opted for a connexional polity and a paid ministry, both distasteful to the Independent Methodists.

The early history of three Independent Methodist societies—those at Stockport, Macclesfield, and Warrington—was more closely linked to the rise of Primitive Methodism. Stockport seems to have harbored two sets of revivalists, at least one of which became the nucleus of an Independent Methodist society. Those members of the New Connexion who had thrilled to the soul-refreshing sessions in Gamaliel Swindells's warehouse in 1797 appear to have found subsequent worship at Mount Tabor Chapel less inspiring. At any rate, when Dow preached in Stockport in 1806, he described his congregation as a band of free-gospel revivalists who had been "driven out from the Kilhamites." At the Independent Methodist conference of 1808, Stockport's delegates, Swindells and Peter Ashley, represented a society boasting sixty-three members, five preachers, and three meeting places.[80] Some among these sixty-three may once have been Wesleyans, the "poor but very pious" revivalists who were the "means of bringing H. Bourne and the Harresehead[*sic*] people more fully into the law of faith." Apparently this element was harried out of the Stockport Wesleyan circuit about 1805. It is likely, though not certain, that they took their "walking prayer meetings" down the road of Independent Methodism.[81]

In 1803 Wesleyan intolerance of lay initiative and cottage evangelism engendered a schismatic body of Christian Revivalists at Macclesfield. The rebels took the name Independent Methodist in 1806. Their *Rules*, copies of which Bunting mailed to his colleagues for their "amusement," carried the motto "Let us walk by the same RULE. We may pronounce those churches happy, however plain and poor, in which 'No simony nor sinecure is known, / Where works the bee—no honey for the drone'." These regulations were reputedly drawn up by Joseph Nightingale, an erstwhile follower of Paine and the author of an unflattering *Portraiture of Methodism*, which later provoked acrimonious pamphlet warfare with the Wesleyans. In the *Portraiture*, published after he broke with Methodism altogether, Nightingale described the Revivalists as "simple, harmless, and well-meaning . . . but enthusiastical and ungovernable to an extraordinary degree." Dow, who likened them to American Methodists, was able to set the Macclesfield society afire with his frontier-style evangelism. Their numbers greatly augmented by this revival, the Independent Methodists built a chapel, which Dow helped to dedicate in November 1806.[82] Proximity as well as personnel united the Macclesfield sect with the future Ranters. Society members from Macclesfield participated in the Mow Cop camp meetings of 1807, and one of them, Mary Dunnel, itinerated for the Primitive Methodists until she and Bourne quarreled late in 1811. The central figure in the Independent society was John Berrisford, the person to whom Bourne dedicated his *Remarks on the Ministry of Women*. Between 1807 and 1813 Bourne was a frequent guest in Berrisford's home; he attended the Independent Methodist conferences held in Macclesfield in 1807 and 1808; and for a time he included its chapel in the Primitive Methodist preaching plan.[83]

Better known as Quaker Methodists, the Warrington Independent Methodists were, as the tag suggests, a mixture of onetime Wesleyans and ex-Friends. The former group seceded from the Old Connexion at the end of the eighteenth century; the latter party, dissatisfied with the sterility of contemporary Quakerism, joined them shortly afterward. Poor though its members were, the society soon managed to erect a chapel, which was used for silent meetings as well as for Sunday preaching. Most members wore Quaker dress, adopted Quaker speech mannerisms, and held Quaker views of the ministery. Until Dow made his headquarters with them in 1805, the Warrington sect was not especially concerned with revivalism.[84] Invited to speak at Warrington after the Independent Methodist annual meeting in 1807, Hugh Bourne became friends with their leader, a chairmaker named Peter Phillips. During the next few years camp-meeting preachers worked closely with the Warrington people and also with the nearby Stockton Heath society, an affiliated band formed by Dow. Both places were listed on the Primitive Methodist plan in 1810, and as late as 1813 Bourne was making appointments for Mary Richardson, a Quaker Methodist evangelist whom he had converted in 1808. Ranter itinerants were still serving the Stockton Heath society in 1817, but in 1830, when their chapel became the birthplace of English teetotalism, it was considered a Quaker Methodist meetinghouse.[85]

The emergence of these Independent Methodist societies demonstrates that the disputes which brought about the Primitive Methodist schism in 1811 were not unique to the Potteries. Similarly, disagreements over revivalism, discipline, and the appropriate limits of lay initiative gave rise to most of the other Independent groups in Lancashire and Cheshire. Yet, despite their common matrix, Primitive Methodism and Independent Methodism developed along separate lines. Some Independent Methodists defected to the Ranters, but most of their societies were still intact in 1820. That more Independents did not join forces with the first Primitive Methodists is probably best explained by their resolute attachment to congregationalism and by their preference for an unpaid ministry.

Such factors as the rigidity of Wesleyan conference discipline, the financial strains within the Old Connexion, and the pastoral shortcomings of its newly professionalized and town-centered itinerancy go far to account for the various Methodist schisms of the late eighteenth and early nineteenth centuries. These problems were in turn related to the political, social, and economic tensions that shaped British life throughout the period. Primitive Methodism grew out of both these contexts, the national as well as the connexional, but the story of its genesis is incomplete without some discussion of contemporary English and American revivalism. It was, after all, pentecostal fires that both energized Ranterism and forged its distinctive character.

Two

Fire from Heaven

The Millennium Anticipated

See how the Scriptures are fulfilling,
  Poor sinners are returning home;
The times the prophets were foretelling,
  With signs and wonders now is come.
      —Camp-Meeting Hymn, 1809[1]

The revivalistic fervor that stirred English Methodism during the 1790s coincided with a spate of millenarian writings and an outburst of apocalyptic frenzy. The 1790s, a decade of social, economic, and political upset, was seen by contemporaries as a period of calamity. Among the poor, Richard Brothers inspired a cult that looked for the dawn of peace, prosperity, and brotherhood once the mighty, overtaken by disasters, had been cast down from their seats of economic, political, and ecclesiastical power. But it was not just the lower classes that breathed this crisis-charged atmosphere. By 1793 the increasingly violent course of the French Revolution, British involvement in war, the uprooting of political and social institutions on the Continent, and the approaching end of the century were leading many to expect an imminent Day of Judgment. Elhanan Winchester warned Parliament that the last of three "woe trumpets" was about to sound, heralding the cataclysm that would usher in the Second Advent, and James Bicheno interpreted the demise of papal authority in France in terms of the Book of Revelation. There were even Anglican bishops who read contemporary events as portents of doom.[2] The rhetoric of Methodist revivalism was often freighted with apocalyptic imagery, and the movement gained impetus from the millenarian climate of the day. Although revivalism and millenarianism sometimes overlapped, the two were not synonymous.

They flourished concurrently in response to the dislocations of the period, and the adherents of both yearned for divine salvation from the snares and hazards of earthly existence. Unlike most of the people caught up in revivalism, however, millenarians expected temporal beatitude to come simultaneously to all who were worthy. Theirs was to be a sudden, collective, and total deliverance accompanied by the obliteration of evil. Some revival enthusiasts may have believed that a terrestrial reign of the just would rise on the ashes of a sinful world destroyed, but for most of them the attractive force of revivalism was primarily personal. It was the individual soul, not the corporate brotherhood, that "got liberty." Any consequent reinvigoration of the local Methodist society was heartily welcomed, but was usually seen as less significant than the private salvation of its members. Furthermore, even those individuals blessed with entire sanctification did not ordinarily suppose that they would live out their days in an earthly paradise.[3]

Some Methodist preachers saw revivalism as a divinely willed means by which the converted might soon be numbered among Mount Zion's hundred and forty-four thousand. John Moon was "led to conclude" that the Yorkshire revivals of 1793–1794 "must surely be a prelude to that glorious conquest of grace which . . . shall take place in the last days; and hence, emminently [sic] preparing for the *grand Millennial* reign of our *redeeming* God. *Amen. Even so*, come. LORD JESUS."[4] These apocalyptic expectations persisted into the early nineteenth century, when Methodist voices were raised in chorus with those of the Southcottians. In October 1801 the Wesleyan *Methodist Magazine* printed an extract from Bishop Hopkins on the millennium, and in 1805 a single issue of the Kilhamite *Magazine* carried three chiliastic articles, one of which compared the "end of the world to harvest." "Time is nearly over," wrote William Bramwell in 1807. "The Revelations are now most clearly explained by matter of fact; and must not those things which are yet to come, be accomplished?"[5] The language of Moon and Bramwell was symptomatic of a general restlessness that was transforming both sober chapelgoers and irreligious sinners into highly combustible fuel for the Spirit. Once touched by its fire, they burned with a zeal for salvation which the Wesleyan conference, wary of the current trend toward "wildness," would dampen only at the cost of schism.

Though imbued with revivalism, the Camp-Meeting Methodists were not much affected by specifically millenarian notions. There were, however, apocalyptic echoes in Bourne's *Collection of Hymns and Spiritual Songs* published in 1809. Asserted one hymn: "These are the days of visitation" when the "Lord will come in clouds and thunder" to "cut his foes asunder" and "hurl them where the damnéd lie." According to another, "Heaven is shaking, earth is quaking, / Mountains fly before his face." But, the faithful assured themselves, "We'll shout above the fiery void, / And tune our harps of gold."[6] For a short time the visionary element which figured in contemporary millenarianism also manifested itself among Bourne's people. From their intercourse with the Magic Methodists of Delamere Forest they learned to attach great weight to dreams and visions. Some of the Forest Methodists fell into trances that enabled them to diagnose the spiritual standing of various leaders. This gift was also bestowed on a few of Bourne's female followers.[7] Once the Primitive Methodist Connexion was established, however, seers and prophecies gradually gave way to the exigencies of governing the societies. Bourne's mature view of the millennium was akin to the "self-help" perspective of Charles Grandison Finney; in the less adventist mood of the 1830s Bourne "scotched at" certain aspects of "flowery millenarian systems." The millennium will come, he told a congregation in Oldham, when Christianity dwells in all. It would only be "brought in by great labours to spread the work," and the faithful "would have to keep it in by like labours" and "sufferings."[8]

The Dynamics of English Revivalism

Once I was holding a Lovefeast and a Local Preacher said to me, 'Sir, We are very dull. If you will give me leave, I will go to the bottom of the Chapel, and set the House on fire all the way up!' . . . [He] began to Shout in prayer . . . and, as he said, he soon had the chapel on a flame—some praying for pardon and others for holiness.

—John Barritt, 1792[9]

The upsurge in revival activity during the 1790s and in the early nineteenth century can be seen as the response of people obliged to live on the verge of the unknown. Like its American counterpart, English revivalism of the period burned brightest in frontier territory. In England these frontiers were figurative, called into being chiefly by the industrial revolution. But there were other ways in which Englishmen were pushing their metaphorical boundaries forward into the untried and leaving the familiar behind. Both its defenders and its antagonists were coming to realize that sooner or later the eighteenth-century political and social order must yield to something new. This awareness induced a sense of uncertainty and flux, which was heightened by a generation of wartime living. Similarly, the irrational carnage of the French Revolution and the wars belied that portrait of human nature so confidently drawn during the Age of Reason. If the "new birth" teachings of Methodism held any promise for a better society in the future, then revivalism was certainly the preeminent means of hastening its arrival. As such, revivalism was a folkish mode of adapting to an altering environment. Essentially a popular movement, it opened a way for even the anonymous poor to enjoy a sense of personal esteem. Whatever the distinctions of wealth or status in English society, these were leveled by sin before the Lamb whose blood had been shed for all. Theoretically, anyone could be "convicted of sin," justified, and sanctified. Anyone might look forward to a day when the story of his spiritual odyssey would be told in a connexional magazine or circulated among the faithful in pamphlet form. Nor were the middle classes immune to the spirit of revivalism. "This blessed work is not confined to the poor," wrote a Methodist itinerant in 1814. "Lawyers, surgeons, and respectable tradesmen have kneeled down and implored mercy with the lowest classes of society."[10]

Generally speaking, Wesleyan revivalism reached its peak between 1793 and 1801. As might be expected, it flourished best in places like Cornwall and the West Riding, areas where Methodism was already firmly established. Only rarely did it penetrate within a seventy-five mile radius of London. The slackening of Wesleyan revival activity after the turn of the century partly reflected conference leaders' growing suspicion of "wildness." The fire of the spirit played havoc with that image of decorum which they were so eager to project. Anxious to ensure connexional solidarity, conference also distrusted the centrifugal tendencies of revivalism. Their experiences at Manchester and elsewhere indicated that revivals were not conducive to docility and that strenuous efforts to impose discipline were likely to breed schism. Yet revivalism did not by any means vanish from the Old Connexion between 1801 and 1821; for example, a wave of enthusiasm surged through a number of circuits during 1816 and 1817. Nevertheless, much of the fervor poured out among Wesleyans during the 1790s was diverted during the first two decades of the nineteenth century into Bible Christian, Primitive Methodist, and various other schismatic societies.

Without denying the influence of such circumstances as economic distress, political unrest, and reaction to events in France, it is also necessary to point out that revivalism operated according to an inner dynamic of its own. Unless certain forces within revivalism itself are taken into account, a fundamental key to its successes and failures is missing. The revivals of the period depended to a marked degree on four factors: the existence of a network of revivalist preachers, at the hub of which was William Bramwell; a desire on the part of society members for an outpouring of the spirit; a willingness among both preachers and people to allow innovations; and some means of communicating revival experiences from circuit to circuit. Injected into the unsettled general climate of the times, these internal elements produced phenomena that struck the editor of the *Arminian Magazine* as new and extraordinary.[11] Mysterious though their origins seemed to contemporaries, the outbursts of the 1790s were generated in situations that duplicated almost exactly those conditions which Finney later identified as likely to promote revivals.[12] This interplay between external events and the inner workings of Wesleyan revivalism was manifested during the major awakening of 1793–1794 in the West Riding of Yorkshire. It can likewise be observed operating over a thirty-year period in the town of Nottingham.

Revivalism in the West Riding, 1793–1795

The revival fires which swept the West Riding between 1793 and 1795 burned in an atmosphere of economic deprivation, political agitation, and government repression. Events in France conditioned attitudes in England. On 20 September 1792 French armies won a psychologically momentous victory at Valmy. The next day in Paris the National Convention assembled and abolished monarchy. With the beginning of the Year I of the French Republic the revolution entered a phase of rapid radicalization. Louis XVI was executed in January 1793; in February the Convention declared war on Great Britain. The Reign of Terror in France coincided with an unprecedented surge of millenarianism and an intensification of war fever in England. Domestic economic problems, already apparent by 1794, took on critical dimensions in 1795. Rain spoiled the harvest in 1793; drought lowered production in 1794; and the extremely long and hard winter of 1794–1795 ended with frost damage to the new wheat crop in March. With trade dislocated by the war and provisions in short supply, prices soared. During the summer and autumn of 1795 food riots were numerous, and claims for poor relief multiplied.

Despite the government's outlawing of Paine in 1792, its condemnation of his remarkably popular *Rights of Man*, and the political witch-hunts of early 1793, radical agitation flourished during the following summer. Late in the autumn English and Scottish delegates gathered in

Edinburgh for a National Convention whose proceedings, though not particularly immoderate, had enough Gallic borrowings to assure the arrest of its leaders. Between the dissolution of this assembly in December 1793 and May 1794 reformers urged a second Convention, this one to meet in England; exchanges between the London Corresponding Society and provincial groups reached new proportions; and sizable crowds thronged to open-air demonstrations, some of which were held in the West Riding. In May, Pitt launched an attack that either temporarily broke up many provincial organizations or drove them underground. Reformers in London, Sheffield, and Norwich were arrested, the papers of the London Corresponding Society were seized, a parliamentary Committee of Secrecy was appointed to scrutinize them, and habeas corpus was suspended. Hunger helped both the London and the provincial societies to emerge reinvigorated in 1795. In November, Pitt called for a Seditious Meetings Act and a Treasonable Practices Act; this provoked a final rash of radical activity that lasted until both measures became law in mid-December.

Broadly speaking, West Riding revivalism attained its highest pitch during the months in which the Reign of Terror was moving toward a climax but before economic pressures grew most severe. In nearly every circuit, revivals were underway well before the repressive measures of 1794 thwarted overt political agitation. Although in some places revivals may have gained momentum from the balking of reformist aspirations during the summer of 1794, it is significant that, except in Sheffield and Rotherham, there were no major awakenings in the immediate aftermath of the Two Acts. Furthermore, in both those circuits the increase of religious zeal late in 1795 and during the first months of 1796 can be largely credited to the influence of William Bramwell. It appears that what chiefly determined the force and the direction of West Riding revivals were various internal factors operating in a general atmosphere of heightened tensions and facilitated by the mechanism of contagion.[13]

The fountainhead of the "new" revivalism in the West Riding was Dewsbury, where Bramwell deliberately promoted a religious awakening in order to overcome lethargy and discord in the society. A firm believer in the effectiveness of female evangelism, Bramwell brought a handloom weaver from Macclesfield, Ann ("Praying Nanny") Cutler, to work in the circuit. He also introduced dawn prayer meetings for the purpose of begging heaven for a revival. The desired outpouring began in November 1792 and within three months produced a hundred new members. Stirred by what they saw at Dewsbury, visitors carried pentecostal excitement to Bradford, Birstall, Halifax, Otley, and Leeds.[14] The revival in

Birstall preceded Bramwell's appointment to the circuit in the summer of 1793. Enthusiasm was at first confined mostly to hearers and other non-members, the regular ticket holders being skeptical of its excesses. His biographer reckoned that, because Bramwell's colleague was opposed to the "confusion . . . frequent on these occasions," the leaders of the society were also antagonistic. On Christmas day, however, fifty persons were converted at a love feast, and all scruples evaporated. The entire circuit was soon alive with revivalism. As at Dewsbury, news of the proceedings drew the curious from afar and thus stimulated fervor elsewhere. The "flame" of zeal was still "glowing" at Easter, and Bramwell nurtured it with family visits and cottage prayer meetings that often lasted until nearly midnight. During his tenure in Birstall the circuit's membership doubled.[15]

Meanwhile, revivalism was sweeping other circuits in the West Riding. Halifax, Otley, Leeds, and Wakefield all experienced awakenings during the year between the Wesleyan conference of 1793 and that of 1794. Furthermore, these were marked by many of the same features observable in both Dewsbury and Birstall. Visitors fresh from a revival at Bradford communicated their enthusiasm to the "proverbially dead" society at Greetland. An itinerant deliberately encouraged the excitement thus aroused; an outburst of ardor duly occurred; and the Greetland members subsequently diffused its energy throughout Halifax circuit. Initially a "sanctification" revival limited to habitual chapelgoers, it quickly developed into a popular activity that converted even scoffers attracted by the noise of the meetings. The "almost indescribable work" won considerable notoriety among the wider public: a company of traveling players advertised an interlude, "the SECRET DISCLOSED, or the Itinerant Field Orator's Fanatical Gibberish, lately delivered in this town, accompanied by all their pious ejaculations, celestial groans, and angelic swoonings, &c., &c."[16] At Otley, Methodists troubled about their "lukewarm" state petitioned the Lord for a revival in the autumn of 1793. The preacher, Zechariah Yewdall, was supportive, and "the spirit of supplication was . . . poured out." It came as something of a surprise to both Yewdall and the faithful that the persons especially affected "seemed most unlikely," being in general "extremely illiterate and ignorant." Like the Halifax revival, the one in Otley circuit was characterized by "confusion" and "irregularity." The ability of women revivalists was again demonstrated—at Otley by Mary Barritt, an itinerant evangelist whose career was promoted by Bramwell.[17] Similarly, Ann Cutler was a "great blessing" at Leeds, where prayer meetings occasionally lasted throughout the night. Dewsbury Methodists had introduced revivalism to the Leeds brethren early in 1793, and their interest was furthered by reports circulated at the annual conference held in Leeds during the next summer. Not until February 1794, however, did the awakening gain significant momentum. By June it had "reached almost every society," and before the wave of enthusiasm crested, 2,000 members were added in Leeds circuit.[18] Revivalism in Wakefield circuit exhibited two familiar attributes: the desired outcome was readily achieved, and the resultant fervor was infectious. In a letter to Thomas Coke, James Wood told how the Wakefield people invoked the spirit for two hours at a watch night, then were gratified as twenty of the petitioners "cried out for mercy." As Wood noted, "this had a happy effect on others, and many were brought under deep convictions by hearing and seeing the happiness of those that had found peace."[19] As elsewhere, when the revival burst the circle of Methodists and became a popular movement, all semblance of propriety vanished.

Between 1793 and 1795 revivalism spread to other places in the West Riding—Keighley, Huddersfield, Rotherham, and Sheffield, for example. It also penetrated York and spilled over into the East and North Ridings. Alexander Mather's remarks about the Hull revival underline notable features also manifested in the West Riding. Interest was sparked by hearing about "hundreds and thousands" being converted in various Yorkshire circuits; the preachers were sympathetic; the members began to pray for an outpouring of the spirit. As was frequently the case, the setting for Hull's first "refreshing season" was a love feast. Mather was aware of the connection between mental attitudes and spiritual consequences. Despite the people's genuine yearning for a revival, their zeal was checked initially by "a too anxious attachment to decorum and order." Later, after this reserve had been broken down, the awakening prospered. Because some of the town's magistrates looked askance at clamorous late-night gatherings, the preachers attempted some "mild regulation." Mather was not the sort of man who challenged authority either in Wesleyan or in civil affairs. Still, he put himself on record as doubting the wisdom of trying to tame revivalism—pentecostal fires were quenched, and the work was impeded for as long as the restrictions were in effect. "Those who have seen extraordinary revivals of religion," Mather testified, "know that it is impossible on these occasions to prevent irregularities."[20]

To untangle the relationship between revivalism and radical agitation in the 1790s is difficult. Even if a comprehensive catalog of revival enthusiasts existed and could be compared name for name to a similar listing of the members of reform societies, the large and anonymous crowds who gravitated to both kinds of meetings would be unaccounted for. When a revival ceased to emphasize the sanctification of a few and became general, sizable numbers came with no real intention of undergoing religious conversion. In a sense a revival session was a lively social occasion. Curiosity and gregariousness doubtless attracted audiences to political demonstrations and revival meetings alike. One itinerant complained that people were far more zealous for the tumult of the meeting than for leading committed lives afterward. The same was probably true of great political gatherings. To make the problem of interpretation more complex, magistrates often assumed that any large assembly, but especially one held under the cover of darkness, was pregnant with danger and indiscriminately condemned them all. The usefulness of parallel timetables is limited. In 1794 a Lancashire preacher, Robert Miller, endeavored to revitalize Bolton circuit, where religion was in a "poor, cold state." On the day before Whitsun his field and street preaching, which had only recently met with opposition, suddenly fired a revival. Within nine days 120 converts were won. How much did this nine days' wonder owe to Pitt's assault on the radical societies in May? It is tempting to assume a cause-and-effect relationship. The same man, however, used identical tactics in Oldham circuit just after Parliament passed the repressive measures of 1795. He was attacked by a mob at Middleton, and not only was there no revival in the circuit, but also "some persons . . . who had formerly been professors of religion" now turned deist. "Previous to their apostasy they were first swallowed up in the vortex of politics, a dreadful snare" into which, Miller admitted, he himself "had once like to have been drawn." Perhaps the renegades from Methodism resented their preacher's aggressive loyalty to the government: his new "political creed" demanded that he "exhort all that I came near" to obey the law and to pray for the king and everyone "in authority."[21]

Comparing the waxing and waning of revivalism with the dynamics of radicalism in Sheffield suggests nothing very conclusive. Relatively free from aristocratic influence, the town had a tradition of democratic independence. The local Constitutional Society was composed chiefly of small manufacturers and workmen in the cutlery industry, and it employed a system of membership tickets and classlike divisions modeled on that of the Methodists. In fact, a "number of Methodists" were reportedly among the organization's 2,000 adherents, while Thomas Cooper, who itinerated in Sheffield from 1792 to 1794, was sufficiently involved in reform agitation for Bunting to allude later to the "odium" attached to his name "on account of his political notoriety when stationed here." Firmly established in 1792, the Sheffield society remained vigorous despite anti-Jacobin pressures during the early months of 1793. In April its members passed a series of resolutions condemning the war, and in May they collected 10,000 signatures for a petition urging manhood suffrage. Later in 1793, Sheffield sent a delegate to the National Convention in Edinburgh and a letter to London criticizing the apathy of its Corresponding Society. If there was a hiatus in Sheffield's radical activity, it came between the summer of 1794 and August 1795, when 10,000 people took part in an open-air meeting on Crooke's Moor. Economic distress no doubt spurred both political unrest and revivalism. By the autumn of 1793 many were jobless or had had their incomes halved by unemployment; by 1795 more were going hungry because of food shortages and spiraling prices. Although Cooper eventually "bid adieu to political inshantments [*sic*]," in 1794, while still under their spell, he led prayers for a revival. The awakening began in a mild way during March, midway between two massive political demonstrations in February and in April; the "scenes of great power," however, were deferred until June—after the town's leading reformers had either been seized or had evaded arrest. Then, according to Cooper's colleague, more than a hundred "found peace" in three days, and many more were "alarmed with a sense of their danger." On one occasion some twenty constables were sent to investigate the uproar caused by the "madness of the Methodists."[22] By August the revival had abated, matching the current slower pace of organized reform. Having drunk a little of enthusiasm and thirsting for more, Sheffield Methodists begged the conference of 1795 to assign Bramwell to their circuit. When he arrived, the virtuoso revivalist "found the town in a turmoil of political agitation and religion at a very low ebb." After a disappointing lull the "work" recommenced, this time on a much grander scale. Within a year 1,250 new members joined the society, and still "the revival continued to advance." Bramwell knew that mere emotionalism would not sustain an awakening for any length of time, and he instituted a carefully designed auxiliary program to keep it alive: local preachers and other members were put to work praying with likely converts; "select bands" petitioned for an increase of the spirit; Bramwell himself visited eight or ten families daily and in his sermons constantly reiterated the promise of instant salvation.[23] Meanwhile, during the autumn of 1796 emissaries from Sheffield carried news of their soul-stirring experiences to Nottingham and so catalyzed the first major revival in that circuit. Two years later, after a final "pentecostal season" at Sheffield, Bramwell himself was appointed to Nottingham.

Wesleyan Revivalism in Nottingham, 1796–1825

Although the population of Nottingham doubled between 1779 and
1821, its boundaries remained virtually unchanged. By the turn of the
century land within the town limits was scarce and expensive, and more
and more people were being forced to live in already crowded slums.
Some migrated to nearby villages ill prepared to absorb their influx. The
dominant industry in the district was hosiery knitting, an occupation
conducted in cottages and small workshops. In 1808 the manufacture of
bobbin-net lace was introduced, and by 1812 well over half of the
employed population of Nottingham was engaged in making either
hosiery or lace.[24] Between 1790 and 1820 the wages of framework knitters declined sharply. During the late eighteenth century even poorly
paid workers were averaging 10s. to 12s. a week, while the most skilled
earned up to 30s.; in 1820 two-needle workers, the most numerous in the
trade, averaged a mere 5s. weekly.[25] Nottingham had a reputation for
turbulence and for radicalism. Food riots, election riots, recruiting riots,
and riots at the assizes were commonplace. During the 1790s the town
was regarded as a center of Jacobinism; beginning in 1811 Luddism
thrived in the neighborhood. After Waterloo neither Major Cartwright
nor Oliver the Spy overlooked Nottingham's possibilities.

At the beginning of the nineteenth century provision for worship
was inadequate both in Nottingham and in the outlying villages. In 1805
St. Mary's, the largest of the town's parishes, had 20,000 inhabitants and
church accommodation for only 2,500. The vitality of Old Dissent had
faded during the eighteenth century: the Quakers and the Independents
had gradually lost members—the latter claimed only forty-one followers
in 1794—while the Presbyterians had drifted into Unitarianism. The narrowness of their salvation theology did not invite mass support for the
Particular Baptists, who in any case were well on their way to becoming
a coterie of aldermen and future Anti-Corn Law Leaguers. In 1800 the
most popular groups outside the established church were the Methodists
and Dan Taylor's New Connexion of General Baptists. Alone among the
Nonconformists they attempted to evangelize the adjacent villages. But
later both the Methodists and the General Baptists temporarily lost some
of their zeal, and when the Ranters arrived in 1815, the missionary field
was theirs.[26]

Methodism had figured in Nottingham life since the third quarter of
the eighteenth century. John Wesley's auditors there had been mostly
lower class, mainly stockingers. When Thomas Tatham joined the society in 1783, it was "not only very small, but very poor and despised."
His parents had protested vigorously, "especially so, as I was about to

commence business." They need not have worried. The fortunes of Nottingham Methodists soon began to rise. By the end of the century Tatham was a prosperous wholesale grocer. Providence had likewise enriched the Kilhamite Robert Hall, a local cotton spinner turned factory owner. In 1815, the year the Primitive Methodists opened their mission in the Broad Marsh slum, pew rents at the Wesleyan chapel brought in £252. The social prestige of chapelgoing had also been enhanced since Wesley's day. About 1802 "several respectable families" forsook the "dull and lifeless" worship at St. Mary's to attend William Edward Miller's more inspiring sermons at Halifax Place Chapel.[27] The days of field preaching were still remembered when the Primitive Methodists opened their Nottingham campaign. Wesley himself had preached in the marketplace as late as 1779, even though the Methodist Tabernacle had been certified for worship fifteen years before. Revivals, too, were a familiar if more recent experience. Except for a brief flurry at Blidworth in 1790, the circuit enjoyed no "extraordinary workings" of the Spirit until late in 1796. Despite its proximity, Nottingham escaped the revival fever that swept the West Riding in 1793–1794. "Ever since I knew them," Mary Strickland Tatham could lament, "this people have been . . . formal, barren, and dead." Their "opposition" and "coldness" had enervated whatever religious passion she had had when she came from Leeds to marry Tatham in 1787.[28]

When a revival did come to Nottingham, its advent coincided with the waning effectiveness of organized radicalism, a deterioration marked by the imminent collapse of the London Corresponding Society. Whether the "chiliasm of despair" helped to account for the increase of 30 percent in society membership during 1796–1797 cannot be determined.[29] What is certain is that some pillars of the local society yearned for a healing awakening. After Wesley's death Nottingham Methodism suffered acutely from disputes about the administration of communion by preachers and, even more, from dissension over lay involvement in connexional government. So much strife led to spiritual torpor. For the first time in its history the circuit's membership decreased. At a love feast in the autumn of 1796 a Derbyshire woman "arose and said, 'the Lord have mercy upon you, for you are the deadest souls I ever met with in all my life'." Only five leaders bothered to attend the October meeting, which instituted weekly sessions to pray for a visitation of the Holy Ghost. Unless "some method [can] be devised to keep the leaders together," worried one, "the society must inevitably be scattered."[30] The Lord did not delay. When Henry Taylor preached in Basford on 9 October, the Tathams marveled at his account of the revival in Sheffield circuit. A few days later they heard a trumpeter in the Dragoon Guards bear witness to his conversion in Sheffield. Mrs. Tatham confided in her diary, "I felt my heart glow within me; it seemed as if the kingdom of God were coming nigh to Nottingham also; at least I desired it might be so." And it was so. On the following Sunday Tatham himself testified at a love feast at Carlton, and the work commenced. On Monday night, after he exhorted any who "felt the love of God" to proclaim it, the Nottingham leaders' meeting resounded with weeping, confessions, and praise. The next Sunday, overwhelmed with a divine vision promising welcome and forgiveness to even the most vile sinners, Tatham interrupted the morning service to communicate the good news. After that, the revival swiftly gained momentum. Within two months the society was infused with zeal, sixty new tickets were distributed, and the members were "cemented together into one spirit."[31]

Besides pointing to the fact that principal Nottingham Methodists were predisposed to revival and thus were susceptible to influences emanating from Sheffield, the Tathams' journals yield a second insight into this awakening. Initially, it seemed a suspicious novelty to some of the faithful. Both conviction of sin and entire sanctification were experienced—"the Lord is manifestly pouring out his spirit upon professors in particular and on the world in general." Revivals that involved converting "the world in general" were frequently tumultuous, a dubious feature in the eyes of a generation of Methodists accustomed to orderly worship and tranquil classes. Once freed from their inhibitions, however, "professors" too were liable to be engulfed in the flood of emotions unleashed at revival meetings. At Nottingham the prejudice against extravagance was dispelled when Henry Longden movingly described how his own doubts were overcome by the evident good work accomplished in Sheffield. Even to Mary Tatham, God's "new" ways seemed "unaccountable." She believed that "most professors of the present day" would "say with the disciples of old, 'We never saw it on this fashion'."[32] Though "strange," the innovation proved "effectual," and once accepted, could be repeated. Three times within the next thirty years the local Wesleyan circuit was infused with holy energy.

The role of preachers was critical. Except in 1796, Nottingham Wesleyans never succumbed to a revival in their absence. The master orchestrator of "powerful seasons," William Bramwell, began a three-year ministry there in 1798. It augured well for revivalism when the conference of 1799 appointed a like-minded itinerant, John Pipe, to assist him. Under their leadership a second outpouring took place. Earlier Bramwell had played mentor to William Edward Miller, who now succeeded him at Nottingham. Also adept at "alarming" sinners and backsliders, Miller brought yet another pentecost to the circuit. In the half decade between

Bramwell's arrival and Miller's departure membership jumped from 1,100 to 2,672. A generation later, during the autumn of 1825, the vigorous salvational preaching of a fourth evangelist, John Smith, triggered a spiritual renaissance that rivaled even the upsurge at the beginning of the century.[33] Apparently, the itinerants' predilections could also work to squelch an awakening. At least twice when the contagion of enthusiasm was abroad, the local Wesleyan circuit remained immune. Despite the ubiquity of revivalism in 1793–1794, Nottingham was not quickened. The superintendent at the time was William Thom, a strenuous advocate of democratic principles—at least as far as Methodist government was concerned. During his two-year tenure the rate of recruitment in Nottingham first slowed markedly, then stagnated. Perhaps Thom was merely indifferent toward winning souls; it may be, however, that his influence momentarily diverted Methodist energies into alternative channels—Kilhamite agitation, Jacobin affairs, or both. The other notable instance in which a revival was deflected from the Wesleyan circuit occurred in 1816–1818, when Nottingham was prompt to respond to the Ranter invitation. The failure of the Wesleyan itinerants to seize this occasion let the Primitive Methodists reap a harvest of hundreds.

The history of Methodist revivalism in Nottingham between 1796 and 1825 reveals that the optimum climate for a religious awakening was attained when four conditions were fulfilled simultaneously: at least one prorevival preacher was ministering in the district; troubled lay leaders, supposing the society to be in jeopardy, were seeking a panacea; most of the ticket holders were amenable; the wider public was suffering anxiety, frustration, or discontent. When only three of these prerequisites were met, a revival was still likely; with just two, it remained possible. If mass conversions were to occur, the last, a general atmosphere of disquiet, was crucial. In Nottingham, as in the West Riding, economic distress was an especially powerful goad to revivalism. For example, the Bramwell-Pipe revival came to its climax in 1800, a year of dearth and extreme privation. The high cost of food brought on another of the town's recurrent bread riots, but, claimed Pipe, "the minds of the people were borne above all," and no Methodists took part in the disturbance. This renewal of fervor was not confined to the poor: "a great concern for religion manifested itself among all ranks." Not only were "many . . . brought out of darkness," but also "several deists renounced their infidelity."[34] There was plenty of anguish but no significant resurgence of Methodism during the Luddite years; however, unemployment, low wages, and high prices unquestionably lent impetus to the Primitive Methodist revival that began to spread through the East Midlands in 1816. The last great revival of the period, the Wesleyan outpouring of 1825–1827, broke forth when, after a season of "unnatural" prosperity arising from a boom in the lace trade, "normalcy" returned "with an awful momentum."[35]

If the revivals in the West Riding and in Nottingham were typical —and there is no reason to suppose otherwise—then the two sets of phenomena can serve as a basis for some generalizations about Wesleyan enthusiasm in England during the late eighteenth and early nineteenth centuries. In the first place, awakenings were most likely to flourish in an atmosphere of tension. This sense of unease might be general, caused by such factors as political ferment, repression, war, and economic disloca-tion; it might be worry about the state of a particular society or circuit; it was often related to both national and parochial conditions, to secular as well as to purely Methodist concerns. Second, the spread of revivalism was largely contingent on the communication of experiences from one place to another. This could happen in a variety of ways: letters ex-changed between preachers or published in Methodist magazines, the periodic reassigning of itinerants, members' travels to other locales, the peregrinations of evangelists like Ann Cutler and Mary Barritt. Third, revivalism could be self-induced when Methodists desired an awakening and were prepared to accept its probable consequences—noise and com-motion. Fourth, the attitude of the circuit preachers conditioned the rise or decline of revivalism among the societies in their charge. Fifth, other circumstances being favorable, a gifted salvation preacher was a potent stimulus to pentecostal excitement. A single itinerant, William Bramwell, figured either directly or indirectly in an extraordinary number of revivals. Bramwell's success derived not only from his efficacy in the pulpit, but even more perhaps from his ability to enhance people's feel-ings of self-worth through home visits and shared responsibility.[36] Fi-nally, the link between radicalism and revivalism is obscure. In general, the economic, political, and emotional climate of the period was con-genial to both movements.[37] When revivalism did fall out of step with popular agitation, the main reason seems to have been that, for reasons entirely intrinsic to Methodism, the inner dynamic of religious en-thusiasm had ceased to operate effectively. The key to the fluctuating fortunes of revivalism lay, above all, within revivalism itself. Taken together these statements constitute a model to which Ranter revivalism also conformed during the first decade of Primitive Methodist history. But before turning to the early years of Primitive Methodism, it is necessary to look at two forces that helped bring the connexion to birth —American camp meetings and the antirevivalistic measures adopted by the English Wesleyan conference after the turn of the century.

The Impact of America: Camp Meetings and "Crazy" Dow

Dow! Dow! why he is a crazy man.
—An American Methodist

Alas! shame! shame! Shall it be published in the
streets of London and Dublin that Methodist
preachers in America have so departed from Wesley
and from their own discipline as to *countenance and
bid God speed such a man as Mr. Dow.*
—Nicholas Snethen, 1805[38]

The vivid descriptions of frontier revivals published in
the Wesleyan *Magazine* "paved the way" for camp meetings in England,
but it was the self-appointed emissary from America, Lorenzo Dow, who
became the "chief means of fully introducing them" to the Methodists of
the West Midlands. A Connecticut Yankee and would-be Methodist
preacher, Dow was so intractable and eccentric that the American conference refused to authorize him as an itinerant. Undaunted, he spent
most of a lifetime traveling across the nation and winning souls as well as
notoriety. Dow was both a millenarian and a republican. In fact, to him
politics and the coming apocalypse were inseparable. "May not the
'Seventh Trumpet' now be sounding, and the 'seven last plagues' be pouring out? . . . Are not all the governments of the old world tyrannical and
repugnant to the 'Law of Nature'?" he demanded in a tract of 1812. A
"JUST JUDGE," he predicted, will "overwhelm the oppressors with an ever-
lasting destruction." Two years later he was *"prophesying and preaching*
the *destruction* of London *(the Mother of Harlots, the Seat of the Beast,
etc.)."*[39]

Dow undertook his first foray across the Atlantic in 1799. Without a
passport and despite a warning that he was a "devilish fool for going . . .
to that disturbed island," the wandering "cosmopolite" made his way to
Ireland. There he held street meetings, alarmed the magistrates, evaded a
press-gang, and made a few converts. From Ireland Dow went to London
where, fearful that he would excite pandemonium, Coke threatened to
"write to Lord Castlereagh to inform him who and what you are, [and]
that we disown you, . . . then you'll be arrested and committed to
prison." Bearded, ragged, and dirty, the prophet returned to Ireland and
eventually embarked for the United States in 1801. Before leaving
Dublin, however, he distributed handbills "among the quality and decent

kind of people"—the lord lieutenant received two copies, the law courts and the stock exchange one each—announcing that "the judgments of God [were] hanging over the place."[40]

Back in America, Dow toured the southern and western states, witnessing and taking part in camp meetings. The frontier revival that had begun in Kentucky at the turn of the century soon swept across a triangle of territory that stretched from western New England to Georgia and across the Appalachians deep into the Ohio valley. American correspondents wrote to Coke telling of four- and five-day camp meetings at which thousands gathered for prayer and preaching in wilderness clearings. Published in the *Methodist Magazine*, their letters fired the imagination of Bourne and the Harriseahead colliers, who eagerly talked of holding a camp meeting on nearby Mow Cop.[41] Although never recognized as an official institution of the American church, camp meetings were for more than a quarter of a century among the most powerful vehicles of frontier Methodism. Francis Asbury once called them the "battle axe and weapon of war" which "will break down the walls of wickedness [and the] forts of hell."[42] Initially interdenominational occasions, camp meetings were most successfully exploited by the Methodists, whose Arminian theology was especially well adapted to revivalism. They reflected the vigor and rawness of frontier life. Rich and poor, black and white, farmer and townsman often came out of curiosity or to enjoy what was, after all, one of few major social events. Both the pious and the scoffers were afflicted with the "falling exercise" and its variations, the "barking exercise," the "laughing exercise," and the "jerks." Usually tents were pitched around a central area in which several preaching stands were erected and a mourners' precinct marked out. Sometimes the sessions lasted until dawn—impassioned exhortations seemed even more dramatic in the flickering light of bonfires and torches. Drunks and rowdies generally disrupted what was already a scene of apparent confusion, and fornication under cover of night was not unknown. But people "got religion" at camp meetings. In 1801, 300 were "struck down" at Cane Ridge, 800 at Indian Creek, and 250 at Stony Creek.[43]

Fresh from these experiences, Dow made another journey to Britain in 1805. Letters of disapprobation preceded him, but they were hardly necessary. Remembering his earlier exploits and leery of anyone who came to peddle the American brand of revivalism, the English conference was not about to sanction this second tour. Dow remained in England until 1807, preaching without a license because his democratic conscience forbade taking an oath of loyalty to the Crown. He was well received in Lancashire and Cheshire, where he ignited revivals among the Independent Methodists. The object of his mission was "to revive street and field meetings *and to introduce Camp Meetings.*" Early in April 1807 he preached at Harriseahead, averring that "for a considerable time in America as much good had been done, and as many souls brought to God at the camp meetings as at all other meetings put together." Bourne was impressed by the "lively and wonderful descriptions of the work which he gave both in the pulpit and in conversation." From Dow he purchased a revival hymnal and some literature on camp meetings. A few weeks later a flag was run up on Mow Cop to guide strangers to the first of many English camp meetings.[44]

In his history of the connexion Hugh Bourne asserted that the origin of Primitive Methodism could not be understood apart from camp meetings and the circumstances that led to them. George Herod, an early Primitive Methodist itinerant, devoted a quarter of his *Biographical Sketches* to Lorenzo Dow. According to Herod, Dow's significance was fourfold. His visit in 1807 both precipitated the decision to hold the first Mow Cop meeting and furnished widespread publicity for it. By printing and selling S. J. Jennings's *A Defense of Camp Meetings* and a similar tract of his own composition Dow supplied both an apologia and a methodology for English camp meetings. Through Dow's instrumentality Paul Johnson, a Dublin physician, participated in a Staffordshire camp meeting in August 1807, "and his visit was a means of bringing the Bournes to a determination to stand by the . . . system, deeming it now to be providential." Finally, Dow facilitated the extension of Ranterism by circulating a *Collection of Spiritual Songs Used in the Great Revival at the Camp Meetings in America,* which he had compiled and had published in Georgia. From the English edition, printed in Liverpool in 1806, Bourne took many selections and incorporated them into the first Primitive Methodist hymnal. Herod, who spoke from long experience as an evangelist, claimed that no one could deny the book's "usefulness in arresting attention, exciting curiosity, awakening sinners, and comforting mourners and believers."[45] Neither can one deny the importance to Primitive Methodism of American frontier revivals or of their strange apostle, Lorenzo Dow.

Conference Wrestles with the Spirit

Many of the preachers of the present day, . . . having become ashamed of the conduct of their brethren who have encouraged noisy meetings, are led to deprive

their people of their Christian liberty and . . . to
check all extravagances . . . whenever they perceive
them beginning to break out.
                                        —Joseph Nightingale, 1807[46]

The Wesleyan revivals of the 1790s provoked a debate
among the preachers which ended in a series of conference minutes
designed to reestablish decorum and to reinforce discipline in the
societies. The tumult characteristic of the new revivalism confronted
Wesleyan leaders with a dilemma. None wanted to stifle the growth of
the connexion or to impede genuine conversions; on the other hand,
revival frenzy did not necessarily entail lasting religious commitment.
During the revival of 1794 the superintendent at Stockport worried
about the "wild fire" that had begun to show itself at love feasts: "My
mind was much grieved at the noise and disorderly behaviour of some
well-meaning persons, . . . who, with their loud 'Amens,' knocking, &c.,
greatly disturbed the congregation." Another itinerant suspected "more
zeal than discretion" among the devotees of revivalism. A third, who acknowledged that violent agitation of the body and outcries might be "un-
avoidable" when "a great number are suddenly awakened at one time
and place," nevertheless warned that "errors" were beginning to creep
into revivalism.[47] According to their superintendent at Manchester, the
habitués of the Band Room were culpable of numerous such deviations:
they clapped their hands, banged on the benches, spoke out spon-
taneously, prayed clamorously, wandered about interrupting others'
devotions and treading on clothes and feet, and generally offended that
deity who "has declared himself the God of order, not of confusion."[48]
Besides disrupting the worship of the more staid members and encourag-
ing ephemeral conversions, revivals won for Methodists an unwelcome
reputation for immoderate behavior. To some ministers, however, the
most distressing consequence of revivalism was its tendency to undermine Wesleyan discipline. In their ardor to save souls, revivalists often
allowed all comers to participate in meetings that were supposed to be
open only to ticketed members. In addition, the system of cottage prayer
meetings fostered by Bramwell and others was both difficult to supervise
and vulnerable to attack from the enemies of Methodism. It was hard to
disprove that those who gathered in private houses were zealous for
salvation and not for sedition. Sometimes, when preachers attempted to
enforce discipline, the lay leaders and the people revolted. Occasionally,
their fellow itinerants balked. Referring to the Kirkgate Screamers, a circuit preacher stationed in Leeds warned, "If a revivalist must be supported by one preacher and two leaders, in opposition to three preachers

and fifty leaders, when he tramples the rules of our society under his feet, and that merely because he is a revivalist, revivalism will soon ruin Methodism."[49]

As might be expected, William Bramwell was an outspoken champion of the revivalists' side of the controversy. In 1796 he issued a circular calling for a renewal of primitive fervor. He was not, Bramwell insisted, a supporter of "what is called RANTERISM or WILDNESS," or of "noise" apart from the influence of the Holy Spirit, but he decried "lukewarmness" and "dead formality." "Beset with opposition from all the powers of hell" (probably personified by his colleagues), Bramwell in 1803 got involved with the Kirkgate schism at Leeds. After his venture with the Screamers ended, he continued to lament the capitulation of Wesleyan Methodism to worldliness and sterile propriety: "The rich, the mighty, sit upon their seats and too frequently usurp improper authority, which damps too much the living flame amongst the simple. Young preachers seek to gain the respect of such persons, to their own destruction."[50]

Wesleyan conference legislation aimed at purging the societies of revivalistic excesses began to appear in 1800. Three years later itinerants were told that people without tickets should not be allowed to attend love feasts and band meetings; furthermore, these gatherings were not to be held without the sanction of the circuit superintendent. Irregular evangelism on the part of women, a potent stimulant of revivals, was severely restricted. "In general," declared the minute of 1803, women ought not to "be permitted to preach among us." A few months after Dow advertised their merits at Harriseahead, the conference of 1807 forbade "what are called camp meetings." The same conference directed that no unauthorized person "from America or elsewhere" be allowed to preach among English Wesleyans.[51] When enforced by conscientious itinerants, this series of minutes greatly weakened revivalism. In the Potteries, where, thrilled by their discovery of the American camp meeting, Bourne and his followers were yearning to reclaim the ungodly, these regulations ultimately produced schism. A Kilhamite historian later chastised the Old Connexion for compelling the camp-meeting enthusiasts "either to cease from attempting to do good, *or to form a separate denomination.*"[52] Like Jacob, conference seemed to have wrestled with the Spirit of God and won. To some, however, it seemed as if the new Israel that emerged from the struggle to journey in divine company was not the Wesleyan, but the Primitive Methodist Connexion.

The "new" revivalism that eventually helped to shatter the unity of the Old Connexion was born in the charged atmosphere of war, economic distress, radical agitation, and government repression. Like its sibling, millenarianism, revivalism fed on the prevalent sense of disquiet and perplexity induced by the uncertainties of the time. The novel element in this new variety of revivalism was its proclivity for overrunning the limits of ticketed membership and society discipline. No mere gentle awakening of souls, this was "wildfire" loosed among the masses. That it burned so lustily owed much to the unsettled climate of the period. What is not so often recognized is that revivalism also operated according to a discernible inner law. Although frequently ignored by present-day social historians, this pattern was perceived and used as a tool to generate revivals by the nineteenth-century American preacher Charles Grandison Finney. Beginning in 1839 extracts from Finney's *Lectures on Revivals of Religion* also served as a handbook for evangelists in the Primitive Methodist Connexion. The energy of the new revivalism was not to be contained within the confines set during the first decade of the nineteenth century by the Wesleyan conference. The most important schism bred by revivalism and the official Wesleyan response to its "extravagances" was the Primitive Methodist Connexion. Chafing under conference restrictions, stirred by Lorenzo Dow and his reports of frontier revivals, and, finally, expelled from the Old Connexion, the Camp-Meeting Methodists of the Potteries would carry revivalism forward under a new banner, that of Primitive Methodism.

Part 2

The Development of Primitive Methodism

Three

The Formative Years

Hugh Bourne was convinced that the Primitive Methodist Connexion "was begun undesigned of man." If its origins owed nothing to human contrivance, he reasoned, then surely God had called the new sect into being. An avowed purpose of his *History of the Primitive Methodists* was "to show the movements of Divine Providence in raising up the . . . Connexion."[1] Bourne's argument hinged on an undeclared theistic premise, but he was right in asserting that no one had deliberately set out to provoke a schism or to found a separate body. Looking solely at human factors, one can see in Primitive Methodism the fairly predictable outcome of unresolved problems within the Old Connexion. Eighteenth-century Methodism had harbored a potential dichotomy: John Wesley had created what was essentially a lay movement, but he had governed it like a benevolent despot. Tolerated so long as Wesley dominated the connexion, this improbable joining of democracy and autocracy came unglued in the hands of his successors. During the troubled quarter-century after Wesley died, social, political, and organizational pressures induced conference to strengthen its inherited authority at the expense of local autonomy. Its efforts to transform the itinerancy into a professional ministry with enhanced power and prestige diminished the importance of local preachers. Imposed on a community that had always prized personal religious experience and dedicated lay involvement over a tightly knit central administration, this policy was bound to excite some opposition. At a time when democratic impulses were stirring society generally, dissatisfied murmurings could easily develop into open revolt. Linked to this conflict at the heart of Wesleyan Methodism were the related questions of revivalism and society discipline. Although camp meetings were the immediate cause of division in the Potteries, much more was at issue. Like most schisms of the period, Primitive Methodism sprang out of a growing incompatibil-

ity between conference authority and local self-government as well as between clericalism and lay initiative.

The likelihood of a split along "primitive" lines became greater as an
influential segment of the Wesleyan population, mostly town dwellers,
grew prosperous and entered the ranks of "respectable folk." Contemporary critics of "modern" Methodism pointed accusingly at such signs
of deterioration as expensive chapels, fashionable clothes, and attachment to wealth and social position. These supposed earmarks of spiritual
decline lay beyond the economic reach of most early Primitive Methodists, who, when they esteemed material poverty in the name of
spiritual riches, made a virtue of their necessity. No doubt the stockingers, farm laborers, and miners who flocked to camp meetings found
some satisfaction in hearing the "new" worldliness denounced. To many
hearers, the summons to recover "primitive" holiness may also have suggested a way of return to an era wistfully remembered as simpler and
happier. The rapid expansion of Wesleyan membership during the war
years overtaxed both the human and the financial resources of the connexion. More and more itinerants neglected rural societies to serve those
in the towns. The personalized "conversation ministry" advocated by
Bourne and practiced by many Ranter missionaries filled a need that
Wesleyan circuit preachers were increasingly unable or unwilling to
meet. Moreover, in times of economic distress poor Methodists often
could not afford to pay the ticket money exacted in most Wesleyan
societies. Some of them turned to Primitive Methodism, which at least
during its formative period required little or no financial support from its
converts.

Finally, the fires of revivalism which raced through much of England during the 1790s and in the opening years of the new century could
not be contained within Wesleyan Methodism. Had conference been less
concerned with decorum and society discipline, had the itinerancy been
less hostile to the idea of open-air preaching and camp meetings, Bourne
and his fellow laborers might have been satisfied to carry on their
evangelism within the Old Connexion. But, confronted with the choice
between maintaining their membership in the Wesleyan society and what
seemed to them a greater good—fulfilling a divine commission to spread
the gospel through camp meetings—Bourne and his band of revivalists
submitted to expulsion. Though by no means the only constituent of the
schism in the Potteries, open-air revivalism was especially important
both because it was the immediate cause of rupture with the parent
denomination and because, along with an emphasis on lay participation,
it would shape the distinctive character of early Primitive Methodism.

Genesis: Camp-Meeting Methodists and Clowesites

Our chapels were the coal-pits, or any other place;
and in our conversation way we preached the Gospel
to all, good or bad, rough or smooth.
—Hugh Bourne, 1801[2]

Primitive Methodism came into being as a separate con-
nexion on 26 July 1811 in the Tunstall kitchen of Joseph Smith, an elderly
ex-Wesleyan; in February 1812 the young community adopted the name
Society of the Primitive Methodists. Although it is anachronistic to
speak of Primitive Methodism before 1811, when the Camp-Meeting
Methodists joined forces with the followers of William Clowes, the
movement began as early as the turn of the century with the homely
evangelism of Hugh Bourne.

Hugh Bourne and the Harriseahead Revival, 1801–1803

Hugh Bourne was almost forty when he undertook the leadership of the
newly founded Primitive Methodist Connexion. Until then his life was
one in which the forces of continuity were far greater than those of
change; its setting was rural, traditional, and relatively circumscribed.
Bourne was born in 1772 on a farm in the same Staffordshire parish of
Stoke-on-Trent where his forebears had lived for generations. When he
was sixteen, the family moved to Bemersley, a larger farm in the nearby
parish of Norton-in-the-Moors. Like his father and grandfather before
him, Bourne learned the wheelwright's trade. Until he joined a Wesleyan
Methodist class at Ridgeway in 1799, he regularly attended Sunday services in the established church at Biddulph, about a three miles' journey
from Bemersley. Before his religious concerns took him to Leeds in 1808
and to London in 1810, Bourne seems to have had little direct experience
of the world beyond the potteries, mines, and moorland farms of north
Staffordshire. Nor did he show any overt interest in the momentous
events which were then shaking the foundations of English society.
Bourne was by no means an unlettered yokel. After learning from his
mother to read and write, he studied for a time with a self-taught scholar,
then attended a Church of England endowed school at Bucknall. When
he was about twelve, he left school, first to work on the farm and to
learn his father's trade, later to live and travel as apprentice to his uncle,

a millwright and engineer. His formal schooling ended, Bourne launched himself on a lifelong program of self-education that included Greek, Latin, French, and Hebrew as well as natural philosophy. But much of his study was given over to religious writings. Although he read books by Anglican divines and seventeenth-century Puritan authors, his ideas were influenced most by Quaker and Methodist works. H. B. Kendall, author of the most comprehensive history of Primitive Methodism, ascribed even Bourne's conversion to books: "By reading, and by reading alone, he was led into the light. . . . His conversion was not directly traceable to any living personal influence whatever. . . . All that men did for him was to lend him the books for which he asked."[3]

Bourne was established in his own business when, early in 1800, an investment in timber took him to the neighborhood of Harriseahead, a colliery village near the Cheshire border. He was twenty-eight, a serious and shy bachelor, who by his own admission was "so bashful as is seldom seen." As a recently enrolled Methodist, he was disturbed because Harriseahead "had no means of grace." Its inhabitants, he noted, "appeared to be entirely destitute of religion and much addicted to un-godliness."[4] A series of timbering and carpentering jobs kept Bourne in the vicinity of Harriseahead for some time. Cut off from the fellowship of a Methodist class, he overcame his usual reticence and gave an account of his conversion to the village blacksmith, Thomas Maxfield. Maxfield had a crony, Daniel Shubotham, a cousin of Bourne's, who worked as a miner at a local colliery. Shubotham vacillated between a vague anxiety about his immortal soul and a distinct pleasure in worldly pursuits. Having learned from the smith that Bourne, though a stranger to the lively delights of cardplaying, drinking, and fighting, was "a safe mon," Shubotham sought him out. Encouraged by his talks with Bourne, the miner was converted on Christmas day, 1800. Shubotham now blazed with an exuberant if erratic zeal to evangelize others. He was a gregarious extrovert whose self-confidence amply compensated for Bourne's diffidence. Together they recruited a second newly converted collier, Matthias Bayley, and set out to spread the faith. Their crusade did not lack publicity, for Shubotham's changed conduct was the talk of both village and colliery. By visiting with prospective converts the trio soon won over four coal miners. The new recruits "were famous talkers for the Lord—they . . . set forth the gospel in conversation, without ceremony, . . . and the converting work opened out among the Kids-grove colliers, and on a large part of Mow Cop God was glorified and sinners were saved."[5]

Cottage prayer meetings were instituted early in 1801. Although

Bourne asked one of the Wesleyan itinerants stationed at Burslem to assign an experienced person to conduct the meetings, none was provided. As a result the Harriseahead prayer sessions quickly developed a style of their own. Chief among their departures from the recommended Wesleyan pattern were the absence of a single leader and a great deal of noise and confusion. After the initial hymn and an opening prayer, a second hymn was sung. Then someone would begin to pray and "in less than a quarter of a minute another would dash off, and so on, untill [*sic*] the whole were exercising with all their faith, hearts, and minds, and with all their voices, and the noise might be heard to a considerable distance." As Bourne saw matters, the innovations were a tremendous improvement. Because they vastly expanded the opportunities for participation, the Harriseahead meetings were livelier than their Wesleyan counterparts and less wearisome for neophytes. The clamor itself was an asset, for even nervous beginners might venture to pray aloud with little fear of being overheard. Weeknight prayer meetings were deliberately kept short so that the workers would be fit for their next day's labor, and all who took part were required to be "correct in their conduct and diligent in the duties of their callings."[6]

Not yet aware that "modern" Wesleyans were "almost entirely out of the converting work," Bourne was eager to acquaint his followers with organized Methodism. The closest Wesleyan class was in Cheshire at the home of Joseph Pointon, about a mile and a half from Harriseahead. Members of Bourne's group visited Pointon's class and began to attend the fortnightly preaching there. Meanwhile, the revival was gaining momentum, and his converts were urging Bourne to preach. He was characteristically reluctant, but finally agreed to do so on a Sunday when no Wesleyan preacher was scheduled for Pointon's cottage. Because the audience was so large, Bourne had to hold forth in an adjacent field, a practice often followed by Wesley, but no longer favored by Wesleyan itinerants. His face shielded by his hand, Bourne floundered until he thought to talk "as if speaking to one person." He ended the sermon with an account of his own conversion and prepared to announce a closing hymn. To his surprise, "the brethren and sisters present opened out a course of mighty prayer and labour with occasional exhortations." Pleased with the fervor of this unexpected finale, he joined in the praying. In retrospect Bourne attached considerable importance to the episode and referred to it as "a camp meeting without a name." The fact that Pointon's dwelling was not adequate to contain the crowd seemed to him a clear sign that open-air preaching was the will of God. The spontaneous outpouring after the sermon convinced him that preaching should always be accompanied by extended prayer services. This greater involvement of the people, Bourne believed, represented a providential "enlargement in Methodism."[7]

Like loosely structured prayer meetings and conversational evangelism, open-air preaching and mass participation in worship would become hallmarks of Primitive Methodism. Another continuing feature which evolved out of the exigencies of this self-help period was what Bourne called "variety in class leading," an invention mothered by necessity when Shubotham refused to be more than nominal leader of the Harriseahead class. The experiment in shared leadership persuaded Bourne that taking turns not only allowed several members to benefit from the experience of leading a class but also enhanced the vitality of the meeting.[8] During the first summer of the revival a deputation of colliers approached Bourne and appealed for assistance in building a chapel at Harriseahead. They promised to contribute their labor and to give what money they could toward its completion. He pledged his support, and the colliers proceeded to dig the foundation. This done, they came to the end of both their technical and their financial resources. Bourne, "ignorant of chapel management," asked the Burslem circuit to adopt the building project. The circuit authorities refused, so he supervised the construction and paid most of its cost himself. Several times during 1801 Bourne requested the itinerants at Burslem to "take . . . into society" the three classes he had organized at Mow Cop, Kidsgrove, and Harriseahead. Not until sometime the following year did they do so, thereby adding about eighty newcomers to the membership roll. The chapel was included on the preaching plan, and sermons were scheduled there twice each Sunday. According to Bourne, "this was over-doing it"; so much formal preaching "seemed to hinder the exertions of the people." Accustomed as they were to "look[ing] to themselves and to God for the conversion of precious souls," this congregation "were keen as fire in their reproofs; and to reprove preachers was like a new thing upon the earth."[9]

Primitive Methodist hindsight would eventually make Wesleyan neglect of the colliers' revival appear salutary because, by throwing the people back on their own resources, it laid the basis for a more democratic leadership and furthered the development of lay participation. At the time, however, Bourne thought that the itinerants were unduly slow to manifest their concern for the converts. In defense of the preachers it should be remarked that the Burslem circuit was a poor one, and that the scene of the revival lay in the hill country on its fringe. In his journals Bourne himself often alluded to the poverty of the district. Writing in 1813, Joseph Sutcliffe, the superintendent at Burslem, described his struggle to make ends meet: "In this neighborhood we have less of the middle classes of society than [there] is perhaps in any other circuit. The gentlemen potters are not distinguished by religion; so the body of our societies are working people, and often deeply in debt." In 1801, the year in which the revival began, the circuit's receipts amounted to less than a third of its expenditures. Given the circumstances, Wesleyan preachers must have felt obliged to husband what little income was available to operate the circuit. Conceivably, the itinerants stationed in Burslem during the early months of the revival were temporarily unable to provide for its fruits. It is also possible that they hesitated to commit any of their meager resources until there was evidence that the conversions would prove lasting.[10]

During the 1802–1803 Wesleyan year,[11] Bourne and the Burslem preachers maintained fairly amicable relations, though Bourne disagreed with the superintendent, Joseph Taylor, as to the proper functions of the itinerancy. Taylor held that preachers should devote themselves primarily to strengthening the existing membership, while Bourne assigned priority to converting the ungodly. In 1802 the revival began to wane. Though members already in the societies did not backslide, no new souls were won. The awakening was brought to a halt, Bourne thought, by a combination of factors: an overdose of preaching instead of prayer meetings, opposition from both the itinerants and their "modern" flocks, and frustration of the revivalists' desire for a daylong outdoor session of prayer and exhortation.[12] The revival at a standstill, Bourne returned to Bemersley. Once settled on the farm, he drew up and followed a plan of his own for conversation preaching at Harriseahead and half a dozen other villages in the circuit.

The Rise of the Camp-Meeting Movement, 1804–1808

Revivalism struck the Burslem circuit with renewed vigor in 1804. Sparked by the Stockport revivalists, the second awakening was more potent and less localized than its predecessor. The pentecost began in September when Bourne and some members of the Harriseahead class made contact with the Stockport group in Congleton. Their zeal proved highly contagious; during a class meeting at Harriseahead the following evening, "there was an extraordinary outpouring of the Spirit; and a very great quickening ran speedily throughout the society. The word was like fire among dry stubble: the work broke out in all directions." Within a short time "there was a reviving in almost every part of the circuit." Enthusiasm continued to spread during the new year. Virtually every society in the circuit felt its effects. At Tunstall the "deadness, which had been proverbial for years," vanished. Even in Burslem, where antipathy toward "wildfire" was strongest, "there was a pretty clamour," and some "prejudices were swept away." The focus of the earlier revival had been on reclaiming the irreligious; this one involved those in quest of entire sanctification as well as mourners.[13] Edward Jackson and William France, the traveling preachers assigned to Burslem in 1804–1805, did not promote the excitement. France was a "determined anti-revivalist" whose preaching stood in need of "a little more animation." Jackson, an elderly man, was more tolerant. He did not approve of the irregularities that accompanied the revival, but he acknowledged that its good effect on people's lives was evident.[14] France was unpopular, and the conference of 1805 appointed William Edward Miller in his place. Miller had been brought into the ministry through the influence of Bramwell, and he had been active in revivals elsewhere. "Expectations were raised," but Miller had "lost the revival spirit." By 1805 he had seen "the propriety of my making a stand for the Methodist discipline." Jackson died in 1806 while Miller was stationed in Burslem, so it is likely that the junior preacher wielded more than usual influence in circuit affairs. During his tenure there he discouraged "variety in class leading" and put prayer meetings on a more formal basis. According to Bourne, Miller "could talk on revivalism as no other travelling preacher had been able to do, and by so doing he could get hold of people's minds and bend them to his own views." Miller was supremely successful at quenching the revival: "upwards of twelve months elapsed without a single conversion taking place."[15]

Among Bourne's followers the cessation of the revival in 1806 rekindled interest in a daylong outdoor prayer session and so fostered the rise of Camp-Meeting Methodism. The novel idea of a "whole day's praying" had been voiced by Shubotham as early as 1801, when the converts at Harriseahead had pressed their leaders to extend some of the livelier prayer meetings beyond the established time limit. "You shall have a meeting upon Mow some Sunday," he had assured them, "and then you'll be satisfied." Shubotham's promise had captured the imagination of the people, and their eagerness had been augmented by the glowing accounts of camp meetings on the American frontier being retailed in the *Methodist Magazine* between 1802 and 1804. The desire to hold a prolonged prayer session on Mow Cop might have been vented and forgotten, Bourne thought, if the Burslem itinerants had encouraged the innovation. By hindering it, the circuit authorities had in fact enhanced its attractions. Until the outburst of revivalism diverted their attention late in 1804, the class members had persistently besought God to *"give us a camp meeting!"*[16] In 1806, the revival spent, both their hopes and their petitions were renewed. The reawakening of interest in an extended prayer meeting on Mow Cop coincided with Lorenzo Dow's second visit to England, a missionary tour meant to publicize the merits of frontier camp meetings. Dow did not come to north Staffordshire until April 1807, when he preached at Burslem, Harriseahead, and Tunstall. Greatly inspired by Dow's message, Hugh Bourne and his brother James accompanied the American to Congleton and there heard his farewell sermon. Armed with pamphlets bought from Dow and resolved to organize a camp meeting patterned on the transatlantic model, the brothers returned to the Potteries.[17]

Bourne expected to hold the first English camp meeting in August at Norton-in-the-Moors, where he had revived and expanded a society abandoned by the Wesleyans, solicited funds for a chapel, and established a Sunday school. His intended strategy was to schedule a three-day session during the annual parish feast and so to counteract the "bad effects" of the wake.[18] The religious activities, he hoped, would provide an alternative alluring enough to preserve the younger members of the society from "being seduced" by the local festivities. When Bourne brought his design before the class at Harriseahead, the people pledged their support, but urged that a gathering on the Mow be held earlier. Thus the camp-meeting movement in England was inaugurated, not at Norton in August, but in Pointon's field on the Cheshire side of Mow Cop in May. Except for the date—the first Sunday on which a sympathetic local preacher was appointed for Harriseahead—this prototypic camp meeting was unplanned. "It was thought best to keep it as secret as possible from the opposers of open-air worship"; nevertheless, "the report flew through the country." On 31 May 1807 visiting spectators and participants arrived from Congleton, Macclesfield, Knutsford, Warrington, Burslem, Tunstall, and elsewhere. A convert who was a sea captain from Hull improvised a flag to mark the site; some people from Knutsford and Macclesfield initiated the proceedings; others erected preaching stands when needed; and volunteers exhorted, led hymns, prayed, preached, and testified as they saw fit. "A most extraordinary variety developed." One group evolved into a "company praying with mourners." Before nightfall, when the session finally wound down, "a work began among the children." Bourne, who estimated that two to four thousand people were present, hastened to print a penny tract recounting the day's events and heralding two future camp meetings. One of these would be held on Mow Cop in July and would last "two or three days or more"; the other would be the assembly he had originally planned as an antidote to the Norton parish feast in August.[19]

The success of the May camp meeting was due in part to curiosity and interest excited by Dow during his recent promotional tour in Lancashire and Cheshire. A number of the speakers at Mow Cop were Independent Methodists among whom he had lived and worked. Some who testified owed their conversion to his preaching. Dow's notoriety was also partly responsible for the itinerants' subsequent attack on the camp-meeting movement. Immediately after Bourne published his pamphlet announcing two more open-air assemblies, the traveling preachers in both Burslem and Macclesfield circulated handbills denouncing them; a few weeks later the Wesleyan conference outlawed camp meetings altogether. The opposition of the itinerants was undoubtedly strengthened by a desire to neutralize persistent charges of Methodist disloyalty to the government. The first camp meeting took place just as Napoleon was nearing the apex of his career. Two weeks after the Mow Cop gathering, he won a decisive battle at Friedland, a victory followed early in July by the treaties of Tilsit, which left the British without a major ally in the war against France. Bourne was fundamentally apolitical. His writings are almost devoid of explicit comment on contemporary issues, and on the rare occasions when he took a public stand on a political matter, he was undeniably conservative. Nevertheless, during the summer of 1807, it was "gravely hinted" that he was "disaffected towards his majesty's government, and that these meetings were got up for political purposes." Whether the estimated two to four thousand at Mow Cop were as innocent of disaffection as Bourne cannot, of course, be demonstrated. Some of the speakers did embellish their testimonies with references to such controversial topics as deism, rebellion in Ireland, the war on the Continent, and the liberties of Englishmen. Those whose views got recorded made their loyalty plain. Obviously, however, neither Bourne nor anyone else was able to monitor all the happenings of the day. Moreover, at a time when almost any sizable crowd was likely to be suspect, how especially vulnerable to misinterpretation would have been a large camp meeting where strangers might randomly come and go and whoever wanted to might deliver an impromptu address.[20]

In 1807 neither the Conventicle Act nor the Five Mile Act had been repealed. Under the terms of the former an unlicensed preacher might be fined £20 and his adult hearers 5s. each. Forewarned in June that charges would be brought against those present should another camp meeting occur, James and Hugh Bourne secured licenses to preach. Hugh also took the precaution of erecting a small wooden "tabernacle" and three tents on Mow Cop so that the campground too could be authorized. Although their import was not recognized then, these actions really marked the beginnings of Camp-Meeting Methodism as a separate sect. The preaching permits were issued to "Protestant Dissenting ministers"; the site became, legally speaking, a Protestant place of worship. Scheduled to coincide with the Wolstanton parish wake, the camp meeting in July attracted an audience not only from the Potteries, but from places up to forty miles away. Bourne counted more than sixty people who were converted during this three-day session. Despite the warnings of their circuit preachers, Wesleyans came "in abundance." Only a handful of these were there to protest the goings-on, and at the next quarter-day meeting they were officially thanked for having remained aloof.[21]

Both the itinerants and the Bournes looked upon the camp meeting planned for Norton in August as the critical test of the movement. The decision to oppose the second Mow Cop meeting had been made locally by the circuit preachers at Burslem and Macclesfield. Before the Norton gathering, however, the Wesleyan conference assembled in Liverpool and banned camp meetings throughout the connexion. Attention was now focused on Burslem circuit as the storm center of a wider struggle between "primitive" and "modern" Methodism. John Riles, the superintendent, returned from Liverpool determined to enforce the interdict. Certain that conference had erred, Bourne was equally resolved to stand by the upcoming camp meeting. Because Riles forbade participation on the part of all local preachers and class leaders, Bourne was hard pressed to find enough volunteers to preach and to conduct the activities. Although society members had been sternly exhorted not to attend, a big crowd did gather at Norton early in the morning of 23 August. Almost in despair because there was "but a small company to support so very large a meeting," Bourne was half prepared to admit defeat when Paul Johnson, a physician from Dublin, unexpectedly arrived and took command. A superb speaker who had worked with Dow in Lancashire and Cheshire, Johnson was a "means of restoring confidence to the meeting," which "went on powerfully" until evening. Monday and Tuesday were equally successful. To the Bournes, Johnson's timely advent seemed providential: they were now absolutely "satisfied that the camp meetings were of the Lord." God, they believed, would either "turn the minds of the conference, or carry on the camp meetings by other means."[22]

Although Bourne had clearly defied the conference minute by holding the camp meeting at Norton, he was not immediately expelled from the Wesleyan society. Instead, both he and James Bourne were treated as pariahs in several places where formerly their labors had been welcomed. Thus freed from many of their usual obligations, the brothers began working in neighborhoods neglected or not yet penetrated by the

Wesleyans. Through family visitation, conversation preaching, and cottage prayer meetings they invigorated existing societies or established new ones at Lask Edge, Tean, Ramsor, Farley, and Wootton. As soon as the weather was favorable, the Bournes demonstrated their commitment to open-air revivalism by launching a new series of camp meetings. The first of these was held in Shropshire on the Wrekin, supposedly the oldest mountain in England. It is likely that the peak was once used for pagan fertility rites. At its crest was a phallus-shaped outcrop of rock known as Balder's Stone, and beneath this, a deep, narrow cleft called the Needle's Eye. According to folk tradition, if a virgin dipped her foot in the water which had collected in the cuplike depression atop Balder's Stone, then "threaded the Needle's Eye," she would wed within a year.[23] Bourne chose to schedule a camp meeting there on the first day of May because "there had existed, time out of mind, an evil custom of multitudes assembling on top of Rekin on the first Sunday in May and spending the day in iniquity."[24] Many inhabitants of this rural region were giving over their first non-working day in May to the celebration of Beltane, a major festival in the pagan year; though they may have been unaware of the ancient significance of their activities, those who annually frolicked on the mountain seem to have been ritually inaugurating the "awakening" phase of the seasonal cycle. A "vast number" were drawn to the camp meeting in May 1808 and at the Wrekin's summit were invited to experience a very different sort of awakening. Again Bourne had timed a camp meeting to divert people from traditional festivities that seemed to him rich with occasions for sin. He long continued to advocate and to practice this tactic. Whenever outdoor revivals served as the entering wedge in breaking down old patterns of leisure, Camp-Meeting Methodism would stand ready to fill the void with alternative pursuits and new forms of association.

Seven weeks and three camp meetings after the Wrekin gathering, the Burslem circuit quarterly meeting finally expelled Hugh Bourne from the Wesleyan Methodist Society. Their action was not unexpected, and, although Bourne's attachment to the Old Connexion was "great," he was "resigned to the Lord's will." William Clowes, who was present at the meeting, said that Bourne's ticket was withheld because he had not attended class regularly. Riles later acknowledged to Bourne that the real reason was his "tendency to set up other than ordinary worship." Despite Bourne's expulsion from Wesleyan Methodism, he and his brother continued to evangelize northeast Staffordshire, preaching and holding cottage meetings in places that lay in a kind of ecclesiastical no-man's-land on the common fringe of the Burslem and Leek Wesleyan circuits. Their aim was simply the conversion of sinners, and they made no effort to form a separate group of societies. The upshot was that the "fruits of their labours usually fell into the Old Methodist Connexion."[25]

Clowes and the Clowesites, 1805–1811

Although Hugh Bourne and William Clowes have generally been recognized as the co-founders of the Primitive Methodist Connexion, both can be more accurately described as men whose zeal for converting others thrust upon them the task of organizing lay people who, like themselves, were not willing to march to the beat of the official Wesleyan drum. The leadership provided by Bourne and Clowes was, of course, a tremendous asset, but without the colliers, agricultural workers, potters, and small farmers whom they called "fellow labourers," there would have been no movement to lead. This dependence on the initiative of other laymen was especially significant in the genesis of the Clowesites.

William Clowes was born in Burslem in 1780. Through his mother, Ann Wedgwood, he could claim kinship with one of the most illustrious families in the Potteries; his father Samuel, however, was a not very enterprising working potter, whom William characterized as "wild and dissipated." Although Samuel Clowes had forsaken religion after reading a "pernicious" book, his wife maintained her allegiance to the Church of England. During his youth William Clowes both took up his father's trade and followed his father's dissolute example. A more proficient and sometimes more industrious potter than Samuel, William spent his non-working hours in dancing, gambling, drinking, and brawling. Marriage did not end his "rake's progress," and he moved restlessly from place to place until in 1808 a narrow escape from impressment in Hull frightened him into abandoning his chums and his debts and returning to Staffordshire. Despite his undisciplined habits, Clowes seems never to have totally stilled his religious conscience. After his encounter with the press-gang, he "prayed that if God would carry me in safety to my native place, I would then serve Him; but no sooner had He preserved me safe to my journey's end, than, among my old companions my promises were forgotten in acts of rebellion." In the interim between his homecoming and his conversion Clowes was the victim of "internal misery," torn between fear for his soul and the urge to "drown my distressing convictions with strong drink."[26]

In Tunstall the revival of 1805 yielded a promising harvest of future Primitive Methodists. James Steele, already a Methodist, now espoused revivalism. Among the newly saved were Clowes, Thomas Woodnorth, James Nixon, and William Morris. Clowes's conversion during a prayer meeting was sudden and complete. He renounced worldly pleasures, drew up and diligently followed a strict set of "rules for holy living," and paid his debts. He also joined a Wesleyan class led by Steele, opened his house to a variety of Methodist functions, and, as a member of a tract society, paired off with Nixon to evangelize a district in Cheshire. The friendship of Bourne and Clowes, which began early in 1805, was based on a sharing of spiritual experiences. Together they made visits to James Crawfoot, the "old man of Delamere Forest," who instructed them in a kind of practical mysticism. In April, Clowes joined the ranks of Bourne's "labourers," and until conference ruled against them, he attended camp meetings. Although, as a Wesleyan class leader, he felt obliged to absent himself from camp meetings for more than a year, Clowes did not break off his association with Bourne. Finally, in the autumn of 1808 he submitted to what he believed to be the will of God and delivered his first sermon in a field near Ramsor. He was a gifted preacher, and in spite of his defiance of the prohibition against outdoor revivals, the Burslem itinerants sought to keep him in the Wesleyan fold. He was invited to preach a trial sermon at Tunstall and subsequently was put on the local preachers' plan for Burslem circuit. Within a few months, however, "much uneasiness began to show itself among certain parties . . . on account of the camp-meetings and my attending them." In June 1810 his name was struck from the preaching plan; in September one of the itinerants withheld his ticket and rebuked his class "for their liveliness in their way of worshipping and praising God; and remarked [that] he supposed they acted as they had been taught." When Clowes inquired what he had "done amiss," he was informed that he had behaved "contrary to the Methodist discipline," and that he "could not be a preacher or leader amongst them unless [he] promised not to attend [camp] meetings any more." Clowes refused. "That I could not conscientiously do, for God had greatly blessed me in these meetings . . . and my motive for assisting in them was simply to glorify God, and bring sinners to . . . Jesus." Earlier in 1810 he had turned down an offer to become a local preacher for the New Connexion. Now, ousted from the Old Connexion, he was without a religious affiliation. Though he advised his classes at Kidsgrove and at Tunstall to choose new leaders, most of the members followed him into exile from Wesleyan Methodism and become the nucleus of a separate body of "Clowesites."[27]

These thirty or forty ex-Wesleyans found asylum in the home of Joseph Smith, an elderly and somewhat eccentric Methodist. The owner of considerable property in Tunstall, Smith in 1787 had donated a building site and had given twenty guineas toward the erection of the town's first Wesleyan chapel. His quarrel with the circuit preachers dated from 1807, when the superintendent had ignored a conference ban on female preaching in order to lure Mary Dunnel away from the Norton camp meeting. Dunnel, an effective revivalist, had been flattered by Riles's invitation to take his appointment in the Tunstall chapel and had failed to appear as scheduled at Norton. Later that year Riles, citing the conference minute of 1803, had barred her from the same pulpit. Indignant at such arbitrary behavior, Smith and James Steele had asked Bourne to join them in a secession. Bourne had "spoke[n] strongly" against forming a separate sect, and Smith had settled for getting his house licensed for preaching. Since March 1808 his kitchen had been the scene of weekly sermons followed by extended prayer meetings. Bourne provided a preaching plan, but Smith determined the rules of conduct in the kitchen chapel and exercised veto power over Bourne's choice of preachers. Before 1810 Clowes had been welcome at the meetings, but because he had for a time obeyed the injunction against camp meetings, Smith did not allow him to preach. Predictably, when Clowes was expelled, Smith vigorously championed his cause: "They have turned Billy out . . . because he could o'er preach 'em; but Billy, for all them, shall preach in my kitchen."[28] Clowes's followers soon began to look upon the kitchen as their "proper place of worship." During this same period James Nixon, Thomas Woodnorth, William Morris, and Samuel Barber also left the Wesleyans and cast their lot with the Clowesites. Clowes himself accompanied Crawfoot and Bourne on a visit to Derbyshire, then alone he undertook a missionary journey into Lancashire. On his return in December 1810 Nixon and Woodnorth proposed that he give up his trade and become a full-time preacher. Because of a depression in the pottery business, Clowes was then working only three or four days a week, but he was earning £1 2s. Nixon and Woodnorth, also potters, offered to pay him 10s. weekly to shepherd the Tunstall society and to open new places. Clowes agreed. During the winter and spring of 1811 he formed several societies, chiefly in north Staffordshire; by July, when they amalgamated with Bourne's societies, the Clowesites possessed an embryonic circuit with Tunstall as its head.[29]

In April 1811 another group of future Primitive Methodists broke with the Wesleyan society in Tunstall. Their exodus was prompted by the expulsion of James Steele, a local preacher and class leader who was also a trustee of the chapel and superintendent of the Sunday school. Smith's cousin and bailiff, Steele had often been present when services were held in the kitchen. Now participation in Clowesite worship became the grounds for ejecting him from the Wesleyan society. Like Clowes, he counseled his two classes to find other leaders. Most of the members refused. The teachers and pupils in the Sunday school were also determined to go with Steele. The new influx of secessionists clearly could not be accommodated in the kitchen. At this juncture John Boden offered them temporary use of a large room which had been built for the storage of earthenware. By the end of April the school had been reopened in the storeroom, and Sunday services were being conducted there by the preachers regularly assigned to Smith's kitchen. In June, Hugh Bourne and his brother purchased land for a chapel-schoolroom. Its erection proved to be the crucial coming together of the camp-meeting people and the followers of Clowes and Steele. According to Bourne, "the house form was chosen in preference to the chapel form, so that, if not wanted, it would just form four houses, according to the plan on which houses are usually built at Tunstall." This "cautious method" was adopted "because it could not be known whether or not the [nascent] connexion would be of any long continuance." On 13 July, two weeks before the Primitive Methodist Connexion came into being, Crawfoot preached the dedication sermon for what came to be regarded as its first chapel.[30]

The Drift toward Connexionalism: Hugh Bourne and the Camp-Meeting Methodists, 1808–1811

Throughout the three-year period between June 1808, when Bourne was excluded from the Wesleyan Connexion, and July 1811, when the Clowesites formally joined forces with the Camp-Meeting Methodists, Bourne and his helpers persevered in their evangelistic labors. They continued to hold camp meetings during the summer months, and, despite the economic necessity of working at their usual occupations, they undertook increasingly systematic visits to villages and farmhouses in north Staffordshire, Cheshire, and Lancashire. Bourne was also ever alert to exploit "openings"—opportunities favorable to the winning of converts. Often, invitations to preach at new places were issued by persons who either had learned of the movement through word of mouth or had witnessed a camp meeting. Sometimes these individuals were Wesleyans who lived in villages where the Methodist cause was defunct or where no class had ever been formed. Sometimes they were society members who disliked "modern" Methodism and felt that the Wesleyan itinerants were neglecting rural districts. Occasionally, a farmer or tradesman, himself not yet "in the way of salvation," thought a dose of vital religion would benefit his neighborhood. Given these circumstances, many people won over to Methodism by the camp-meeting missionaries did not have a strong attachment to the Old Connexion. Bourne's fraternization with the Independent Methodists and with the Magic Methodists also diminished the probability of negotiating a peaceful return of the camp-meeting enthusiasts to the Wesleyan body.

Bourne's association with the Independent Methodists began in May 1807, when a number of them came to Mow Cop to assist with the first camp meeting. In July, Bourne traveled to Macclesfield, where he lodged with John Berrisford and attended the Independent Methodists conference. At this meeting "one of the main matters was arranging for an interchange of preachers to promote variety." Before returning home Bourne inaugurated the exchange by visiting the Quaker Methodists at Warrington, the Dowites at Risley, and an independent society at Runcorn. It was expected that Mary Dunnel of Macclesfield would reciprocate by lending her revivalistic powers to the camp meeting at Norton. At the next annual meeting Bourne and the Independent Methodist delegates aired their views on the legitimacy of preaching by women. At the urging of Berrisford, Bourne wrote and published a pamphlet, *Remarks on the Ministry of Women*, which argued that the Bible had authorized, and John Wesley had used, women to spread the gospel. Later in the summer of 1808 Bourne met in Warrington with James Sigston of Leeds, formerly a leader of the Kirkgate Screamers, Paul Johnson, and Peter Phillips, the central figure in the Quaker Methodist society. Their object was to promote revivals in England by printing and circulating the autobiography of a popular American evangelist, Benjamin Abbott. Between 1808 and 1811 Bourne and some of his fellow revivalists continued to meet with and to preach among the Independent Methodists. But, though these contacts may have strengthened Bourne's early prejudice against a paid ministry, they exerted no significant influence on the future shape of the Primitive Methodist Connexion.[31]

The impact of their intercourse with the so-called Magic Methodists was greater, chiefly because for a time both Bourne and Clowes looked upon Crawfoot as their spiritual mentor. A rustic mystic and until 1809 a Wesleyan local preacher, Crawfoot held monthly prayer meetings at his cottage in Delamere Forest. Those who frequented the sessions often had visions or fell into trances, phenomena that earned them their sobriquet and gave rise to the rumor that they "used magic or were in league with Satan." Bourne and Clowes made their first joint visit in 1807, heard Crawfoot preach, saw a farmer's wife "go into vision," and listened to a man who "spoke good things, but he dabbled in politics and then he was quite out." During the evening Crawfoot tried "to open some matters in the scriptures" which Bourne and Clowes did not then "fully understand." Initally, Bourne reacted negatively to Crawfoot; nevertheless, he stopped at Delamere Forest after his tour among the Independent Methodists. While he was there, a female seer predicted that, unless he took up preaching as a vocation, he would never be blessed with visions. This intelligence may have contributed to his later decision to expand his missionary labors.[32]

As their pilgrimages to the "old man of the forest" grew more frequent, Clowes learned to "bring down the high power" through prayer. Already able to armor himself with divine protection when traversing the "haunted domains" of the terrifying "Kidsgrove bogget," Clowes now assisted in exorcising the devil from an elderly woman in Harriseahead. In 1809 he discovered that he had the "gift of laying on of hands." Bourne increasingly experienced premonitions and dreams laden with spiritual symbolism. During a bearbaiting he "felt the spirit of the wake dash upon me . . . and I bore the cross awhile, till . . . the spirit said that my desire should be granted." The wake festivities were duly rained out. On another occasion Bourne interpreted his dream about an ugly black dog drowning in a deep pit as a sign that a Ramsor woman thought to be "in witchcraft" would be liberated from the "bond which binds her." During this period he often felt called to a certain place or had a "divine intimation" of someone's call to preach. The "vision work" practiced by the Magic Methodists began to manifest itself among some of the camp-meeting women. Although he did not much publicize it, Bourne himself had a few visions. In 1810 he and Crawfoot journeyed to London, where they called upon Joanna Southcott, the aged prophetess who in 1813 would announce herself to be supernaturally pregnant with the child destined to prepare the way for Christ at the Second Advent. Bourne concluded that "Joanna was in witchcraft." The pair were more favorably impressed by their interview with a woman who, after having been run over by a horse and carriage, had made a marvelous deathbed recovery. Before her "miraculous restoration," the victim had seen Bourne and Crawfoot in a vision and, while in a trance, had witnessed "glorious things."[33]

Crawfoot was poor, and in November 1809 Hugh and James Bourne undertook to pay him 10s. weekly for ministering to the societies in their care and for opening new places. Bourne was able to reconcile this with his belief in free gospelism by regarding the small salary as a private act of charity. Though until the middle of 1810 Crawfoot was directed to guide new converts into existing connexions, hiring him was in fact a step toward forming a separate organization. At the quarterly meeting of the Northwich Wesleyan circuit held in December, Crawfoot was taken to task for having preached at the Quaker Methodist chapel. That he had also been employed as an itinerant missionary by the Camp-Meeting

Methodists did not help his situation. Soon he was cast out of the Wesleyan society, and his name was crossed off the preaching plan. In 1813 Crawfoot and the Primitive Methodists came to a parting of the ways. His influence, however, long survived his estrangement from the connexion. Although he was uncouth and uneducated, Crawfoot seems to have possessed impressive mystical gifts as well as an extraordinary ability to communicate his insights. Not talented as an open-air revivalist nor even very adept at pulpit oratory, he was a compelling speaker and a perceptive listener when it came to spiritual discourse with a handful of people. More than twenty years after Crawfoot's removal from the connexion, Bourne published an article in which he acknowledged his debt to the "old man" and the Magic Methodists of Delamere Forest. From them, Bourne wrote, he had learned how to carry on the "conversation ministry" more effectively and how to talk and pray with mourners. The Forest Methodists had also taught Bourne to share vicariously in the spiritual sufferings of others and to practice "exercising faith in silence." They believed that it was best to refrain from discussing "immediate religion" until, through faith, the "power of God [descended] to attend the words." This was "quite new" to Bourne, but he came to understand that "the plainest words accompanied by the . . . power of God would have an effect; but the most skilful words, if not so accompanied, would have no effect."[34] Because Crawfoot's preaching career in the connexion was so brief, it was Bourne and Clowes who served as the conduits through which these teachings passed from Delamere Forest into the mainstream of early Primitive Methodism.

The camp-meeting missionaries had no fixed rounds. Compared to the orderly circuits of Primitive Methodism in its later bricks-and-mortar stage, their efforts lacked plan and continuity. The explanation for this is twofold. First, Camp-Meeting Methodism was a lay movement. Except for Crawfoot, none of its missionaries was a full-time salaried preacher;[35] by necessity evangelism was done in the time remaining after the demands of the workweek had been met. Second, and perhaps more important, the aim of the Camp-Meeting Methodists was not to form a sect, but to awaken sinners and to supplement the labor of others. As they saw it, their task was to hold camp meetings, to extend Methodism, and to minister to societies that were not being adequately served by the Wesleyans. As a result, their itineraries were not firmly set in advance. Sometimes an individual missionary would take the initiative in opening a new place; more often, the work was begun in response to an invitation. Such requests might come at any time and from as far as thirty or forty miles away. When the cause was introduced into virgin territory, the usual procedure was to attract attention by holding an open-air service, then to meet with any who were interested inside a cottage or house made available by some favorably disposed person. If the camp-meeting people had been asked to come into the neighborhood, the session out of doors might be omitted. The attempt to raise up a society might fail, and the evangelists would then abandon the place for a more promising one. Or it might succeed, in which case the missionaries would preach, make cottage visits, and conduct prayer meetings until such time as the Wesleyan circuit was able and willing to take full pastoral charge of the young society. Of the societies that were nurtured by the Camp-Meeting Methodists between 1808 and 1811, only a dozen were listed on the first printed plan of the Primitive Methodist Connexion.

Hugh Bourne seems to have covered more territory more systematically than any other camp-meeting missionary. Not only was he indefatigable, but he had somewhat greater financial resources than most of the others. Apart from what he called his "Cheshire round" (chiefly Independent Methodist societies), Bourne's most regular visits were made to villages and farms in the area between Cheadle and the Derbyshire border. That the cause thrived here was partly due to the steady encouragement given by various "respectable" families who opened their "substantial" farmhouses for meetings. The societies formed in this district were regarded as an informal circuit with Ramsor at its head. When Clowes joined Bourne to work in "Ramsor circuit," the pair soon gained a reputation for invincibility. One of the two would talk earnestly with a potential convert while the other prayed without pause. Thanks to their efforts, a supposed witch was freed from her "bond," and it was said "there had not been such men on earth since the days of the apostles." A farmer at Ramsor "got to entertain such an opinion" of the missionaries that, confident they would pass it, he put them to the test of converting a local woman. Liberated within the evening, she immediately invited Bourne and Clowes to "come to her house on the morrow to take a cup of tea, and to convert her husband." Her spouse, won over next day, became a local preacher and a class leader. Success bred success, and "the news soon spread rapidly and extensively that there were two men in the country that could convert anybody."[36]

During 1810 and 1811 missionaries also pushed eastward toward the Dove and into the Churnet valley. Societies were formed in Staffordshire at Froghall, Alton, and Rocester. Visitors who had traveled to a camp meeting held at Ramsor in 1810 were so impressed by the eloquence of Mary Dunnel that numerous invitations to preach were forthcoming. As a result, she, Bourne, and Crawfoot began evangelizing southwest Derbyshire. Their way in this neighborhood had been prepared by Elizabeth Evans, George Eliot's aunt by marriage and the prototype for Dinah

Morris, the heroine of *Adam Bede*. Despite opposition from "professing Christians and pastors," the camp-meeting preachers were able to form societies at Roston, Hollington, Boyleston, and Rodsley.[37]

During this period Bourne also undertook missionary forays into south Staffordshire, through northeast Shropshire in the vicinity of Market Drayton, and through north Cheshire and Flint. While traveling in south Staffordshire in 1810, he recruited John Benton to the camp-meeting movement. According to Bourne, Benton "had been brought up in ignorance and had not much command of language," but "his zeal was great." On account of one or both of these characteristics, Benton was "much opposed" by his fellow Wesleyans. One of them had denounced his preaching as a "scandal on the cause of Christ," claiming, "you have had no learning, you do not understand grammar." On a subsequent occasion, when Benton was exhorting a crowd of colliers, his discourse was interrupted by groans and shrieks as "some fell from their seats; and the whole assembly was thrown into consternation." Promptly closing his Bible, Benton left the lectern to pray among the mourners. As he moved through the congregation, he encountered the man who had scoffed at his preaching "standing and looking on with amazement. Said Benton to him, 'This is grammar!'"[38] Though Bourne described him as a collier, Benton owned an interest in a coal mine as well as some land and houses. Thus he was able to mission at his own expense and later, while a Primitive Methodist preacher, to refuse his appointments and defy the connexion's moratorium on moving into new areas. In 1811 he made a brief attempt to awaken London, then left the metropolis to open some places in the Black Country. These he put into Bourne's charge when he took his place on the Primitive Methodist preaching plan in September.

Beginning in 1829 the quarterly tickets given to members of the Primitive Methodist Connexion proclaimed, "First camp meeting held May 31, 1807; first class formed March 1810." The last half of this statement is somewhat misleading. The class referred to was at Stanley, a village about four miles from Bemersley. This was not, of course, the first to be raised up by the camp-meeting enthusiasts; the societies at Harriseahead, Kidsgrove, and Norton, as well as several in the vicinity of Ramsor, all antedated it. What made Stanley unique was that it was the first of Bourne's societies to feel the impact of a stiffened Wesleyan policy toward ministering in tandem with the camp-meeting missionaries. When it was proposed that the Wesleyans and Bourne's evangelists "labour jointly" at Stanley, the superintendent at Burslem insisted the Wesleyans "would have it all in our own hands . . . or else have nothing to do with it." The ten members of the class refused to accept this condition. "Then . . . you mun lay your hands off it," countered their spokesman. Bourne interpreted the situation as a "manifest proof" that the camp-meeting people were now being called by God to form a separate connexion. "From this time their views were changed, and the great reluctance to taking upon them the [total] care of societies was removed."[39] It was in this sense only that the little class at Stanley, formed in March 1810 and disavowed by the Wesleyan itinerants two months later, was "first." To assign it primacy as the earliest Primitive Methodist class not only suggests a premature date for the connexion's birth but also diminishes the importance of the contributions made by Clowes and Steele. As Clowes explained, their followers and the Camp-Meeting Methodists "stood in separate and detached parties" until the summer of 1811, and, though they readily lent each other assistance, Clowesites and Bournites "pressed after the salvation of sinners in separate lines of action."[40]

In March 1810 Bourne drew up plans for both the Staffordshire and the Cheshire-Lancashire missions. Neither of them provided a schedule of preaching appointments. Of the eleven places included on these plans only Stanley, Risley, and Runcorn were designated as camp-meeting classes; the remaining eight were looked upon as preaching stations because their societies were officially either Wesleyan or Independent Methodist. Although by September the Camp-Meeting "Connexion" counted 136 members, quarterly tickets were not introduced until June 1811. It was the supposedly Wesleyan society at Ramsor that urged the "propriety, and even necessity" of using tickets. Bourne feared that this would be the undoing of free gospelism: "Tickets will cost something . . . ; you know there is no money gathered in the societies," he told Francis Horobin. When the Ramsor farmer volunteered to pay the printer's bill, Bourne capitulated. The model for these first tickets was borrowed from Wesleyan Methodism. Like Wesleyan tickets they bore a quotation from the Bible. The verse chosen—"But we desire to hear of thee what thou thinkest; for as concerning this sect, we know that everywhere it is spoken against"—has a tentative quality. It also suggests that the Camp-Meeting Methodists identified themselves with the early Christian community. They too were a tiny minority in an alien world, and they too had been summoned to spread the gospel in its original simplicity. Bourne believed it was not the tickets, but "zeal for the Lord of hosts" that held the camp-meeting people together. He described the members as "timid" and their bond of union as "in some degree secret," adding, "the idea of the connexion's soon breaking apart was usually rather strong."[41] While the tickets were being printed Bourne worked out a preaching plan for Stanley, Ramsor, Tunstall, and five other places. This time the plan listed specific preaching appointments for two salaried preachers, Clowes and Crawfoot, and for thirteen local preachers including Steele. The directive appended to it revealed a "primitive" Methodist responsiveness to lay opinion: "If any other person be present whom the congregation wishes to speak, the wish of the congregation must be complied with."[42] Because the plan provided for both Clowesites and Camp-Meeting Methodists, *de facto* union was achieved when it went into effect in June 1811. By then all ties with the Wesleyan Connexion had been severed; a site for a chapel in Tunstall had been chosen; class tickets had been issued; and the nucleus of a full-time ministry had come into being. Formal merger with the Clowesites was at hand.

Exodus: The Fashioning of the Primitive Methodist Connexion, 1811–1816

I cannot pretend that Seth and Dinah were anything
else than Methodists—not indeed of that modern type
which reads quarterly reviews and attends in chapels
with pillared porticoes, but of a very old-fashioned
kind. They believed in present miracles, in instantaneous conversions, in revelations by dreams and visions;
they drew lots and sought for divine guidance by
opening the Bible at hazard . . . ; and it is impossible
for me to represent their diction as correct or their
instruction as liberal.
                    —George Eliot, *Adam Bede*, 1859

The first general meeting of the Primitive Methodist Connexion convened in Joseph Smith's kitchen in July 1811. Drawing on the wisdom learned from past experience with determined lay folk, those present agreed to appoint their preachers "where [they would be] best received and most likely to be useful." Tighter control over preachers was instituted: henceforth, "when planned they should not be free to pick and choose their appointments but just to go in the fear of God and fulfill them."[43] The most important decision taken at the meeting was partially to abandon free gospelism, a significant departure from the practice of the camp-meeting group. In his history of the connexion, Bourne cited two reasons for the new policy. First, because of a depression in the pottery industry, Woodnorth and Nixon were no longer able to support Clowes, who, just to keep out of debt, privately practiced such self-denials as dining on bread and water and selling his featherbed. Nor were the Bournes' resources adequate to meet the needs of a growing connexion. Second, many of the members wanted to pay ticket money. Bourne did not explain why the urge to give was so strong that previously some had refused to join because "they had no opportunity of regularly subscribing to the support of the cause." According to Clowes, gratitude was their primary motive. Perhaps the notion of self-help so as to maintain personal dignity also played a role. Certainly, a quarterly assessment was the custom among Wesleyans and Kilhamites, and some people may have felt that contributing to the Primitive Methodist coffers would both legitimize its status as a connexion and accord them a place in the ranks of "real" Methodists. A third factor, not mentioned by Bourne or Clowes but undoubtedly influential, was that the Tunstall members were considerably more wedded to "methodistic" discipline and organization than were the Bournites; to them ticket money betokened good order. The general meeting either shared or deferred to Bourne's conviction that the poor ought not be denied society membership simply because they were unable to pay. The assembly agreed to introduce regular collections for the support of the ministry, but it made these voluntary. Money was to be given to "proper persons" (presumably local stewards), who were to hand it over to Steele, the newly appointed circuit steward. It was anticipated that the payments would be small and that the sum collected would not cover expenses: "what fell short" was to be "made out by private subscription."[44]

Even though the measures passed in July clearly established the principle that lay people who could afford to should assume responsibility for supporting their ministers, its actual practice was hindered by a lingering attachment to free gospelism on the part of Bourne and others. The 14s. per week allowed to Clowes and Crawfoot were subsistence wages. Beginning in October 1811 money donations and gifts in kind were counted as part of their weekly compensation. As late as 1834 a member of the New Connexion described the circumstances of a Primitive Methodist itinerant as "far below that of an ordinary mechanic." Writing almost half a century after the connexion was formed, Walford noted that circuit preachers were still "labour[ing] under the disadvantages . . . of a narrow-mindedness" inherited from a time "when they used to inculcate the doctrine of a free gospel," saying, " 'We do not want your money but your souls'." Walford implied that the tenacity of this attitude was mainly due to Bourne's influence: "more than once" he had disputed with Bourne about the "impropriety" of not paying more than the too-scant allowance that "he thought so abundant."[45]

The preaching plan for the last quarter of 1811 listed seventeen places, all in Cheshire and north Staffordshire, and seventeen preachers.

Only two of the societies mentioned, Ramsor and Stanley, had camp-meeting origins. Clowes's class at Kidsgrove balked at joining "Hugh and James Bourne's connexion," but Tunstall was assuming primacy as the circuit town, and between 1811 and 1816 the people there had a dominant voice in shaping connexional policy. The remaining thirteen societies also belonged to the former Clowesite circuit. The young sect soon baptized itself Society of the Primitive Methodists. The name was chosen after Crawfoot told how in 1790 he had heard Wesley exhort his fellow laborers to "go out . . . into the streets and lanes" and to "preach the gospel" wherever "there is an open door," wherever there are "two or three under a hedge or tree." "This," their elderly founder had reminded them, "is the way the primitive Methodists did." Wesley's words had deeply impressed Crawfoot, and when summoned to answer for his irregularities, he had told the Wesleyan authorities, "if you have deviated from the old usages, I have not. I still remain a primitive Methodist."[46] By February 1812 the just christened connexion had doubled the number of its preaching places. Bourne had won back some societies in Derbyshire that had followed Mary Dunnel when she "set up for herself" in 1811. Benton's classes in the Black Country had also affiliated with the Primitive Methodists as had five erstwhile camp-meeting societies—Alton, Rocester, Cauldon, Wootton, and Risley.[47]

The Wesleyan conference of 1811 stationed Joseph Sutcliffe in Burslem. Sutcliffe, who worried about the chances of salvation for sleek grocers occupying pews in the pillared chapels of "modern" Methodism, "laboured and struggled" to heal the "serious schism" in Burslem circuit. "I cannot wholly requit [sic] my predecessors of haste or inexperience in that business," he confided.[48] During his two-year tenure as superintendent, Sutcliffe convinced the stewards and leaders to invite the secessionists back into the Old Connexion. After consulting their societies, the members of the Primitive Methodist quarter-day board resolved unanimously "that we should remain as we were."[49] By the time they rebuffed the Wesleyan peace overtures the Primitive Methodists had acquired a good deal of administrative paraphernalia. Regular quarterly meetings were being scheduled; printed plans and tickets were in use; a quarterly collection was provided for; stewards and class leaders had been appointed.

Crawfoot was suspended from preaching in February 1813. He then withdrew from the connexion, taking with him a few societies, the last two of which, Cauldon and Waterfall, rejoined the Primitive Methodists about 1830.[50] The issue of authority raised by the Crawfoot imbroglio was settled in 1814 when Bourne was elected to fill the newly created office of superintendent, a position that he continued to hold until 1819. The year 1814 also saw the completion of a code of rules. Several months earlier a committee had been named to draw up "regulations for the whole body." Its members, which included Bourne and Steele, had agreed that formulating rules for the entire connexion was "too weighty" for three men to undertake. Instead, preliminary drafts had been made and read to every society, comments solicited, and "objections and improvements" incorporated. In January 1814 the final version was approved by the quarter-day board and sent to the printer. Bourne himself had discussed the proposed regulations with almost every person in the community. There was, he wrote, "scarce a member but gave his opinion on them before they were completed." Of this early venture into participatory democracy he remarked, "it is probable there never was an instance of rules being made in the way these were."[51] Had Cobbett or Cartwright applauded this innovative process, Bourne would have been horrified. To him it had no political implications; the crux of the matter was that the rules impinged on the fate of individual human souls. If salvation were an intimate affair between a man and his God, then each person had a right to be consulted. Nevertheless, because they counseled the members to be like their Lord, "no respecter of persons," the regulations themselves were inherently egalitarian. Whether the first Primitive Methodists were aware of it or not, the fundamental spirit of their rules was at odds with the notions of privilege then pervading Britain's social and political order.

Until 1819 the geographic limits of Primitive Methodism changed very little except on its Derbyshire frontier. The connexion's exodus from the Potteries was distinctly an eastward movement—through Derbyshire, along the valley of the Trent toward Nottingham, and into Lincolnshire and Leicestershire. The chief reason for lack of growth in other directions was what Bourne referred to as the "Tunstall non-missioning law." This was a course backed by Steele and other former Clowesites, who argued that early gains should be consolidated before further expansion was attempted. Their fear of overextending the connexion may have derived partly from the fact that Tunstall experienced a revival in 1813.[52] A minority held that the sect's vitality depended on evangelizing new areas, and they vigorously opposed the ban. Bourne privately shared the latter point of view, but at the same time he tried to be impartial and to keep relations harmonious between the two groups. Later he commented that "the suspension of the missionary labours produced a season of deep anxiety and painful experience," because "the societies instead of prospering more prospered less." The connexion appeared so weak that "some thought . . . [it] would absolutely break up." In Staffordshire and

Cheshire, where majority opinion prevailed, the non-missioning law was adhered to; in Derbyshire, however, "a period was put" to its stultifying effects. There, beyond easy reach from Tunstall, "a few enterprising individuals" ignored the moratorium and resolutely pushed east.[53]

One of those who rebelled was John Benton. As early as 1812 Benton refused his preaching assignments in order to open fresh territory in the hill country east of Leek.[54] He also rejected the larger of Bourne's hymnals as unsuitable for the mission field. It was, he said, "too much like the [Wesleyan] Methodist hymn book. The people wanted something new; besides, half a crown was too much money for the people to pay." Benton added a few of his own rough but sprightly compositions to Dow's *Collection of Hymns and Spiritual Songs* and had a thousand copies of this shorter and cheaper book printed. In October 1813 Benton asked the connexion to take charge of the societies he had formed in northeastern Staffordshire and western Derbyshire. He gave Bourne directions for going into "his circuit" and moved on to mission elsewhere. Clowes was sent to cultivate what Benton had sown. The worth of the non-missioning law was hotly debated at a meeting of the quarter-day board held at Tunstall in 1814. Benton was present, and when the majority again affirmed that "the Connexion had already a sufficient number of stations," he "gave notice that it was his duty to get souls converted and [that] he would not be tied any longer." He returned to Derbyshire and began marshaling an army of "praying labourers." "John Benton was like something let out of prison," Bourne observed. The converts at Mercaston, Weston Underwood, and Turnditch "joined [him] heart and hand."[55] Their first conquest was Belper, where by loudly singing in the streets they won for a generation of Primitive Methodists the name "Ranters."

To a great extent the immediate future of the connexion was shaped by what took place in the villages of south central Derbyshire during the first half of the decade. Here was the real matrix of the Primitive Methodist revival that began to sweep through the East Midlands in 1816. Bourne regarded these Derbyshire outposts with special affection. Not only were they a useful proving ground for techniques no longer acceptable at Tunstall but also territory in which new members were bursting with unquenchable zeal to spread the gospel. Bourne was the first of several missionaries who worked in the district between 1811 and 1816. In 1811 he entered Mercaston, a village badly served by the Church of England, abandoned by the Wesleyans, ignored by other Nonconformist denominations, and tagged "Hell Green" by its inhabitants. Within the year Primitive Methodist societies were formed there and at Hulland, Turnditch, and Weston Underwood. Benton also toured the region with Eleazar Hathorn, a former deist and army officer, who had lost a leg while fighting in Spain. Popularly known as "Eleazar of the wooden leg," Hathorn was an effective revivalist and a favorite preaching companion of Benton. Another evangelist, John Wedgwood, freelanced in the area during 1812. Soon afterward Wedgwood attached himself to the Primitive Methodists, but, like Benton, he continued to finance his own missions and, therefore, was never very amenable to discipline.[56] When Clowes met with the Primitive Methodist classes in 1813, he found them prospering. Bourne had recently instituted a tract society whose members paired off to distribute free religious literature from house to house. Where the pamphlets were well received, three or four members would follow up the opening by holding brief prayer meetings. Intended as an agency for gaining converts, the Religious Tract Visiting Society also developed into a training school for new talent. Five of its veterans became local preachers, and two of these, John Harrison and Sarah Kirkland, also served as itinerant missionaries. By 1814, the year that Benton and his lay recruits entered Belper, Derbyshire Primitive Methodists were already building chapels and organizing Sunday schools.

A market town in 1780, Belper by 1814 was fast becoming an industrial center as well. The manufacture of textiles was largely responsible for the twentyfold increase in Belper's population during the forty years after 1780. In 1821 fully a third of the inhabitants were employed in the Strutt cotton works, and many others derived their incomes from selling food, clothing, and supplies to the mill workers. Although the town's chief employers certainly did not conform to the infamous image of hardhearted, tightfisted mill owners, Belper and its neighborhood were a "focus of popular discontent and the headquarters of organized conspiracy" from Luddite times to the eve of the First Reform Bill.[57] Not everybody in Belper welcomed Benton and his lay volunteers. The first time he preached in the market square an adversary climbed onto a butcher's roof and tried to dump a bucket of waste over his head. Undaunted, the preacher and his missionary troupe undertook a series of visits to Belper. Their open-air meetings and singing processions stirred considerable interest and produced a number of conversions. By 1817 Primitive Methodism had made enough of an impact on Belper so that Strutt, "perceiving a decided change wrought by our instrumentality, in many of his work-people," provided building materials for a chapel and sold the society a site at a shilling per yard.[58]

Both Methodism and disaffection toward the government flourished in the Belper area in the years after Waterloo, but the level of enthusiasm each provoked varied from time to time. The Wesleyan circuit enjoyed a revival in 1815 and 1816, partly because the superintendent, his wife, and the junior traveling preacher all worked to promote it; the circuit's membership doubled during their two-year stint. Much of the "high evangelistic fervour" they aroused drained away during the next six years. The total of 1,200 reported in 1816 remained static through 1818, dropped by 110 in 1819, then hovered around the 1,000 mark between 1820 and 1822.[59] There are no Primitive Methodist membership figures available for the period; however, the cause seems to have prospered from the time of the Primitive Methodists' arrival in 1814 to at least 1817. In the autumn of 1819 the Belper society underwent a "gracious visitation," the effects of which were felt "chiefly among young people, and more especially among children." Early in October "hundreds" participated in a love feast. This revival not only continued into the spring of 1821, but it also spread through mid-Derbyshire and inspired local Primitive Methodists to mission part of the High Peak region as well.[60] The years between 1815 and 1820 witnessed first an upsurge of political agitation (1816–1817) that reached an apex at the time of the Pentridge rising in June 1817, then its subsequent reorientation into constitutional reform, and finally its demise at the end of the decade. If there was a negative correlation between revivalistic and revolutionary fervor, in the case of Wesleyan Methodism this would explain only the circuit's decline after mid-1816 (as potential converts and backsliders joined radical societies instead). But the Wesleyans did not gain members after the disheartening experience of Pentridge or even after 1819. It is possible to argue that, while the Ranters did not profit from the failure of the rising in 1817, they did benefit from the aftermath of Peterloo. Their revival, however, was well under way before Parliament passed the repressive legislation of December 1819.

The second major town in the county to attract the attentions of Primitive Methodism was Derby, opened by Sarah Kirkland early in 1815. A native of Mercaston, Kirkland had been convinced of sin by William Bramwell, had lapsed during adolescence, and was reawakened by Bourne in 1811. In 1813, at the age of nineteen, she took her place on the preaching plan. Her first convert was a Gypsy, who took upon himself the role of herald whenever his band was encamped where she was evangelizing. The notoriety attached to being both a "girl-preacher" and a Ranter no doubt helped Kirkland draw large crowds, but it was her extraordinary gifts as a revivalist that ensured her success as a missionary. So popular was she in Derbyshire that the people there offered to pay her salary in order to keep her from being sent elsewhere. Soon after she preached in Derby, a society was formed and regular services were scheduled.[61] In 1816 Derby was made head of the connexion's second circuit.

The creation of Derby circuit was a direct consequence of a revolt against the moratorium on expansion and the conservatism at Tunstall. In addition to the non-missioning law, Steele and his supporters had tamed camp meetings almost to the point of dullness. Having been "trained for the sanctuary and not for the field pulpit," and convinced that "a well-conducted camp meeting should be confined to the delivery of well-arranged discourses," these ex-Clowesites opposed the use of "praying companies" and of multiple preaching stations. Bourne advocated brief exhortations interspersed with praying, reading, and singing; a variety of concurrent activities; and the participation of a host of "praying labourers." All of this, he thought, had the advantage of "bringing many talents into action." He had observed a loss of spontaneity in the camp meetings, and he deplored their deteriorating efficacy as instruments of revivalism. In 1814 Benton reversed the pattern by restoring the "old style" at Belper, but the real turning point came as a result of the camp meeting conducted by Bourne and Benton at Mercaston in June 1816. Like the camp meetings held before 1811, it followed the pattern which had developed on the American frontier. The people in Derbyshire were thrilled with the seeming innovation and would no longer tolerate the disapprobation of Tunstall. "So the Lord, by means of this Mercaston camp meeting, opened out a new line of proceedings," wrote Bourne. The effect of this system and "other matters" soon "caused a cry in the new converts, 'We will not be under Tunstall'." The issue was referred to the quarter-day board, and, rather than risk a secession, its members elected to form another circuit. To Bourne these pivotal events of 1816 were "like a new founding of the Connexion." With about 700 members in Staffordshire, Derbyshire, and Cheshire, Tunstall circuit was the more numerous of the two. It was out of the smaller Derby circuit, however, that Primitive Methodism emerged reinvigorated to conquer Nottinghamshire, Leicestershire, and Lincolnshire.[62]

In 1816 the Society of the Primitive Methodists was still a relatively small sect. Since its founding the connexion had roughly quadrupled in size, having grown from 200 adherents in 1811 to about 800 five years later. Thus far its evangelistic activities had been confined almost entirely to north Staffordshire, an adjacent section of Cheshire, and the southern half of Derbyshire. Nearly all its societies were located in villages. Even Tunstall, the administrative center of Primitive Methodism, had a population of less than 1,000 at the beginning of the nineteenth century. A majority of the members belonged to the lower—though not to the lowest—strata of English society; especially in Derbyshire and in east Staffordshire, however, there were a significant number of independent farmers who had cast their lot with the Primitive Methodists. The missionaries had met with occasional opposition, but encounters with serious persecution were yet to come. At the time Derby circuit was formed, Primitive Methodism stood on the verge of a period of rapid expansion. Already it had evolved most of the missioning techniques that would prove so successful in the immediate future: camp meetings, the "conversation ministry," cottage prayer sessions, street singing, and open-air preaching. In three important ways Primitive Methodism had departed from contemporary Wesleyanism: it was firmly committed to lay rather than ministerial ascendancy; it placed less emphasis on discipline than did the parent body and encouraged revivalistic "excesses" no longer tolerated by the Wesleyan conference; it operated on a far smaller budget and made minimal financial demands on its members. Half a decade after amalgamating, Primitive Methodism retained distinct traces of its dual origins, a condition that would persist until 1819. Dominant in the Potteries and in Cheshire, the ex-Clowesites valued consolidation more than expansion, sound organization and a diligent pastorate more than evangelistic enterprise. Though concerned to win souls, they were unwilling to neglect established societies in order to form new ones. Bourne, Benton, and Wedgwood, on the other hand, held that the vitality of Primitive Methodism depended on continually expanding the connexion's boundaries. Existing societies would be quickened, they believed, if the members got involved in the work of pioneering new missions. The converts on the Derbyshire frontier embraced this idea with an enthusiasm that refused to be contained by the non-missioning law. Augmented by the experience of the Mercaston camp meeting in 1816, the zeal to evangelize propelled these lay volunteers across the border into Nottinghamshire, where they initiated the Ranter revival of 1816–1818. Its energy renewed and its early ethos restored, the camp-meeting element in Primitive Methodism would no longer dance to tunes piped in Tunstall. As a result of their insubordination, the connexion was able to exploit opportunities for growth that would make it by mid-century the largest non-Wesleyan body in English Methodism. In 1851 the Primitive Methodist Connexion would number 106,074 adherents, a membership more than a third as great as the Wesleyan total.

Four

The Conquest of Canaan, 1816–1819

The Revival in the East Midlands

Perfection without any bounds was her theam. . . .
I hold with sanctifycation attainable. . . . But to hold
forth the hight of perfection to a purmiskes multitude
. . . and [to arouse] that uncommon zeall that many
call wild fier, it seemed to jar and grater something
simelor to putting hot iron into cold water more of
confeusion than younity of spirit.
                    —Diary of John Glover, Derbyshire, 1808[1]

The penetration of Primitive Methodism into the East
Midlands was as unplanned as the connexion's origins. Far from being a
centrally directed evangelistic strategy, the thrust into new territory was
initiated by a scattering of individuals, each working independently of
the others and all contravening the ruling of 1814 against further expansion. Typically, much of the original impulse came from lay persons.
The first to arrive was Sarah Kirkland, who had been persuaded by
Robert Winfield that the hungry framework knitters of Nottingham
might yield to female preaching. Accompanied by the Derbyshire farmer
and his daughter, she opened her mission on Christmas night, 1815. Although Bourne had tacitly approved the eastward advance, he did not
preach in Nottingham until the following August. By then a "surprising
work" was already in progress. Kirkland was graduated to the status of
itinerant, the first of many Primitive Methodist women to be officially
recognized as professional ministers. Ripe for revival, Nottingham in
1817 replaced a less-flourishing Derby as the head of a circuit whose
perimeter was expanding into the counties of Lincoln and Leicester.
Previously undermined by unauthorized missions in Derbyshire, the

Tunstall ban was now altogether defunct. Bourne concluded that the *fait accompli* marked a triumph of divine wisdom over excessive human caution.[2]

The Primitive Methodists reached the East Midlands just as food shortages, postwar unemployment, depressed wages, and soaring prices were stirring widespread discontent with the established social and economic order. According to one of their Nottinghamshire proselytes, George Herod, it was also in 1816 that Luddism fused with leveling, and "the minds of thousands were . . . excited with disaffection towards government." Herod observed that the Primitive Methodist evangelists were able to win a hearing partly because both their dress and their dialect betokened lower-class origins. The unorthodoxy of their approach was likewise a great asset. Had they been immediately recognizable as evangelists,

> it would have been said—"Oh, it's some Methodist preacher; it is nothing new." But the course adopted led to a different result. . . . When the preacher had collected the people in the open air by lively singing, they waited in eagerness to hear if he would tell them something new. And when he commenced his fervent and energetic prayer . . . deploring their wretched and miserable condition as a result of their transgression, an influence was often brought to bear on them that caused them to reflect. But especially when he read out his text and began to portray the character, conduct, and circumstances of his hearers, his word . . . often reached their consciences, and many saw the error into which they had fallen, and the danger of mixing with infidel and political companions—and so forsook them and became valuable members of society.[3]

As Herod's account makes clear, novelty alone gave Primitive Methodism a decided advantage. So long as a new Moses did not represent religion in its familiar guise, desperate and hungry people were eager to take up the search for milk and honey. Similarly, when Oliver the Spy promised the capture of Canaan in 1817, his words found a ready audience. Usually the missionary began by stressing what was uppermost in the minds of his hearers—the intolerable misery of their existence. Then, unlike either the false or the true prophets of radicalism, he would thrust the burden of guilt back onto his audience. "Getting liberty," he would assure them, was not to be achieved by overthrowing Lord Liverpool's government, but by conversion and sanctification. The tactics of the evangelists were predicated on an awareness that hearsay and curiosity would attract huge crowds of potential converts. The name "Ranters" itself provoked interest. "Inquire for the 'Primitive Methodists'," wrote Dow, "and you could not find what you wished, but on inquiry for *Ranters*, anyone could tell you." Bourne noted that "if it was given out for a Ranter-preacher to preach, the neighbourhood and often a part of the country would usually come together." Herod recalled that Ranterism was a "new topic" of discussion for the groups that collected on street corners to talk politics. The word retained some of its former revolutionary connotations. A "wicked man," who spent his Sundays drifting from one public house to another, discovered that the Ranters had come to his village. Assuming that the newcomers were radicals "under a feigned name," he hastened to hear them. Disappointed when insurrection did not figure in the sermon, he resolved to attend a class meeting, for there the preacher would surely relay to trusted initiates "some private communication . . . about a general rising." The quest eventually led to his conversion.[4]

Although the Primitive Methodists habitually employed dissident Wesleyans to help create an opening wedge, the apostolate was primarily directed to persons outside the pale of organized religion. A too-careful scrutiny of tickets, they believed, would lessen opportunities for conversion. To deny nonmembers entry into a class meeting might be tantamount to denying them salvation. Similarly, the early missionaries did not institute band meetings, admission to which was selective and carefully controlled by well-disciplined Wesleyans. Another departure from conventional Methodist practice was the outdoor love feast. In the East Midlands this originally intimate and often emotional exercise was expanded into a colossal assembly where everyone was welcome. The first of these affairs was deliberately sited at the junction of the Nottingham-Newark highway and another thoroughfare. The innovation was an immediate success. A vast crowd of people gathered on Priest Hill to celebrate their fellowship in Christ, and so many invitations to preach ensued that several more itinerants had to be rushed into Nottinghamshire. It may have been this giant love feast that impelled one county magistrate to write an alarmed letter to the Home Office about meetings of thousands of Ranters on the commons, wastes, and lanes.[5] Natural social impulses favored the Primitive Methodist cause. At a time when traditional forms of community recreation were beginning to disappear, a camp meeting or an open-air love feast offered a new and entertaining way to break the work routine, to exchange gossip, and to mingle with friends and strangers. Even non-Methodists were apt to travel several miles in order to join in the activity. Frequently, they carried back curiosity-arousing accounts of their experiences and thus played harbinger to the missionaries who followed.

The actual dynamics of Primitive Methodist expansion during the "great revival" cannot easily be charted, partly because the movement was always subject to a variety of centrifugal forces, and partly because the sect kept no systematic records of its progress. Any attempt to correlate the response to their mission with economic conditions or with political behavior must begin by reckoning with three factors. First, the mammoth open-air exercises that won the greatest notoriety were almost always held during warm weather. Often they were scheduled as counterattractions to wakes or fairs. During the winter months most sessions took place in cottages, barns, or warehouses and were not so well publicized. This seasonal element makes dubious any facile conclusions about the short-term waxing and waning of Primitive Methodist vitality. Second, it is very difficult to draw a line between the pious sheep and the radical goats. Methodist congregations generally included both members and a fairly regular but ticketless body of "hearers." A Ranter meeting was also likely to attract many who were merely curious as well as some who came only to harass. Even people who joined the society were not necessarily apolitical or antiradical. Especially during periods of rapid growth, it was difficult to identify and withhold tickets from those whom Bourne considered "improper persons." Nor were the missionaries always eager to do so. While some Primitive Methodists followed Bourne's example and disavowed politics entirely, not all were convinced that membership in the society precluded a commitment to radical agitation. Doubtless, there were also many who were concurrently but superficially involved in both Hampden Clubs and Ranter revivalism, or whose interest fluctuated from the one to the other.

A third problem is raised by the issue of free gospelism. By 1816 connexional leaders had opted against it, but organization was loose and discipline lax. Many advocates of an unpaid, nonprofessional ministry considered themselves Primitive Methodists until they were pressed to collect contributions. Several in the vanguard of the East Midlands campaign won followers by preaching free-gospel Christianity. Rather than submit to the practice of paying class and ticket money, they and their converts often severed their rather casual ties to Primitive Methodism. Although he did not secede from the connexion, John Wedgwood vexed Bourne by refusing to ask for "ordinary collections or class money." Wedgwood's ally and frequent preaching companion, John Benton, likewise espoused free-gospel views. By June 1817 Nottingham circuit was riddled with free gospelism, and its "pecuniary concerns" were "very crooked." Clowes arrived at the end of August and began a campaign to undo the mischief, but he was only moderately successful. Especially in the mining district along the Derbyshire border and in the industrial villages around Nottingham, free religion was too deeply rooted to be wholly eradicated. The effort to do so usually entailed the loss of individual members and sometimes of entire societies. By the autumn of 1818 circuit finances were "almost reduced to a wreck." During the previous year Wedgwood and Benton had pressed into northern Leicestershire and had seriously infected the new territory as well. The dramatic revivalism that accompanied the advent of Ranterism in the East Midlands was never repeated; on the other hand, the subsequent decline in Primitive Methodist numbers does not necessarily imply an abandoning of the religious quest in favor of a political one.[6]

The Awakening of Nottinghamshire

When the Ranters reached western Nottinghamshire, local Methodism was suffering malaise. Although she had heard that religion was "very low" there, Mary Tatham Oastler encouraged her mother to believe that many "would enter heartily into the work of God" if only "the way were made plain." But in 1816 neither the Wesleyans nor the Kilhamites were prepared to convert Nottingham's "swinish multitude." Sarah Kirkland was. Not bold enough to preach in the marketplace, she opened her mission in a small room belonging to some ex-Wesleyans. After one of them proclaimed that she had recently dreamed of a young woman "coming out of Derbyshire" who was garbed like Kirkland, rumor recruited hundreds of inquisitive hearers, and the preaching had to be transferred to an abandoned factory. Soon "it became the talk of the market people that if they would go to the room in Broad Marsh, they would get converted."[7]

The Primitive Methodist revival was flourishing well before radical agitation reached fever pitch. Confined to Broad Marsh during the winter of 1815–1816, the awakening overspilled the slum during the following summer. On 2 June an estimated 12,000 people thronged to the Nottingham raceground for a Whitsun camp meeting. The society at Bulwell, formed after Kirkland preached from a cart in a nearby field on the following day, was sixty strong by the beginning of July. On 11–12 August large numbers flocked to open-air meetings in Hemphill Lane and Bulwell Forest; then, not yet weary of praying and preaching, they came to hear Bourne, who visited Bulwell on 13 August. A "great multitude" also greeted him in Nottingham, where a "glorious time" was had in the factory room. Kirkland moved on to Ilkestone (Derbyshire) and sparked a "great revival" among the colliers there. At Hucknall Torkard she found "much temporal and spiritual destitution, coupled with alarming political disaffection." Soon, however, a Primitive Methodist society with sixty or seventy members was holding services at the Seven Stars Inn. Kirkland's highly successful missionary tour also included several

other mining and manufacturing villages in southwestern Nottinghamshire and the adjacent part of Derbyshire.[8]

Economic distress became exceptionally severe in the autumn of
1816. November brought the first issue of Cobbett's "Twopenny Trash,"
the widely circulated "Address to the Journeymen and Labourers." While
Henry Hunt was denouncing corruption at Spa Fields in London, Hampden Clubs and Union Societies were multiplying in the Midlands. The
neighborhood of Nottingham was in a ferment compounded of Luddism,
reform agitation, and want. On 9 June Luddites demolished a dozen
point-lace machines in New Radford. Their trial in August caused
"intense" excitement among the working classes, "most of whom deeply
sympathized with the Luddites." Confronted with an "organized and
infuriated" armed crowd, the jury acquitted them. So much alarm was
generated by the trial that the government considered making Newark
instead of Nottingham the assize town. In September the mayor convened a meeting to address the prince regent concerning the "terrific local
pressure on the inhabitants . . . arising from the state of utter destitution
of many thousands of the working classes." By November, when James
Towle of Basford was executed for frame-breaking at Loughborough in
the previous June, the price of wheat had risen to over 76s. per quarter.[9]

Religious enthusiasm mounted as misery increased during the winter
and spring of 1817. During this period Benton opened Bingham, and,
despite opposition from the local church party, a "very large" society
was formed. He visited some of the industrial villages where Kirkland
had preached in 1816 and introduced the cause in other places. Benton
estimated that 1,000 people heard his sermon at Car Colston Green in the
spring of 1817. When Bourne preached at Nottingham in May from
Isaiah 43:2 ("When thou walkest through fire, thou shalt not be
burned"), he called the occasion "one of the greatest times I ever had."
Oliver the Spy was also touring the district in May. Whether the outdoor
love feast at Priest Hill took place before or after the abortive rising set
for 9 June is not recorded, but two weeks after Pentridge the "work was
going on well and rapidly." According to Herod, a "more extensive
revival than [Benton] had ever witnessed" broke out in June. Wedgwood, John Heath, and John Hall were urgently summoned into Nottinghamshire to assist Benton, who was unable to visit all the places from
which he had received invitations to preach. Clowes attracted a crowd of
2,000 in the marketplace at Bingham, and he reported that within the
space of two months fifty-two members had joined the new society at
Blidworth. In September he could exclaim, "Such a field for labouring
I never saw! All around the country—east, west, north, and south—they
are crying 'come and help us'."[10]

The revival was still vigorous well into the spring of 1818. In March

Bourne observed that the "converting work" was proceeding rapidly—
"hardly anything could stand before it." Thousands were said to have
thronged to a camp meeting early in April. Making a final journey to
England during the summer of 1818, Dow applauded Ranter successes in
Nottinghamshire: "I found they had been the means under God of turning many from darkness to light." Herod was struck by Dow's "odd"
appearance and noted that the "strangely clad" American advocated republicanism as well as salvation. The fact that Dow was foreign, looked
peculiar, and argued against monarchy probably enhanced his attraction
as a speaker. "Hundreds" heard him at East Bridgford, and he addressed
a huge crowd in the open air at Bingham.

By the time of Dow's visit, however, the awakening in Nottinghamshire had lost some of its fire. Although enthusiasm had not yet abated
among the society members at Nottingham, Hucknall Torkard, and
Ilkeston, nowhere was Primitive Methodism still provoking the general
excitement and dramatic conversions that had characterized its first appearance in the region. It would have been more remarkable if the flame
of revival had continued to burn high. Presumably, by the late summer
of 1818 most of the combustible consciences in the vicinity had already
been ignited.[11]

Herod claimed that 1818 was the year in which Primitive Methodism "took deep root" in Nottinghamshire. His assessment was probably
based on the fact that it was then that the first significant attempt was
made to consolidate the fruits of the revival. Previously, in the absence
of a printed plan scheduling itinerants for weekday appointments, each
preacher had simply assigned himself and had tried to inform the others
of his whereabouts. Nor before 1818 had much attention been paid to
organizing converts into classes or societies. Harrison welcomed the
effort to do so: "This step was judicious, for it was the means of establishing order."[12] Lack of discipline was compounded by the havoc being
wrought by free gospelism.[13] The Tunstall circuit, which had been under-
writing the mission to the East Midlands, could no longer afford the
burden of paying debts incurred elsewhere. In September a circuit committee was appointed to deal with Nottingham's financial crisis. As the
only body authorized to act on a circuit-wide basis between quarter-
days, the new committee proved so useful that what originated as a local
and temporary expedient soon became an integral part of connexional
government. Bourne valued circuit committees because they served as a
"means of filling up a chasm . . . in discipline."[14] For the laity they meant
expanded opportunities to learn the techniques of administration. One
early result of enhancing the already democratic nature of Primitive
Methodism was the introduction in 1819 of parliamentary procedure at

the meetings of quarter-day boards and circuit committees, a usage quickly adopted by the entire connexion.

In January 1819 illness forced Bourne to relinquish direct supervision of all but the Tunstall circuit. By the time he withdrew, revivalism had spent its energies in the immediate vicinity of Nottingham and was flowing into new territory. Such rapid expansion demanded more sophisticated administrative machinery, and in March 1819 the circuit was divided into branches. Membership figures for this period are somewhat misleading because growth was occurring in the branches, not at the center. These branches rapidly matured into independent circuits: Hull in June 1819; Scotter, Sheffield, and Derby in March 1820; Lincoln in September 1820; and Grimsby in December 1820. The decline of the revival in Nottinghamshire was evidenced, however, by the fact that preaching vocations from the circuit fell sharply after 1820. In 1828 the *Primitive Methodist Magazine* listed 142 active itinerants who had entered the ministry before 1825. Nottingham had provided 60 percent of those called before 1820, only 10 percent of those who took up preaching between 1820 and 1822, and just 4 percent of the remainder.

The Opening of Leicestershire

Like the evangelizing of Nottinghamshire, the Primitive Methodist advance into Leicestershire was self-initiated by preachers eager to win souls and well aware that social unrest and economic deprivation were creating a climate favorable to revivalism. Late in the summer of 1817 John Benton, John Heath, and John Wedgwood pushed out of Nottinghamshire and into the neighborhood of Loughborough. Other evangelists soon followed, and by the late spring of 1818 the Loughborough section of the Nottingham circuit plan listed sixteen places, eight regular preachers, and ten preachers "on trial."[15] In September the Leicestershire societies were formed into a separate circuit, partly on account of the troubles in Nottingham, but also because the missionaries in the frontier territory were reaping such a rich harvest of converts. The initial focus of their attention was Loughborough and the villages south and east of the town. Apart from agriculture, the chief means of support in the district were framework knitting and hosiery-making. As in Nottinghamshire, the triennium after Waterloo was here a period of economic crisis during which political agitation enlisted the support of General Ludd. The average annual expenditure for relief in the county between 1813 and 1815 was £106,427; during the following three years it mounted to £133,675. In 1816 Luddites destroyed fifty-five lace frames in a midnight attack on the factory of Heathcote and Boden at Loughborough. In consequence, Heathcote transferred his bobbin-net lace manufacturing operation to Somerset, thus creating considerable unemployment in Loughborough. Six men found guilty of frame-breaking were hanged at Leicester in April 1817; drilling in preparation for the "general rising" planned for 9 June began shortly afterward. At Countesthorpe, a village of 740 people, nearly all of whom depended on framework knitting, a barn was converted into a storehouse for ammunition. Not long after the revolution had plainly failed to materialize, the Ranters reached Countesthorpe, and "all the leading men belonging to the Levellers" were "convinced of sin." The house where these mourners promptly held their first prayer meeting "was crowded to excess," but, when the opening hymn was ended, "there was not one to be found" who knew how to pray. Soon, however, the "two principal Levellers obtained the remission of their sins . . . , and then they were enabled to pray without a book." Both forsook radical agitation to become Primitive Methodist local preachers.[16]

Loughborough, with 7,500 inhabitants in 1821, had grown extremely rapidly during the wars with France. The impetus for this population boom was an increase in the demand for cotton hosiery, the recently introduced manufacture of mohair and worsted hosiery, and, above all, the making of patent lace on the newly invented "Loughborough machine." The advent of the first Ranter preachers during the crippling depression induced by the shutdown of Heathcote and Boden and only a few weeks after the Pentridge rising generated a fresh topic for discussion in the pubs and lanes of the town. For some, the missioners' message reawakened hope, affirmed self-worth, and provided an alternative structure of values. By the time that Bourne paid his first visit in January 1818, Loughborough's converts had been organized into a society; by May they had erected the first Primitive Methodist chapel in the county, a heavily mortgaged structure which the impoverished members were later obliged to give up because they could not meet their debts.[17]

Except for Quorndon, a manufacturing village also famed for its hunt, the Primitive Methodists encountered very little overt persecution as they evangelized northern and central Leicestershire. On the contrary, in 1818 Clowes found that "the spirit of conviction had extensively gone abroad among the people." "Indeed," he commented, "the whole country appeared to be on a move." John Benton, the archetype of Ranter village missionaries in this early period, was able to empty some Anglican churches when he preached on Sundays. John Harrison, who was not apt to exaggerate numbers, recorded that a docile crowd of 1,000 people listened to him preach at Hoteby on the night of 12 May 1818. "Hundreds" from his audience walked him part of the way back to Leicester afterward. "Some hundreds" gathered in the street to hear him at Thrussington; 300 came for a daybreak exhortation at Queniborough; 2,000 congregated on the moor at Coleorton; and another 1,000 attended his outdoor sermon at Shepshed. Typical of Harrison's tour in Leicestershire was a visit to Elstone, "where the gospel plow had not been set in for a great length of time." He and another preacher excited curiosity by singing through the street, addressed the crowd they attracted, and left accompanied by many who begged them to return.[18]

Missioning activity at Syston in January 1818 illustrates the displacement by Primitive Methodism of customary forms of rural recreation. Syston was opened by George Hanford, a Sileby lace manufacturer, who during the early 1820s played a prominent role in connexional government. Approached on Plough Monday by costumed "plough bullocks" from Syston begging money for revelry in the public house that evening, Hanford refused. Instead, he gave an unsolicited sermon. " 'Oh'," the mummers retorted, " 'you are a Ranter, by your preaching'." Asked if Syston had any Ranters, they replied, " 'No! . . . and if they ever come there, we'll kill 'em'." Thus challenged, Hanford assembled a band of Primitive Methodists from Sileby, traveled to Syston, and argued down the local clergyman, a farmer, and a lawyer who summoned a constable. He then preached to the audience that had assembled on the village green. The upshot of Hanford's mission was that on a subsequent Plough Monday only one of the "bullocks" was willing to participate in the traditional rites. When queried about the demise of the usual festivities, the solitary reveler explained: " 'Why, the Ranters have been to our place and [have] broken up the gang! . . . They are folks that go about singing and praying, and standing on greens, in market-places, at the stocks, or anywhere they can get, and telling people they must give up getting drunk, fighting, dog-fighting, gambling, fox-hunting, ploughbullocking, and all such things. . . . [All] have turned Ranters but me, and so I've come to tell you!' " According to one perhaps biased account, Primitive Methodism ultimately replaced both pubs and plough bullocks in Syston.[19]

Primitive Methodist missionaries did not reach Leicester until March 1818. First to preach there was John Benton, who confessed that he had felt reluctant to enter the county town, preferring instead to evangelize the surrounding villages. Its prosperity tied to the manufacture of stockings, Leicester almost doubled in population during the war years; in 1821 it had slightly more than 30,000 inhabitants. When the Ranters arrived, Methodism had not yet made much impact. This was partly because older forms of Nonconformity, especially Baptists, were well established in Leicester, and also because the diocesan clergy had evangelical inclinations.[20] Robert Hall, the eloquent minister of the Harvey

Lane Baptist Chapel, gave his blessing to the Primitive Methodist mission in the town. Asked whether the Ranters "ought to be put down" on account of their "irregular practices," he pointed out that Jesus, the apostles, the Protestant reformers, and Wesley were all "very irregular," and added, "There must be something widely different from mere irregularity before I condemn."[21] Benton's coming, preannounced by a derogatory caricature displayed in the windows of several stationers' shops, stirred heated arguments for and against Ranterism. This anticipatory discussion no doubt helped to swell the crowd when he finally spoke at Belgrave Gate. Wedgwood, Clowes, and Harrison soon followed Benton to Leicester. Their audiences too were sizable: Clowes urged 2,000 people at Belgrave Gate to "acquaint yourself now with Him and be at peace." On a single day Harrison addressed "several thousand" at Orchard Street, 5,000 at Horsepool Street, and 8,000 at Frog Island. Meanwhile, two other preachers were at work elsewhere in the town. The next morning Harrison preached near West Bridge to the "largest congregation I ever had."[22] The response to the Primitive Methodist message was great enough so that the connexion was hard pressed to find experienced leaders to take charge of the classes formed; one man, William Goodrich, was responsible for four classes with a combined total of almost 300 members.[23]

Camp meetings were perhaps the single most important means of advertising Ranterism in Leicestershire. Many of them were scheduled to coincide with parish feasts, a stratagem that Bourne had employed much earlier in Staffordshire. Wakes, Bourne maintained, were "seasons of much leisure," and camp meetings were "well calculated to fill up that leisure." A "diversity of pious exercises," he declared, "engages the people extensively and brings their talents very generally into action." To achieve the desired variety and participation Bourne advocated "short and lively" preaching "intermingled with singing, prayer, praise, exhortations, reading or speaking experiences, relating anecdotes, [and] reading short and striking accounts of the work of God." This model was successfully copied at Barlestone, where, he claimed, it prevented improprieties, drunkenness, and altercations. The Barlestone camp meeting was a protracted one: "Nearly the whole of the inhabitants were constantly engaged in religious exercises . . . [from Sunday] until Thursday in the wake-week." Phenomena previously unknown in England, though characteristic of American revivalism, emerged in Leicestershire during 1818–1819. At a second camp meeting at Barlestone onlookers witnessed some instances of "falling," a fairly common occurrence during awakenings on the American frontier. Another event familiar to Americans but so far not attempted in England was the outdoor meeting at night. This innovation was first tried in November 1818 at Hinckley. So dramatic was the scene created by the flickering of candles and lanterns that the experiment was repeated at Burbage a few days later; the meeting here "looked brilliant and dazzling, and the whole had a striking appearance." Another American practice was introduced at a circuit camp meeting in Charnwood Forest, where a horn was used to signal the transition from prayer sessions to sermons. This assembly was also the first to employ a "permanent praying company" exclusively devoted to mourners. Publicized in the *Primitive Methodist Magazine*, the new techniques were soon widely used by Ranter evangelists.[24]

Leicestershire Primitive Methodists were instrumental in bringing to birth the connexional magazine. An abortive effort to publish a quarterly periodical was made by Bourne in 1818. The first twopenny issue, dated April, was sold "for ready money only." The quarterly was not a financial success. Bourne paid for both its initial and its final (July) numbers. At a meeting in Leicester in November 1818 an itinerant, Robert Culley, spoke on behalf of "the friends in this circuit," suggesting a presubscribed threepenny monthly instead. Bourne submitted the matter to one of the stewards, Joseph Skevington of Loughborough. Encouraged by Skevington, Bourne and others began to solicit subscriptions, and on 11 January 1819 the first issue of the *Methodist Magazine for the Year 1819, Conducted by the Camp-Meeting Methodists Known by the Name of Ranters, Called Also Primitive Methodists* was sent to press. When Bourne fell ill a few days later, William Goodrich of Leicester assumed the task of editing the periodical until August. Despite his poor health, Bourne contributed articles to the eight issues edited by Goodrich and published at Leicester. When in 1820 he was himself appointed editor, he brought out three "substitutes" for the months missed during the autumn of 1819. Volume 2 of the now rechristened *Primitive Methodist Magazine* (1821) was printed in various towns; beginning in 1822 it found more permanent headquarters in Bemersley.[25]

According to a report entitled "State of the Connexion, Michaelmas, 1820," which was included in the first volume of the *Magazine*, the revival was still flourishing in Leicestershire, and the Loughborough circuit was expanding. By June 1821, however, one hostile observer claimed that "the Ranters have bawled themselves out of breath in this neighbourhood and, I think, are losing ground. They have chanted and shouted till the people take no more notice of their noise."[26] Perhaps economic factors contributed to the waning success of the mission in Leicestershire: in the spring of 1821 the hosiery trade revived after a period of unemployment and wage reductions during the preceding winter. But one reason for diminished enthusiasm, as in Nottinghamshire earlier, was simply that the novelty of Ranterism for the merely curious had worn off. The half-converted lapsed into inactivity, while a more committed minority became the nucleus of those societies which remained intact.

The peak of the revival in Nottinghamshire lasted a little more than two years—from 1816 to mid-1818; in Leicestershire the awakening began during the summer of 1817 and persisted through 1820. During 1817 and the first nine months of 1818 seventy-five towns and villages were evangelized and scheduled for regular Sunday services. An equal number of local preachers and exhorters were "raised up."[27] Some of the initial gains proved to be ephemeral, as both secessions and backsliding took their toll. More stringent enforcement of discipline with regard to class attendance and the payment of ticket money shrank membership rolls earlier swollen with the names of free gospelers and those in whom the flame of religious zeal burned erratically. The keeping of accurate records itself yielded more realistic numbers than the sometimes illusory estimates claimed during the height of the revival. By 1823, after some members once counted as part of either Nottingham or Loughborough had been incorporated into other circuits, the combined Primitive Methodist population of the two older circuits was slightly more than 5,000. It was, however, primarily during the waning phase of the East Midlands revival that Nottingham circuit was reaching out to establish missionary branches in Lincolnshire and Yorkshire.

The Rural East Midlands: Ranters, Persecutors, and Enclosures

> His voice rang like thunder, his eyes flashed fire, he stamped with both feet, he waved his arms over his head, then over the people near him, froth fell from his lips . . . , as he spoke of the devil throwing the wicked into hell like a man throwing faggots into a bonfire. It was awful. During the same service some were weeping and some shouting and praising God.
> —Description of William Braithwaite, ca. 1819[28]

Until the spring of 1819 Nottingham was the center from which virtually all Ranter evangelistic activity emanated. Except for a mission to Sheffield opened in 1819, these endeavors were directed eastward and northward. The bearers of Primitive Methodism achieved varying degrees of success. Especially en route to Lincolnshire and in the southern two-thirds of that county, the missionaries faced considerable hostility, which they were only sometimes able to overcome. In some parts of the eastern West Riding of Yorkshire they found a lukewarm reception or attracted modest but not always lasting support. In northern Lincolnshire, the Marshland district, and the East Riding of Yorkshire, however, Primitive Methodism won substantial and enduring victories.

Whereas the "great revival" was primarily centered in towns and in mining or industrial villages, most of the new territory opened from Nottingham between 1817 and the end of 1819 was more strictly agricultural. From one-third to one-half of this farmland was enclosed during the sixty years preceding 1820. One consequence of these acts was often to reduce marginal cottagers and smallholders to the status of wage-laborers. Perhaps more important from the standpoint of Primitive Methodist expansion, enclosure also deprived such people of their sense of personal worth and of their place as self-sustaining members of the village community. Stripped of customary common rights, they became social inferiors dependent on the pleasure of their "betters." But enclosure *per se* was only the most obvious facet of a more general and long-evolving process, the capitalization of agriculture. In pursuit of profit the larger landowners consolidated, expanded, and improved their holdings, imposed short-lease policies, and practiced rack-renting. Unable to benefit from economies of scale, small farmers were increasingly less likely to survive, particularly when the agricultural boom of the war years collapsed after 1815. Former small owners and tenants were thrust into a labor force already enlarged because of population growth and now further augmented by discharged soldiers and sailors seeking employment. The work for which they competed offered diminished security as hiring by the day, week, or task gained popularity among employers. Abandonment of the traditional pattern of hiring at annual fairs not only meant that many farm laborers were without income during slack seasons; it also eroded personal ties. Landowners felt less paternal responsibility for the welfare of a rural proletariat than they had shown for longer-term laborers with whom they were better acquainted. In workers so regarded, resentment quite naturally displaced deference, especially when these employers dramatized their wealth and superior status by building neoclassical mansions. Potentially advantageous for the spread of Primitive Methodism, this situation could also be detrimental: the shamed poor of the countryside were often eager to demonstrate their discontent by embracing an alternative to the established church, but defensive parsons and gentry were frequently just as anxious to thwart the intrusion of Ranterism.

The sect first met with significant opposition in the prosperous farming region that stretched south from Newark into the county of Rutland. Within this area lay the extremely fertile Vale of Belvoir, whose riches George Crabbe had contrasted to the poverty of his native east Suffolk. Here "Plenty smiles," Crabbe had observed in 1783, but "alas! she smiles for few— / And those who taste not, yet behold her store" were like slaves who mine gold: "The wealth around them makes them doubly poor."[29] The principal landowner in the Vale was John Henry Manners, the duke of Rutland, who was himself sympathetic toward Wesleyan, but not necessarily Primitive, Methodism.[30] A majority of the clergy and squirearchy across the entire district were ill disposed toward Methodism in general and vehemently set against the revivalistic kind. Tumult accompanied the introduction of Ranterism into a number of neighborhoods, and often the uproar was instigated by clergymen. For example, at one village the "lower sort" were well plied with drink and set to ringing the church bells in order to drown out Wedgwood's exhortations. Not adept in the art of ringing, they cracked the largest bell, a mishap which gave rise to the notion that, if the parson were to use this means of frustrating the Primitive Methodists a second time, the steeple would fall.[31]

Although persecution of the missionaries was a constant factor, the outcome of their efforts varied from place to place. The history of Ranter evangelism in the region both shows the sort of resistance the preachers encountered and yields some insights into why at times such opposition was surmounted. The Nottinghamshire villages of Tythby, Shelford, and Car Colston lay within less than five miles of one another, but Primitive Methodism fared differently in each of them. Obliged to delay his outdoor sermon at Tythby because its 500 inhabitants were all at church when he arrived, John Harrison finally assembled a large but "stiff-necked" congregation. "I could not move these formal professors," he confessed, "and to all appearance God did not—so I left them."[32] Tythby remained immune to the revival spirit. Next day Harrison was welcomed at Shelford, where one of the villagers had already opened his stud-and-mud cottage for preaching. About the same size as Tythby, Shelford was part of the hereditary estate of the earl of Chesterfield. His steward tried but failed to rid it of Ranters by evicting their host, whose dwelling stood on a strip of waste land facing the parish church. Offended by the continuing presence of the Primitive Methodists, the church party had the ground enclosed and demolished the "eyesore." A similar scenario was followed after another cottager let the missionaries use his house. When the Ranters moved to a third dwelling, its occupant was brought before the bench for harboring their services. Because the case against him was legally unsound, the magistrates had to dismiss it. Subsequently prevented from purchasing a building lot, Shelford's society members bought a canal boat, which they towed downriver from Nottingham, anchored in the Trent, and made into a chapel. Persecution merely bred antagonism among the people and thus increased support for the Primitive Methodists. Eventually, their opponents concluded that the Ranters were "incorrigible" and could not be eradicated, though "we may pull half the village down."[33] At Car Colston, the "center of a number of villages where clergymen resided, who were decided enemies to dissenters, and great supporters of fox hunting," the local squires were persuaded to disrupt an open-air meeting. The attempt failed chiefly because they were dispersed by a member of their own class, William Lockwood. A former Wesleyan itinerant who espoused revivalism, Lockwood had married a wealthy property owner in the district. He continued to champion the Primitive Methodists, and Car Colston Green, which was strategically located along the Fosse Way, became a popular site for large Ranter gatherings.[34]

Whether or not Primitive Methodism took root in a given locale was largely contingent on the evangelists' success in finding a haven for preaching. The influence of Lockwood may have counted for something in village affairs, but it mattered not at all in the market town of Newark. When he tried to speak from his gig, a clergyman ordered the fire brigade to turn its hoses on him. Although several missionaries sought to establish a society in this bastion of Toryism, at first none of its 8,100 residents would open their houses to the preachers.[35] At Kinoulton the church was in ruins, the incumbent a nonresident, and attendance at Anglican worship sparse. Kinoulton ought to have been congenial soil for Ranterism. It was not. Benton was stoned and a dangerous bull was set upon him; another missionary was driven out of the village. One key to this failure appears to have been that the people of Kinoulton knew their vicar was empowered to punish offenders against the church without the consent of any other authority.[36] Benton, Wedgwood, and Harrison were all greeted with volleys of rotten eggs, filth, and stones at Bottesford, a small town which Harrison christened "Little Sodom." Benton noted that Bottesford lay in the shadow of Belvoir Castle, the seat of the duke of Rutland, and that its inhabitants were "under the influence that sprang from the aristocratical and High Church party." Nevertheless, as at Shelford, some were bold enough to defy the establishment. A house was offered for preaching, and the Ranters soon succeeded in "raising a considerable interest." In 1829 they enlarged their "well attended" chapel; by 1836 almost one-tenth of the population was enrolled in the Primitive Methodist Sunday school.[37] At Redmile, a village near Belvoir Castle, the preachers were assaulted, and, "none daring to open a door," they forsook the place. A woman whose family was one of the few who were not dependents of the duke was later converted at a camp meeting. She asked the Ranters to return, and, with a meeting place now secured, more and more people flouted the status quo and joined the society.[38]

When, in 1817, Wedgwood was arrested and imprisoned at Grantham, the episode was significant for three reasons. The incident, which occurred at the beginning of the Primitive Methodist mission to Lincolnshire, drew Clowes to the East Midlands and so into direct contact with the revival. This, Clowes's initial exposure to the impact that Ranter evangelism could have on great numbers of hungry and disaffected people, enlarged his vision of the role that Primitive Methodism might play. The episode also provided the sect with its first "martyr." Released on bail after his two weeks' incarceration, Wedgwood hastened to a camp meeting at Buckminster, where he was hailed as a popular hero. Finally, the Ranters learned a valuable lesson at Grantham: aristocratic patronage was not always an asset. The arrest of Wedgwood convinced a local baronet, Sir William Manners, that supporting the Primitive Methodists was a splendid way to vex the town's corporation, which had rejected his candidate in the last parliamentary election. To this end he had a stone pulpit for Ranter use erected near Grantham's guildhall. The people, however, were suspicious of the Primitive Methodists' "entanglement" with aristocracy and until 1835 were deaf to their message.[39]

As they progressed through Kesteven and into the section of Lindsey nearest to Lincoln, the missionaries continued to encounter opposition from both the church and the landed interest. This was the part of Lincolnshire best provided with churches, but not necessarily with resident clergy. According to a contemporary observer, "rusticity and ruthlessness" characterized its laboring population, a description which agreed with that recorded in the late 1790s by Richard Watson, a native of Lincoln. As a young Wesleyan local preacher, Watson had found people in the surrounding villages indifferent to religion, spiritually ignorant, and "strenuously opposed to all attempts to instruct and reform them." Here clergy and gentry still were able to stir up a hostile crowd. Lincoln itself was a stronghold of Anglican resistance to "unlearned and non-ordained" Methodist preachers. In 1811 a prebendary of the cathedral had called them "mean and illiterate, silly boys, idle, ignorant, profligate mechanics, without any religious information or any attachment to anything that is good." Despite injuries from a barrage of stones, Clowes and Wedgwood held forth for twelve hours midway between the cathedral and the castle yard. They did manage to win some converts during this first visit, and a laborer offered his house for meetings. In 1819 a chapel was opened "with a display of hysteria which struck [one] beholder as akin to a brawl," but it was soon lost to the connexion. For the next twenty years the fortunes of the Primitive Methodists in Lincoln were usually at low ebb. The city headed a struggling circuit, but many of the societies formed between 1817 and 1820 did not survive infancy. Consequently, the area had to be evangelized again several years later.[40]

The pattern of gains and failures in Kesteven and the adjacent corner of Lindsey was similar to that in the eastern parts of Nottinghamshire and Leicestershire, and for the same reasons. This was also true in Holland and in the fen country of southeastern Lindsey, territory that was opened late in 1819. If anything, Primitive Methodism fared less well in southern Lincolnshire than it did in Newark Hundred or the Vale of Belvoir. Not only did the landowning element take more extreme measures against the introduction of Ranterism, but also, even where conversions occurred, the rate of backsliding was higher and the resultant dissolution of societies more frequent. Such ephemeral enthusiasm may have been partly due to geography—south Lincolnshire lay farther from such centers of revivalistic energy as Nottingham and Loughborough. Basically, however, it appears that Ranter efforts in the region were premature in two respects: most members of the establishment were still too defensive to admit the possibility that Primitive Methodism might serve as a "taming" force, and a majority of the lower orders were not yet prepared to challenge their influence. The missionaries who visited Kesteven, Holland, and southeastern Lindsey a decade or more later reported less persecution and greater success.[41]

The victories in north Lincolnshire more than compensated for the somewhat disappointing results obtained from early missions in the southern two-thirds of the county. During Victoria's reign an Anglican cleric recalled being told as a child that this district was a "very rough place where people did what was right in their own eyes, there being no strong body of clergy or of gentry, or towns of any importance to check headstrong and corrupt tendencies."[42] The lack of these traditional elements of control may have facilitated Ranter evangelism. North Lindsey had larger parishes, fewer churches, considerable pluralism, and many absentee clergy. Even those parsons who were resident had often been set apart from the poorer elements in their flocks, a consequence of the enclosures that had enhanced their status while proletarianizing smallholders, cottagers, and agricultural workers. Another asset enjoyed by the Primitive Methodists in northern Lincolnshire was that their way had already been prepared by such Wesleyan revivalists as the Moselys, Mary Barritt, and, most recently, John Oxtoby. An illiterate laborer, Oxtoby in 1818 had accompanied a local farmer on a missionary tour of the villages around Louth and Grimsby. Though ignorant of theology, "Praying Johnny" had soon eclipsed his partner, a Wesleyan lay preacher. With impassioned exhortations and cries of "Fleear [floor] 'em, Lord! fleear 'em, Lord!" Oxtoby had brought weeping penitents to their knees in cottages and farmhouse kitchens across north Lindsey. When in 1819 he joined the Primitive Methodists, the connexion benefited directly from his powers as a revivalist.[43] Another especially effective conversion preacher who helped to evangelize northern Lincolnshire was William Braithwaite. Known as "Hell-fire Dick" on account of his vivid rhetoric, Braithwaite, like "Praying Johnny," became something of a legend in the area.[44]

The missioning of northwestern Lindsey was begun at the inland port of Gainsborough on the Nottinghamshire border. Singing "Stop, poor sinner, stop and think," Braithwaite and a companion advanced on the marketplace in December 1818. The future Chartist Thomas Cooper "ran out with a crowd of neighbours" to hear the two men "called 'Ranters'." Then fourteen, Cooper was among those who were "greatly affected." Along with a dozen other youths and some adults, he joined the society. Several of his fellow members were "poor men who knew little of books, but who found happiness in prayer and in hearing others read and preach about the goodness of God." During his brief continuance as a Primitive Methodist Cooper heard many "loudly earnest young preachers" and attended prayer meetings which often lasted until midnight.[45] Six months after the town was opened, Gainsborough branch of Nottingham circuit employed seven preachers and included twenty-seven villages situated in a territory that stretched eastward from the Isle of Axholme almost to Market Rasen. A measure of Ranter success in the district was the gathering held on Hardwick Hill in June. "Thousands" were present, and the event was later ranked as one of the sect's "historic" camp meetings. In March 1820 Scotter—only a village but more strategically located than Gainsborough—was designated as head of a newly independent and steadily expanding circuit whose plan by 1821 would boast forty-four preaching places.[46]

Northeastern Lindsey likewise proved hospitable to Primitive Methodism. Informally missioned by two women during 1818, the vicinity of Market Rasen was also visited by Harrison in May 1819.[47] Ready to exploit these openings which had been made unofficially, the next quarterly meeting at Nottingham appointed a full-time itinerant, Thomas King, to this, the future Grimsby circuit. King took up his duties in August, and it was probably he who presided over an outdoor assembly near Caistor that reportedly attracted between three and four thousand people, most of whom were "farmers' servants, day labourers, and village mechanics."⁴⁸ Within eighteen months there were more than fifty preaching sites and over five hundred members in a circuit encompassing the area from just west of the Lincoln Wolds to the North Sea and from Alford north to the Humber. The autumn of 1820 had signaled the start of an "uncommon revival of religion, such as is seldom known in this part of the country." At "drunken" Thoresby, for instance, the society organized in September was eighty strong by February, and Covenham gained fifty converts between January and April.⁴⁹ Described in 1821 as in a "very flourishing state," the circuit was headed by a port town that was beginning to recover some of the well-being it had enjoyed as a center of fishing and trade during the era of the Hansa. Hurt by the rise of Hull in the seventeenth century and crippled by the silting up of its own harbor, Grimsby by the end of the eighteenth century had housed fewer than 1,000 persons. A new harbor had been opened in 1800, and, by the time King arrived on Halloween, 1819, the population had tripled. The place was ripe for the advent of Primitive Methodism. There were only ninety-nine members in its Wesleyan society; neither the Baptist nor the Independent cause was vigorous; and the Anglican clergyman had to serve Clee as well as Grimsby. On occasion, the promise of a free pint at the White Hart was used to swell attendance at the parish church.⁵⁰ King preached both in the marketplace and from a wheelbarrow on a piece of waste ground that later came to be called "Ranters' Wharf." The eight members of the class he formed met in a stable until the autumn of 1820, when, augmented by more than seventy new ticket holders, they transferred their place of worship to a warehouse. The society waxed with the growing prosperity of the town, and in 1836 the vicar of Grimsby himself was a "hearer." Even when local families rose on the social scale, the children and grandchildren of the first converts did not forsake Primitive Methodism to join a denomination considered more fashionable.⁵¹

Their obituaries in the connexional magazine reveal that the members of the Ranter generation in Scotter and Grimsby circuits came from the same kind of backgrounds as their counterparts in south Lindsey. The majority were farm workers or servants. Such phrases as "poor but industrious" appear frequently; less usual are references to people like the "respectable farmer" from East Stockwith whose daughter was a "prood lass with her fine earrings." Some among the early Primitive Methodists in north Lindsey were threatened with unemployment if they continued to support the sect. A wagoner, George Smith, ignored his master and became a local preacher as well as steward, trustee, and treasurer of the chapel in Bishop Norton. John Bell, an agricultural laborer at Brattleby, also refused to be intimidated. When discharged he became first a local preacher and later an itinerant. On the whole, it appears that, smarting from the social and economic impact of enclosures, the lower classes in northern Lincolnshire were readier than those in the south to defy the squirearchy. They were probably also emboldened by the fact that there were fewer resident clergy to buttress the opposition of the large proprietors.[52]

Sometimes enclosures resulted in the creation of numerous smaller holdings rather than domination by one or two great landowners. This situation was advantageous for Primitive Methodism because it increased the likelihood of discovering independent sympathizers. For example, in the parish of East Halton, enclosed between 1801 and 1804, fifty-seven people were awarded land. Among these were seven who received more than one hundred acres, twenty-two whose holdings amounted to between ten and one hundred acres, and twenty-eight who got tracts of less than ten acres. East Halton had a Primitive Methodist society by 1819, and by 1828 the members had opened a two-room chapel which, unlike most Ranter places of worship, occupied a choice site on the main street of the village.[53] Similarly, the cause prospered at Haxey, a parish with many small owners.[54] Occasionally, the failure of the Church of England to provide adequately for the population provoked a major landowner into sponsoring the Primitive Methodists. There was no church at Crosby, so the Anglican lord of the manor, Sir Robert Sheffield, built a Ranter chapel in its stead.[55]

An index of the comparative fortunes of Primitive Methodism in northern and southern Lincolnshire is provided by the membership statistics reported in 1823, the first year that these figures were broken down by circuits. Lincoln circuit, which covered considerably more than half of the county, claimed 664 members. Scotter circuit and its progeny, Brigg and Marshland, counted more than double that number. Grimsby and its daughter circuit, Louth, together had a total of nearly 600. There were, then, almost three times as many Primitive Methodists in north Lindsey alone as there were in southern Lincolnshire, an area not quite twice as large. It is symbolically important that the entire administrative district was placed under the headship, not of a major town, but of a village—Scotter.[56]

The Evangelizing of Eastern Yorkshire

On the very day of my entering into Hull I preached in the evening in an old factory in North-street. . . . On the day following I took a walk down to the pottery by the Humberside, where I had worked upwards

of fifteen years before . . . I then returned, and took a
walk up and down the streets and lanes in which I
had formerly wrought folly and wickedness. It
brought to my recollection the time and place when
captured by the press-gang, and other circumstances
of dissipation and riot. O, what gratitude filled my
soul when indulging in the contrast! . . . I am now a
sinner saved by grace, and a missionary of the cross.
                                    —William Clowes, 1819[57]

The opening of Kingston-upon-Hull was of crucial significance for the expansion of Primitive Methodism in the North of
England. Not only was Hull one of the great evangelistic triumphs of the
Ranter period, but also it soon became the headquarters for missionary
campaigns that extended through much of Yorkshire and northward into
Durham, Cumberland, and Northumberland. Not content with these
endeavors, leaders at Hull sent evangelists to Cornwall, Kent, Hamp-
shire, London, and even the United States.

In 1821 about 42,000 people lived within the area that constitutes
the modern city of Hull. Since the formation of the Hull Dock Company
in 1774 and the subsequent modernization of the port, whale fishing had
yielded economic priority to shipping and commerce. Hull had a long
tradition of evangelical religion and liberal politics, and Wesleyan Methodism was firmly rooted there. In 1814 Thomas Thompson, a prominent
Wesleyan layman and an M.P. for Hull, reported that on one Sunday in
October the new chapel, the fourth in the town and the largest in England, could not accommodate the crowd of more than 4,000 persons
who gathered to attend the service, "so mightily does the desire to hear
the word of God prevail in this place."[58] Revivalism had figured in the
history of local Methodism as early as 1794, when the tide of religious
zeal then sweeping the West Riding had spread into Hull. Again in 1798–
1799 and in 1816 revivalism had struck the Wesleyan circuit.[59]

Women played a prominent role in the group of revivalists who
were instrumental in bringing Primitive Methodism to Hull. One of
them, Hannah Woolhouse, was a Wesleyan class leader who aspired to
preach. This ambition, frowned upon in the Old Connexion, was encouraged by her husband, a sack and sailcloth manufacturer who had
heard Sarah Kirkland at Broad Marsh. Late in 1817 Hannah Woolhouse
and another woman journeyed to Nottingham, rented lodgings, participated enthusiastically in the revival there, and returned home to publicize Ranterism. In December 1818 Woolhouse appeared at the quarterly
meeting in Nottingham and requested that the Primitive Methodists send

a preacher to Hull; "she shewed that the work of God at Hull and its dependencies was going on powerfully, and she thought it her duty to . . . attend the stationing." The itinerant dispatched to Hull was Clowes, who reached the scene of his erstwhile profligacy in January. At a factory there he found two classes awaiting his arrival and eager to be received as Primitive Methodists.[60] Among those present to welcome him was John Oxtoby, who, after having incited the "great revival of 1818" among the Wesleyans of northern Lincolnshire, had just begun awakening the villages on the opposite side of the Humber. The fifty-two-year-old farm laborer volunteered to assist by, as he put it, "picking up the birds that Clowes shot." In practice this meant accompanying Clowes and praying with mourners stricken by the preacher's words.[61] In addition to the classes at Hull, Clowes found would-be Primitive Methodists ready to be organized into societies in seven villages along the estuary. In March the widely circulated report of a love feast to be held at Hull drew people from as far as twenty miles away. Individuals allowed to enter without tickets were converted, and this convinced Clowes that "it was necessary to be firm in discipline but not to tighten the reins too much." Some who attended testified that "such a love feast they had never enjoyed before; others wept and praised God, who had in his providence mercifully sent the Ranters to Hull."[62]

By March congregations were already outgrowing the space available in the factory, and the society began building a chapel on Mill Street. The services held to celebrate its opening in September sparked a "great revival" during which "some of the outcasts of society became reformed characters."[63] The impetus generated by the novelty of Ranterism was sustained by the distribution of tracts, the organization of praying bands, and the systematic use of the "conversation ministry." Open-air services were held in the most neglected and disreputable neighborhoods. Thanks to the cooperation of the borough magistrates, preaching and prayer meetings were only occasionally interrupted by troublemakers. Moreover, in Hull, not only were the Primitive Methodists ordinarily immune from persecution, but also a larger than usual number of "respectable" townsfolk joined their societies. Within six months of Clowes's arrival, Hull had achieved circuit status, and by September 1819 it claimed more than 400 members. In June 1820 the circuit, which "extended rapidly and was very prosperous," was divided into seven branches; nine months later forty itinerants were at work in Hull and its missionary branches, and circuit membership had reached 4,845.[64]

The demand for missionaries in the East Riding was so great that the first itinerants sent to assist Clowes—John and Sarah (Kirkland) Harrison—usually worked independently of each other. During the early spring of 1819 Sarah Harrison undertook an evangelistic tour through the countryside northwest of Hull. When her husband visited the area in July, he found that "the sound of the Ranters . . . had gone over this part of Yorkshire." He estimated that seven or eight hundred heard him preach at Market Weighton. At Stamford Bridge the entire population was "on a move"; some of the villagers "were laughing, some weeping," while "others [were] praying as they walked down the street."[65] Harrison's optimism was justified. Traveling preachers assigned to Pocklington branch during the autumn and winter of 1820–1821 reported such tidings as a "glorious revival" at Allerthorpe, "prospering" societies at Bubwith and Bugthorpe, and some "hundreds" in attendance at Riverbridge. In February 1821 a correspondent noted of the by then fully fledged Pocklington circuit: "The work is rolling along here in a wonderful manner; souls are getting saved almost every day."[66]

Although an inexperienced itinerant ventured on a premature and largely unproductive mission to the Wolds late in 1819, this almost exclusively agricultural part of the East Riding was not systematically evangelized until 1821. The Wesleyans were "doing good work" in the region when Clowes first entered Driffield, its chief market town, but they had not yet extended their labors beyond the "fringe of the great forest to be cultivated." Once the initial prejudice of the Wesleyans toward Ranterism was overcome, there was little friction between the two connexions. The absence of antagonism proved fruitful. According to one of the major proprietors in the district, by midcentury "most of the religion between Malton and Driffield [was] to be found amongst the Methodists." The Primitives won some converts among the more substantial farmers, but their main appeal was to the craftsmen, the agricultural laborers, and the tenants or yeomen who grew grain and raised a few sheep on the small farms then prevalent in the Yorkshire Wolds. So successful was Primitive Methodist evangelism there that Driffield eventually headed the most numerous country circuit in the connexion.[67]

The missioning of the Yorkshire coast, begun in 1820, was marked by two characteristics. First, in the closed communities of these seaside villages, conversions came from every class or not at all. At Bridlington Quay revivalism caught the imagination of merchants and shipowners as well as of fishermen, scullery maids, and laborers. Second, religious enthusiasm tended to be periodic. Flamborough gave ready acceptance to Primitive Methodism, and the village was a "hotbed" of revivalism for the next half-century. Between awakenings, however, the cause languished. At Filey, where Wesleyan Methodism was struggling to survive and the influence of the established church was "almost a negative quantity," the inhabitants resisted conversion until 1823. Then Oxtoby ignited a "remarkable revival" that "laid the foundations of a strong cause" and worked a "moral revolution" among the fishing folk. By the autumn of 1822 Bridlington branch had nearly 400 members and employed three traveling preachers. Yet within two years much of the early excitement had cooled; by 1824 Bridlington was a "complete wreck" and had to be evangelized again by the more stable Driffield branch.[68] The foothold secured in the region between Bridlington and Filey did serve, however, as the base for further missioning efforts which during 1821 spread Ranterism up along the coast as far as Whitby in the North Riding. By that time much of the rest of the North Riding had also been opened by itinerants sent from Hull.[69]

In most cases the predominately agricultural eastern part of the West Riding proved less responsive to Primitive Methodism than did the East Riding. By 1822 two rural circuits (Brotherton and Ripon) as well as a missionary branch (Tadcaster) had been formed on the western borders of Hull. Farther south, Doncaster circuit was the product of Nottingham's mission to Sheffield. Marshland circuit, an outgrowth of Scotter, lay partly in Lincolnshire. The West Riding was Wesleyan territory, and Ranterism appears to have prospered least where the Old Connexion was strongest. The reverse was also true. Primitive Methodism flourished in Marshland, which the Wesleyans had begun to abandon a few years earlier. Relative to population density, the Ranters were weakest in Doncaster, an area that boasted thriving Wesleyan societies.[70] Tadcaster branch grew initially, then began to decline as losses in the villages, formerly "comparatively vigourous," took their toll.[71] In the middle Aire and Ouse valleys Wesleyan revivalism and informal evangelism carried on as recently as 1816–1817 had created a climate favorable to the Ranters, who arrived in 1819. But in this, the future Brotherton circuit, the Wesleyan itinerants wisely allowed scope for such lay enterprises as the preaching of Sammy Hick, "the village blacksmith"; consequently, most of the enthusiasm engendered was contained within their own societies. One exception was Knottingley, the haven of a secessionist group which had started as an offshoot of the Leeds Kirkgate Screamers. Another was Ferrybridge, where the class met in a boarding school whose master was to be the point of contact between the Primitive Methodists and the band of revivalists who invited them to Leeds.[72] Ripon encompassed a very large area reaching from the boundaries of Tadcaster and Leeds in the south to Middleham in the North Riding and from Nidderdale eastward to the Hambledon Hills. Because of its size Ripon was considered a demanding assignment: one itinerant claimed to have walked 2,400 miles during his three years there. The circuit was extensive, much of it was thinly populated, and the membership of 507 reported in 1823 indicated that efforts in the region had been reasonably successful.[73]

The introduction of Primitive Methodism into York in May 1819 contrasted sharply with the missioning of Hull. At Hull, entered by invitation, Clowes had been greeted by classes eager to join the connexion; at York, evangelized out of a sense of duty, he expected to encounter difficulties. Supposing that he would be denied permission to preach and jailed if he did so against the wishes of the lord mayor, Clowes judged it better not to ask. While he was holding forth in the marketplace, his audience was surrounded by a troop of cavalry, which he suspected had been sent to arrest him "under the idea that I was a radical speaker, inciting the people to rebellion."[74] Although Clowes was allowed to finish his sermon and depart without incident, the itinerants who followed him were likewise apprehensive about preaching in York.[75] The reluctance felt by these pioneers of the York mission probably sprang from a realization that the venerable capital of the North epitomized the sort of place that had been shown to be "barren and rocky soil" for Primitive Methodism. Once the second largest city in England, York in 1819 was a market town of 20,000, which had not yet been touched by the industrial revolution. As the administrative center not only for the county but also for the then very extensive jurisdiction of the archbishop of York, it was a bastion of both civil authority and ecclesiastical influence. York Methodists were among the most conservative in the Wesleyan Connexion. They had turned a deaf ear to the Kilhamites during the 1790s, had chosen not to receive the sacrament in their own chapels until 1815, and still avoided scheduling services during the hours set for worship in the established church. The society was well endowed with prosperous members, and very few would stray into the Ranter fold.[76] In 1820 York's Primitive Methodists hired a small chapel in a deteriorating neighborhood. The fact that two farmers from Elvington stood surety for the rent suggests that the members themselves were not considered good financial risks. The early state of the society matched its chapel site; a person who joined in 1822 found it "in a low and feeble condition." York became a branch of Hull circuit in 1820 and, somewhat prematurely in the estimation of its first superintendent, was made a circuit two years later. The village societies fared somewhat better than the one in the town. When preachers were able to report such tidings as congregations of more than 1,000 or the accession of seventy-two new ticket holders within a quarter, this was largely a measure of success in the countryside.[77]

Quite different was the fate of Primitive Methodism in Marshland and Holderness. The former was a lowland tract extending from the northwest corner of Lincolnshire into the West Riding and including the Thorne Waste. Traversed by the lower reaches of the Ouse, Aire, Don, and Trent rivers, it was sparsely settled, almost devoid of manufacturing, and, before improved methods of fertilization were introduced in

1821, not very productive.[78] There was some precedent for Methodist revivalism in the region. Just before the turn of the century William and George Mosely had aroused considerable fervor in Marshland. Many of the converts won by the "praying colliers" later lapsed, however, because societies were not formed or did not last.[79] This was the Old Connexion's Snaith circuit, but during the postwar years its societies were not very well served. Of the seventeen still in existence in 1817, only six were scheduled for preaching every Sunday. The Wesleyans had already abandoned a number of places, perhaps for financial reasons.[80] The Primitive Methodists had two advantages. First, their evangelism was cheaper than Wesleyan pastoral care: their itinerants were paid much less, and they relied more on lay workers and self-financed preachers. Also, when Marshland was opened late in 1819, Primitive Methodists in nearby Scotter were fired with zeal to spread Ranterism. Undeterred by poor roads and a scattered population, they moved into the new territory. Within little more than two years twenty-six societies were formed, and by the summer of 1823 Marshland was an independent circuit with 447 members.[81]

Holderness, a peninsula between the Humber and the North Sea, had been recognized by the Wesleyans in 1807 as a place needing the attentions of their Home Missions program.[82] In the middle of the next decade, however, their funds and evangelistic energies were diverted into overseas missioning schemes. Wesleyan retrenchment in Holderness opened the way for Ranter success. In April 1819 John Harrison extended the Primitive Methodist frontier into this "dark, benighted part" whose two Wesleyan preachers were "a supply inadequate to its need but burdensome to its finances."[83] The people of this farming district had been introduced to revivalism by "Hell-fire Dick" Braithwaite, who had come to the district independently the year before his appointment as a Primitive Methodist itinerant to Scotter. Harrison was welcomed with offers of money, a building site, and the use of a Calvinist chapel as well as four barns "emptied by their proprietors on purpose for us to preach."[84] A year later, Clowes and another preacher sparked a revival in Holderness, which was soon reinforced by the quickening effect of a camp meeting at Keyingham, one of three such sessions held in conjunction with the connexion's first annual meeting at Hull.[85]

Just as Primitive Methodism prospered in areas such as Marshland and Holderness and languished in places like York and Lincoln, so too it took root in the High Peak of Derbyshire while making little impact in the environs of Chesterfield. Chesterfield had "many genteel families," and both the town and the surrounding countryside were well served by the Church of England. Nottingham's mission to the vicinity, begun in

1819, won only 237 adherents in a period of four years. Members of the small society in Chesterfield were mostly very poor, and, when they eventually tried to build a chapel, "no site could be obtained within the borough."[86] Evangelists converged on the High Peak from three directions—Sheffield, Belper, and Macclesfield. Launched with a camp meeting at Bradwell in 1819, the mission from Sheffield was responsible for 200 conversions in a period of twelve weeks. "I never saw such a work before!" one preacher exclaimed of the response to Ranterism. Like Holderness, the thinly populated Peak region had earlier been designated as one of the Wesleyan Home Missions. Again like Holderness, the field was clearly "ripe unto the harvest," but the Wesleyans were not prepared to reap it. When it became a circuit in 1823, Bradwell alone claimed a total of 522 Primitive Methodists.[87]

Less than four years after the first classes were formed in Kingston-upon-Hull, the connexion had gained almost 11,000 members in the territory missioned by Hull circuit. "When I look at the work in Yorkshire, it is amazing! Many chapels are built . . . and hundreds of souls brought to God," marveled William Clowes.[88] Some of this remarkable success can be attributed to the energy and initiative of Clowes himself. Much, however, depended on the fact that Hull's far-ranging evangelism was partly subsidized by the connexional Book Room (whose ledgers were the Bournes' worry rather than his). Clowes was therefore able to pay a large and mobile army of missionaries to work in the North of England.[89] Vocations to the ministry were plentiful. Because wages were low during the infancy of Hull circuit, it was no great sacrifice for a laborer to abandon his job in order to answer the call to preach. Clowes was also an efficient administrator. He maintained firm discipline and demanded strict accountability from his itinerants, and he restationed them frequently, a wise tactic in so extensive a circuit. The positive thrust of this strategy was twofold: it enlivened the societies by assuring variety, while presenting the preachers with constantly renewed challenges. The timing of the northern campaign was another asset, for the Ranters were superb at village evangelism, and urbanization had not yet begun materially to affect the region being missioned. Lastly, Primitive Methodism was able to take advantage of current weaknesses in the Wesleyan Connexion brought about by financial strains, neglect of rural societies, and dissatisfaction on the part of some laymen. In 1819 the superintendent at Hull was vexed by a series of problems: Wesleyan Methodism in his circuit was suffering because of the difficulty of collecting both ticket money and contributions to the missionary fund; the stationing of itinerants in the towns and "only just preaching in the country" was the "real cause of the increase of the *Ranters*"; trustees who owned chapels were "threat-en[ing] the preachers with calling in the Ranters . . . if their will is opposed."[90]

The rapid advance of Hull circuit was acknowledged when the town was selected as the site of the connexion's inaugural conference in 1820. During the first week of May, Ranters preached nightly in the streets of Hull as well as in the local chapel. Three camp meetings were held simultaneously—one in Holderness, one across the estuary in Lincolnshire, and one in Hull itself. Thousands attended the camp meeting in Hull; a dozen praying companies were employed, and "the harvest was truly plenteous." The climax of the conference was a love feast on the night of 9 May. At this gathering "the work had so broken out [that] the meeting could not be concluded." The congregation outstayed by five hours its formal dismissal at nine o'clock. Consonant with the Ranter experience in the East Riding, all the worship services held in conjunction with the annual meeting were "remarkably successful," and a "great number" of converts were won.[91]

The missioning both of the rural East Midlands and of eastern Yorkshire between 1817 and the close of the decade manifested a fairly consistent pattern. Primitive Methodism was welcomed in places neglected by the church, especially when such locales were also not sufficiently provided with Wesleyan preaching and pastoral oversight. The Ranters were well received in towns with a liberal and Nonconformist tradition like Gainsborough and Hull or in those experiencing a sudden spurt of growth like Grimsby. Urban centers of Tory and Anglican influence, such as York, Newark, and Lincoln, were almost totally resistant to Ranter enthusiasm. In agricultural areas where Wesleyan Methodism was firmly established, the Primitive Methodist evangelists encountered attitudes ranging from indifference to moderate interest. Further, these responses varied more or less inversely with the differing degrees of Wesleyan strength. Not only the negative social and economic impact of enclosures, but also the size and number of holdings awarded in a given parish affected the fortunes of Primitive Methodism in the countryside. Finally, much depended on whether alienation on the part of rural laborers, cottagers, and smallholders had developed to the point where some would refuse to be intimidated by the clergy and the squirearchy.

The Reinvigoration of Tunstall Circuit

[Wedgwood, wearing] an Indian handkerchief tied round his head . . . , took his stand at the side of a brick-kiln. The congregation was very large for a place so thinly populated. . . . A respectable man whom I knew stood looking down on a company of mourners who were down on the ground, crying out for mercy. . . . He said, "Before I would demean myself as these people are doing there, I would have my hand cut off." . . . It was not long before he was on the ground, crying earnestly for mercy like the rest.

—Thomas Bateman, Cheshire, 1819[92]

While Primitive Methodist evangelists who ignored the Tunstall non-missioning law were expanding the sect across the East Midlands and into Yorkshire between 1816 and 1819, growth in Tunstall circuit remained virtually static. Renewal began after a complaint was made at the quarterly meeting in December 1818 by the societies around Ramsor—an area that had originally been missioned by Bourne and in which the members had always been less amenable than those in the Potteries to policies set in Tunstall. The board directed that a committee study the ills of the circuit. Their diagnosis, pronounced at the next quarter-day, traced the "root of all the evils" to the modified style of camp meetings used in Tunstall circuit since 1816. These assemblies consisted almost entirely of sermons, which not only wearied the listeners but also absorbed the energies of the preachers and caused them to neglect other responsibilities. Feeling slighted, the people withheld ticket money and contributions. Worse yet, according to Bourne, the "pious praying labourers were continually thrown [into] the background and trodden underfoot," and their "talents [were] constantly buried." The trend toward verbosity had spread beyond the camp meetings and was also afflicting class meetings and prayer meetings. Deprived of the opportunity to participate, the people's enthusiasm flagged, and almost no new preachers were recruited. The Tunstall quarter-day board responded by passing a series of regulations which "swept away" the "long tedious exercises." Thereafter camp meetings were to be modeled on those being held in other circuits. Prayer meetings, class meetings, and preaching services were to be limited to an hour's duration or less, and the role of preachers and class leaders was confined primarily to orchestrating the active involvement of everyone present.[93]

Although James Nixon, Thomas Woodnorth, and a few of the local preachers initially resisted the new regimen, the circuit steward, James Steele, had been convinced by Bourne of its efficacy, and he lent his considerable influence to implementing the regulations. A successful camp meeting at Wrine Hill on 29 May 1819 demonstrated the worth of the revised system. At the June quarter-day "it was found that the circuit was rising out of its crippled state, and that it had begun to revive in almost every part." This recovery gained momentum during the next nine months; between March 1819 and March 1820 the circuit added more than 1,000 members. Continued growth during the subsequent year was celebrated by holding the connexion's second annual meeting at Tunstall.[94] The Wesleyan Burslem and Newcastle-under-Lyme circuits also enjoyed an "outbreaking of God's work" during 1820–1821. The *Methodist Magazine* attributed this revival to the happy consequences of following the guidelines on pastoral work laid down at the Liverpool conference of 1820. While these practices undoubtedly did have a positive impact, the renewal in Burslem circuit had begun as early as Christmas, 1819—the month after the Six Acts were passed. Also, trade in the Potteries was depressed during 1820 and 1821.[95] The changed tactics adopted by both the Wesleyans and the Primitive Methodist Tunstall circuit seemingly were put into effect at an optimal time.

The prohibition against opening missions also became defunct in Tunstall during 1819. Initially the ban was not formally retracted. Instead, as in the East Midlands, it was simply ignored by a few enterprising individuals who financed their own efforts. Eleazar Hathorn undertook to extend Primitive Methodism into Lancashire; Sampson Turner acted as the sect's self-appointed agent in the Black Country; and John Wedgwood determined to evangelize western Cheshire. Launched in the spring of 1819, Wedgwood's preaching tour exemplified the manner in which the injunction forbidding aggrandizement was replaced by a policy of vigorous expansionism. Immediately triumphant, the "Cheshire mission" carried him through a rural district in which outsize Anglican parishes were being badly neglected by their clergy. According to Thomas Bateman, one of many converts made by Wedgwood during this foray, "religion was at a fearfully low ebb," with few Methodists, few Dissenters, and not many churches. Although Cheshire was "noted as a High Church and Tory county," recalled Bateman, there was very little persecution of or opposition to the Ranters.[96] In fact, though the majority of people won over in western Cheshire belonged to the laboring classes, there were also a "number of respectable families who early identified themselves" with Primitive Methodism and "became its stay and support."[97]

The revival began at Easter and sped through the countryside west of Nantwich. Chorley Green was the spot par excellence for the "converting work." Rumor promised that, if only they would come there, the "greatest sinners" would surely be "affected," and mourners, "no matter how heavy their burdens," would certainly be liberated. Usually the anticipated results were achieved. On "many occasions," Bateman remembered, Wedgwood had no need to preach at all, because penitents began "to cry for mercy during the first prayer, or singing . . . and so mighty was the power resting on the people that not one was left standing; all were on the ground praying for themselves or for each other, for justification or sanctification." Often hundreds would gather at the village green "even on a week night," and at one especially moving session 200 persons were "in distress."[98] The quarter-day board at Tunstall formally annexed the territory in June 1819. Wedgwood had not bothered to form classes, preferring instead to evangelize when and where the spirit beckoned. During the summer he pressed on toward Chester and into the peninsula of Wirral, while three less-flamboyant itinerants sent from Tunstall organized his converts into classes and drew up preaching plans.[99] The cause continued to prosper under their direction; new places were opened, and members flocked into the societies. When Bourne came to southwestern Cheshire the following autumn, he found that demands for preaching were far outpacing the supply of preachers. At the suggestion of Bateman and another lay worker, the quarterly meeting in March 1820 designated the "Cheshire mission" as Burland branch of Tunstall circuit. Eighteen months later, when Burland itself became a circuit, there were eighty societies listed on its preaching plan.[100]

As early as 1820 it was clear that the growth brought about by Tunstall's abandoning of the non-missioning law called for a more sophisticated administrative apparatus as well as for smaller rounds that could more easily be visited regularly by the itinerants. In March, Tunstall circuit was divided into six branches—the home branch, Ramsor, and Burton-on-Trent in Staffordshire; Burland and Preston Brook in Cheshire; and Belper in Derbyshire. Evangelism in the Black Country had met with such success that Darlaston was put at the head of its own circuit. Attached at first to the home branch, the mission to Lancashire flourished so vigorously that in 1821 Manchester became an autonomous circuit. Preachers from Belper branch and some enthusiastic society members from Macclesfield aided the Bradwell missionaries working in the High Peak, and together they laid the foundations of Winster circuit. Two years after Burland achieved independent status, its extensiveness and the more than 900 members in it warranted the creation of Chester circuit as a separate entity. The county town itself was one of the few places in Cheshire where even Wedgwood had failed to gain a hearing. Although the "boy-preacher," Thomas Brownsword, had attracted a crowd of 500 in March 1821, other evangelists sent during the year had been harassed by rowdies. By December, however, Bateman could exclaim, "The work prospers much in this ancient city now. Thank God!

After a storm there comes a calm!" Ultimately, Chester, like Grimsby, was a place in which Primitive Methodism came to have a "recognized prestige" and to "wield considerable local influence." Also, as in Grimsby, the descendants of the first society members continued to maintain their families' allegiance to the connexion.[101]

The reinvigoration of Tunstall circuit was the consequence of several factors: the ending of the moratorium on new missions, the curtailment of sermons to allow for broadened participation by the people, and a readiness to pursue the offensives initiated by self-appointed evangelists like Wedgwood, Turner, and Hathorn. In some places the failure of the movement for political reform and the repression that followed may have created a climate favorable to the spread of Primitive Methodism. Certainly, much of the ground opened from Tunstall lay in counties identified by one of the Six Acts as disturbed—Lancaster, Derby, Chester, and Stafford. In geographical terms the renewal of Tunstall meant expanding the connexion east to the frontiers of territory missioned by Hull and Nottingham circuits, west as far as Wales, north into Lancashire, and south into Worcestershire. Within less than five years Primitive Methodist numbers multiplied more than tenfold. Before its reawakening, Tunstall circuit had claimed 690 members; by 1823 there were 7,178 Primitive Methodists in the parent circuit and the ten new circuits that had so far sprung from it.[102]

The "great revival" in the East Midlands chiefly affected the working classes in manufacturing towns and industrial or mining villages. Except for Hull, the advance of Primitive Methodism into eastern Nottinghamshire and Leicestershire, Lincolnshire, eastern Yorkshire, and western Cheshire was primarily a rural phenomenon. By the end of the decade Ranterism had also embraced the challenge of evangelizing three other kinds of communities: the mining and ironworking Black Country, the textile villages of the West Riding, and factory towns such as Macclesfield, Leeds, and Manchester.

Five

Confronting
the Philistines:
The Black Country,
Textile Villages,
Factory Towns

The Ranters are labouring to turn the world upside
down. . . . We have people in our circuit who are just
the very sort of matter they like to work upon. They
have got some of our members and will get a few
more, I expect. . . . It seems a sort of religious fever is
crossing the country. They boil—they boil up—they
boil over, and I expect will put the fire out and sink
down into cold water again.
    —A Wesleyan Itinerant, Bradford, 1821[1]

During 1819 Ranter missionaries took up the task of
evangelizing the Black Country, the textile villages of the West Riding,
and some of the burgeoning factory towns of Yorkshire, Cheshire, and
Lancashire.Their experience in the three types of communities manifested some common features. In all three Primitive Methodism attracted
converts almost exclusively from among the victims of industrial
capitalism—miners and ironworkers suffering because of a severe depression which struck the area around Birmingham in 1819; textile
workers whose status and incomes were deteriorating under dual pressure from the putting-out system and a contracted but fluctuating

117

market; mill "hands" who lived and labored in crowded, dirty, and for them culturally sterile towns such as Leeds and Manchester. In some of the urban settings class antagonism affected the advance of Ranterism. Both by the proletariat and by the propertied, the sect was identified as working-class. Eighteen-nineteen was the year of agitation for "radical reform," of Peterloo and its sometimes revolutionary aftermath, and of the Six Acts. Because the places being evangelized were in districts where disaffection toward the government was rife, the early progress of Primitive Methodism was intertwined with political developments. Finally, especially in the West Riding, many of these towns and villages lay in territory where both Wesleyan Methodism and the Methodist New Connexion were already a significant influence.

The Black Country

When John Benton joined forces with the Primitive Methodists in 1811, he had brought as his dowry a few societies in south Staffordshire, some of which were still intact in 1819. During the early spring of that year Sampson Turner, a society member at Cannock Lane, launched a missionary drive into the populous Black Country. Aided by three other men, one of whom was a Wesleyan local preacher regarded as having "too much fervour and too little discretion," Turner generated a revival out of which Darlaston circuit issued only twelve months later. It was to become "one of the most powerful and procreative circuits of the Connexion."[2]

Turner and his assistants—all "men of standing and business ability" —did not look like typical Ranter preachers. It is surprising that, carrying walking sticks and clad in dress coats and top hats, they were able to gain so great a following. Letters written by Wesleyan itinerants stationed in the area indicated that, in the words of one, "the times [were] awful." Their concerns included the disintegration of a society in West Bromwich after an ironworks closed and threw its members out of work; hardships caused by stagnation of trade along with rioting sparked by attempts to lower wages in the collieries around Dudley; "bad trade, infidel reformers," and a "considerable" decline in collections at Birmingham.[3] In fact, the times were propitious for conversions to Methodism. Between 1819 and 1823 the combined numbers in the Wesleyan Connexion's five Black Country circuits rose from 4,184 to 5,910. The Primitive Methodist Darlaston circuit, which did not even exist in 1819, claimed 1,551 members by 1823. Even the New Connexion's not very prosperous Birmingham and Wolverhampton circuit grew from 120 in 1815 to 431 in 1821.[4] Both Wesleyans and Primitives benefited from the fact that the Church of England had failed to provide adequately for the vastly increased population in the region; both faced opposition from the adherents of older, non-Methodist denominations as well. Efforts to purchase chapel sites were thwarted; preachers were arrested; attacks on them were abetted or ignored.[5]

Harassment simply worked to popularize the Primitive Methodist cause. In March 1820 Tunstall lent the newly formed Darlaston circuit a pair of itinerants, James Bonsor and Thomas Brownsword. Early in July, Brownsword and two local preachers were arrested at Stourbridge and committed to the county jail at Worcester. As a result, "multitudes" were drawn to a "vast meeting" at the raceground on the following afternoon, and "this was the introduction of . . . [Primitive Methodism] to Worcester." In an addendum to Brownsword's journal Bourne commented, "This imprisonment caused a considerable sensation." Four weeks later, Bonsor was taken into custody after preaching at a camp meeting held during the parish wake at Bilston (where the vicar was a magistrate) and again in the marketplace at Wolverhampton. During his incarceration he prayed with his fellow prisoners and preached to the "many people [who] came to visit me and brought food." Released next day, Bonsor promptly delivered two more open-air sermons in Wolverhampton. He was later fined at the Stafford sessions but, instead of paying, told the magistrates they should give him "something for my trouble." Both confrontations with authority "turned out to the furtherance of the gospel and the enlargement of the circuit."[6]

While the arrests and jailings attracted publicity and sympathy, it was preaching in the streets and coal pits, holding camp meetings and outdoor love feasts, carrying on the "conversation ministry," and establishing networks of cottage prayer meetings that made possible the vitality of Primitive Methodism in the Black Country. In September 1820 the work of evangelism was "going on rapidly," with "hundreds added." In December, Tipton had five classes and 130 members in society, the chapel at Dudley was "well-filled," and there was a "glorious time" at a love feast in Wednesbury.[7] The early converts memorialized in the *Primitive Methodist Magazine* were mostly miners and ironworkers, several of whom were killed in pit or foundry accidents. For some, membership in the society gave new meaning to their lives and enhanced their self-esteem. One previously illiterate iron puddler learned to read so that he could study the New Testament and improve his effectiveness as a class leader and local preacher. Another, who lost his job in an ironworks, found employment as a collier and held daily prayer meetings at the pithead.[8]

During the early 1820s the Wesleyans, following the guidelines on pastoral work laid down at Liverpool, engaged in much the same activities as the Primitive Methodists and for much the same class of people. In Wolverhampton circuit most of their places of worship were cottages or hired rooms, and the "genteel" few were outnumbered by their working-class brethren. The same was true in other Old Connexion circuits. Nevertheless, Primitive Methodist gains in the Black Country did not reduce Wesleyan totals there. It is possible, though, that conversions in the towns offset Wesleyan losses in rural neighborhoods. Faced with financial difficulties, the Wesleyans began paring expenditures by cutting back their corps of traveling preachers. First to feel the impact of this retrenchment were small societies in the country, and it was, of course, village evangelism at which the competition excelled. At least one Wesleyan itinerant feared that personnel reductions would bring "great evils in those places from which preachers may be taken." Presumably his circuit, Wednesbury, was among those "infested with" Ranters "waiting" to take over "feeble flocks" about to be abandoned by the Wesleyans. To some extent, the main focus of Ranter efforts lay to the west and north of Birmingham and Dudley, the two most numerous Wesleyan circuits. Although the Primitive Methodist circuit had outposts as far afield as Worcester and Cannock Wood, most of its societies were contained within a rough triangle drawn from Wednesbury through Wolverhampton to Stourbridge, then back via West Bromwich to Wednesbury.[9]

Unlike some areas in which initial enthusiasm was mighty but transitory, Primitive Methodism in the Black Country continued to thrive. In the autumn of 1821 Darlaston opened a mission that stretched from northeastern Worcestershire to Radnorshire in Wales. This Hopton Bank branch also prospered and three years later became a separate circuit. A decade after it was formed, the by then contracted Darlaston circuit had seventy local preachers, 1,226 members, 1,542 pupils enrolled in eighteen Sunday schools, and forty preaching places within a ten-mile radius of the town.[10]

The West Riding of Yorkshire

The Primitive Methodists approached the woollen manufacturing districts east of the Pennine Chain from two directions. Evangelists sent from Nottingham moved northward from Sheffield, while others from Hull advanced south via Leeds to the vicinity of Dewsbury. Undertaken in response to the urging of John Coulson, the Sheffield mission yielded six circuits in the West Riding within a period of less than five years—Sheffield (1820), Barnsley (1821), Wakefield and Halifax (1822), Doncaster (1823), and Huddersfield (1824).

A Wesleyan since his conversion by Bramwell, Coulson shared his mentor's disenchantment with "modern" Methodism. After meeting Clowes while on a business trip to Hull, Coulson switched his allegiance to the Primitive cause, and in March 1819 he secured the appointment of a missionary for Sheffield. This preacher, Jeremiah Gilbert, left no account of his first nine months there, but the plan for December 1819–February 1820 listed only eleven engagements per week—scarcely the abundant harvest reaped when Nottingham and Hull were opened. Perhaps, caught up in the widespread constitutionalist activity before Peterloo and its more violent aftermath, most working people in the district were not yet ripe for revivalism. Certainly, it was during this period that Clowes, seeking to win converts at Dewsbury, further north in the West Riding, "found the minds of the people so much exercised with the politics of the day, that the story of the cross had but little charm for them."[11] Gilbert met with greater success after the repressive Six Acts were passed in December (Sheffield gained circuit status six months later) and especially after the abortive rendezvous of radicals at Grange Moor near Barnsley in April 1820. Sheffield was a circuit town for both the Wesleyans and the Methodist New Connexion. A Wesleyan traveling preacher assigned to Sheffield in 1818 had reported that the town and a few of the villages were prosperous, but, he had added, "this is not generally the case. The distress of the poor . . . is not yet terminated."[12] A mild awakening at that time was followed by two years in which membership decreased slightly. Pointing in 1820 to the severely depressed economy in the neighborhood, another Wesleyan itinerant ascribed these losses to emigration and to the inability of the people to pay ticket money—"possessing a little native pride, they have . . . absented themselves."[13]

The first Primitive Methodists working in the Sheffield mission were subjected to almost no rough treatment from the crowd, but they were repeatedly annoyed by clergymen who sent sometimes reluctant constables to arrest them. Gilbert was brought before the bench half a dozen times in little more than a year. His usual response, imitated by the preachers appointed soon thereafter to assist him in the growing mission field, was to sing a hymn that began, "Wicked men I scorn to fear," to insist on being driven to the site of his hearing, there to advise the magistrate concerning the relevant statutes, and, when imprisoned, to regale his audiences later with the tale of his adventure. The people, he observed, "seemed to pay more attention to me when I was a prisoner than when I was a free man." Once, after being jailed and taken to court, Gilbert resumed the sermon interrupted by his arrest. "There were a great many more to hear than there had been before," he commented.[14] Unlike both Wesleyan and New Connexion leaders, with their protestations of loyalty and their admonitions to be patient under affliction, Gilbert was accurately gauging the popular temper in this section of the West Riding. Sympathetic readers of Hone's *Political House that Jack Built* probably lent a readier ear to Gilbert and his colleagues, who openly challenged authority, than they did to the likes of Jabez Bunting.[15]

The converts won in this part of Yorkshire were almost entirely from the working classes.[16] Many were Wesleyans or Wesleyan backsliders. Frequently, their lives had been dislocated—by the need to move in search of work, by personal or family tragedy, by economic privation. Typical was George Buckley, a native of Warrington who lost his employment as a fustian cutter first at Manchester, next at Huddersfield, and finally at Halifax. He joined the Primitive Methodist society in Halifax when it was formed in 1821 and later became a chapel trustee. At the time of his death in 1834 Buckley's job was to post bills for printers.[17]

The traveling preachers often, and the local preachers and class leaders nearly always, came from the same background as the other early converts in the region. William Taylor was a potter who had been laid off when depression affected the Staffordshire industry. He migrated to Yorkshire, worked briefly at the Don Potteries, failed to find a job back in Tunstall, and returned to the West Riding, where he became the chief evangelist to the Barnsley area. A second itinerant, Thomas Holloday, was one of nine children in the family of a shepherd. A twenty-two-year-old farm servant when he was converted in 1819, Holloday described himself as unemployed and impoverished.[18] Samuel Kirk, a Wesleyan who had fallen away as he moved about in quest of field work, was reconverted when curiosity led him to a Ranter meeting at Aughton in 1820. After unsuccessfully looking for employment in Lancashire, he settled in Sheffield and became the leader of one of the town's three classes. When he turned local preacher, he was earning only 6s. weekly. Son of very poor parents, George Taylor was a weaver. Soon after he finished his apprenticeship in 1820, he "drank deeply" of the "pernicious principles" of some radical associates. Within a year, however, and apparently attracted by the sense of community among the Primitive Methodists, he joined the society at Barnsley. In 1821 he became an exhorter and later a class leader. Twelve thousand people reportedly attended his funeral in 1826.[19]

At a time when some rural Wesleyans were feeling neglected by ministers whose energies seemed increasingly absorbed in the towns, the

Primitive Methodists were engaged in an aggressive missionary campaign directed primarily at the villages. George Chisholm and William Taylor, for example, spent an entire week in one colliery village near Barnsley, preaching by day in the coalpits and holding nightly meetings that lasted until after midnight. The journals kept by itinerants working in the Sheffield mission, especially those of Gilbert and Taylor, indicate that they were sensitive to the needs of individuals and willing to devote time to them. Some like John Day of Flockton sought out the Primitive Methodists because they were dissatisfied with "various occurrences" among the Wesleyans. At Royston, where "God's word began to run like fire among dry stubble" in January 1821, local Wesleyans welcomed what they perceived as a return to old ways and averred that "there had not been such a revival" in their neighborhood "since the time [of] holy Bramwell."[20] In some places Ranter activity stimulated Wesleyan efforts. A Primitive Methodist awakening in the handloom-weaving village of Skelmanthorpe provoked a "holy rivalry"; camp meetings, preaching services, cottage prayer meetings, and house-to-house visitations "were followed by such an outpouring of the Spirit as Skelmanthorpe had never seen."[21]

Camp meetings were held at least as early as June 1820, but at first their importance was secondary to the role played by street preaching, cottage evangelism, and the opening of village missions. During the spring and summer of 1821, however, there were at least seven major camp meetings in what had by then become the Sheffield and Barnsley circuits. The gathering at Wolfstones near Thong in April advertised the Primitive Methodist cause in the Huddersfield area, and that held on Greetland Moor in August served the same purpose for the territory around Halifax. Ten thousand people were said to have come to the former; Gilbert reckoned that an equal number attended the latter.[22] The most impressive camp meeting of the summer was held on Mexborough Common in June. Some newspapers reported an assembly of 20,000 or more; according to Bourne, there were "more than ten thousand" people, sixteen praying companies, and "hundreds . . . converted to God." The hero of this occasion was Thomas Holloday, who, arrested for street preaching in Halifax on 27 May, had compounded his offense by continuing his sermon from a window in the constable's house. The "multitude of people" thronged outside were dispersed with difficulty, and Holloday spent the ensuing week in the Wakefield House of Correction. Aware of his assets as a "martyr," fellow Primitive Methodists posted bail on 2 June and hurried him to Mexborough in time to speak there.[23]

Gilbert's original sphere of evangelism, though based on Sheffield, had extended over northeastern Derbyshire and the southeastern corner of the West Riding. By September 1820 Primitive Methodism was advancing northward and generating so much enthusiasm that several more itinerants were sent to the mission. Initially, the focus of much of their activity was the vicinity of Barnsley and Wakefield. Appointed within a few months of the failed rising that was to have emanated from Grange Moor, the missionaries found their efforts quickly rewarded. After an increase of 400 members during the first quarter of 1821, Barnsley achieved autonomy and accelerated its evangelizing of territory to the north and northwest, districts that within the next triennium became the Wakefield, Halifax, and Huddersfield circuits.[24]

According to a "chiliasm of despair" interpretation, the Ranters ought also to have triumphed in Huddersfield in 1820. Not only was this not the case, but, even when a delayed revival did break out, it was at first primarily the Wesleyans who benefited. The town of Huddersfield was introduced to Primitive Methodism little more than three months after a beacon was lit on Castle Hill to signal the local beginning of a general rising. Halted by the presence of a troop of cavalry and three companies of infantry, the march on Huddersfield had disintegrated.[25] The failure of the insurrection did not immediately thrust disappointed croppers and weavers into the waiting arms of the Methodist societies thereabouts. In fact, for Old and New Connexion alike, the reverse was true.[26] Nor did the Primitive Methodists enjoy an immediate victory in Huddersfield, though a sizable crowd did collect to protest the imprisonment of Taylor and his female colleague in mid-July 1820. Except in the Holmfirth Valley, the fervor released by the camp meeting at Wolfstones in 1821 worked chiefly in the Wesleyan interest. A likely explanation for this is that the itinerants assigned to Huddersfield in 1818 had launched an energetic program of village evangelism aimed at strengthening existing societies and forming new ones. Using such Ranter tactics as cottage meetings and adopting a more lenient attitude toward revivalism than that currently sanctioned by conference, Wesleyans in Huddersfield circuit had already established a network of havens congenial to souls awakened by Primitive Methodist efforts.[27] During 1821–1822 Wesleyan Methodism recouped more than half the losses suffered in 1820. Meanwhile, the Ranters "laboured without any apparent success" in this "sad place for infidelity."[28] Primitive Methodism had taken hold, however, in the Holmfirth Valley, and it was growth there that in September 1821 warranted the establishing of a Nether Thong (later Huddersfield) branch of Barnsley circuit.

In contrast to Huddersfield, where Ranterism had a slow gestation, the mission to Halifax flourished from the start. The decision to open the area was made at the March 1821 quarterly meeting in Barnsley; just a year later Halifax was an independent circuit boasting twenty-three preaching places. By the time the Primitive Methodists arrived, both Wesleyan and New Connexion Methodists had taken pains to improve their rural pastorates. In 1819 the Wesleyans had "judiciously divided" their itinerants between town and countryside, a step which gratified the local stewards because, henceforth, the preachers "could be more among the people and visit the villages." The Kilhamites had created an apparatus for home missions and put the area around Halifax at the head of their list of districts needing attention. All three Methodist connexions gained members between 1821 and 1823. The revival set in motion by the camp meeting on Greetland Moor in August 1821 was still potent among the Primitive Methodists in January 1822. Excitement also spread through the Wesleyan Halifax and Sowerby Bridge circuits during the autumn and winter following this camp meeting. In Sowerby Bridge the renewal occurred after the expulsion of "many for non-attendance and other causes." The Ranters were particularly successful in this circuit, but not necessarily because of the Wesleyan purge: many of the "hundreds" who came regularly to their services at Sowerby Bridge were said to have "seldom attended any place of worship before." Their progress in Halifax circuit, however, may have been fueled partly by discontent felt by Wesleyan local preachers, described in 1819 as "appear[ing] to be jealous and envious" of the itinerants. The vitality of Primitive Methodism in the town of Halifax was acknowledged when Ebenezer Chapel, built in 1822, was fixed as the site of the connexion's annual meeting in 1824.[29]

The missioning of Leeds furnishes a good example of early Primitive Methodism as it encountered a population beginning to undergo the stresses of urbanization and industrialization—twin forces that would radically alter the face of much of the West Riding. During the Napoleonic wars a traveler had recorded his impressions of Leeds on the flyleaf of a book at a local inn: "The Aire below is doubly dyed and damned, / The air above with lurid smoke is crammed; / The one flows streaming foul as Charon's Styx, / Its poisonous vapours in the other mix." In a second stanza this critic had lamented that "wasted life and broken health" were the "penalty" exacted for the riches being accumulated by the town's entrepreneurs.[30] The emblematic sheep on the "Leedes Armes" pointed to the historic importance of wool in the local economy. Eighteenth-century Leeds had been a major center for the domestic system of producing woollen goods. When the Primitive Methodists arrived in 1819, it was a rapidly growing factory town, ill prepared to absorb the influx of rural workers who were migrating there in search of employment in its textile mills. Although population continued to swell—the growth rate was 47.2 percent during the next decade—the self-perpetuating governing body established by a seventeeth-century charter persistently ignored the deteriorating quality of life in Leeds.[31] The east-flowing Aire and some of its tributary becks were used to carry off sewage and factory wastes, and, because the terrain on which Leeds was built sloped downward toward the southeast, the least sanitary neighborhoods were in the eastern and southeastern parts of town. It was here among the mill workers and in the outlying weaving villages that the Primitive Methodists scheduled much of their preaching and formed most of their societies.

Methodism was a significant force in Leeds. Early in the reign of Victoria, the vicar of Leeds, Walter Farquhar Hook, would call it "the established religion" in his parish.[32] There was also a vigorous tradition of popular revivalism in and around Leeds that dated back to the awakenings of 1793–1794. Encouraged by Bramwell, this enthusiasm in 1803 had burst the confines of Wesleyan discipline and had produced the schismatic Kirkgate Screamers; in a tamer and more acceptable form it had aroused village Methodists as recently as the visit of Gideon Ouseley in 1816. Less conspicuously, the revival spirit was being nourished by laymen like those who in September 1819 wrote to the "Ranter Preacher, Hull," asking that a Primitive Methodist missionary be sent to Leeds.[33] The self-appointed task of these revivalists was to bring religion into the slums of the town. The appeal of Wesleyanism in such quarters must have been somewhat diminished when the circuit's superintendent decided in 1819 to reinstate the long-abandoned practice of grouping members into classes according to their social and economic status. He also adhered rigidly to the stance of unquestioning political loyalty adopted by the Wesleyan conference and was proud to proclaim that, despite the "distress of the times" and the ubiquity of the "infectious doctrines of sedition and infidelity," not one of the Wesleyan Methodists in Leeds circuit had been "seduced."[34] The town also headed one of the most numerous circuits in the New Connexion, but by 1819 the official policies of Kilhamite Methodism were being shaped by the propertied laymen who dominated connexional government, and they enjoined their poorer brethren to shun political agitation and to accept hardship patiently.[35] One asset enjoyed, however, by both varieties of Methodism as well as by the older Nonconformist denominations in Leeds was that all had been solidly established there before the advent of Ranterism, and "this was in many respects a disadvantage to [the Primitive Methodist] cause."[36]

The fifteen young men responsible for bringing Primitive Methodism to Leeds learned of the connexion from a derogatory article in the Hull *Rockingham*. According to the newspaper, the Ranters were a communistic as well as a revivalistic sect, and their preachers (who wore

sturdy shoes and corduroy smallclothes) "had eaten up the whole substance of several farmers." Told that there were Ranters at Ferrybridge,
the group sent a pair of delegates to hear them. One of these, John
Verity, was invited to preach at an outdoor meeting. When the Wesleyan
authorities at Leeds discovered that he had done so, he was summarily
dismissed from his post as a class leader. Spurning the admonition not to
"join with these divisionists who were going about only to tear and rend
the Wesleyan societies," Verity and another revivalist, Samuel Smith,
appealed to Hull for a Ranter missionary. Promised that one would be
sent as soon as possible, they drew up a preaching plan for their fellow
evangelists. Clowes undertook the assignment, and by the time he
reached Leeds in November, the volunteers had already won one
hundred converts and had organized half a dozen societies.[37] Many who
heard Clowes's first sermon judged it to be "the 'right old sort of stuff',"
and "went away rejoicing." Clowes then hired a room in a warehouse
and dispatched the town crier to advertise the Ranter presence in Leeds.[38]
His arrival marked the beginning of a triennium during which Primitive
Methodism made "amazing progress" in the vicinity. After little more
than a year as a branch of Hull, Leeds became an independent circuit.
None of the thirty-five places included on its first plan was further than
seven miles from the center of town, and most would eventually be considered part of metropolitan Leeds. Some of the weaving villages responded especially well to the Primitive Methodist gospel. John Coulson,
the first superintendent of the circuit, remarked of the weavers, "We
were very successful among them." In 1822 the Leeds society erected a
chapel on Quarry Hill to replace its former rented place of worship—an
old factory on East Street in the Bank, one of the most squalid parts of
the town.[39] The future looked so bright in December that the quarter-day
board decided to use the £20 surplus in the treasury for missioning
London.[40]

Such optimism was unwarranted. Not only was the effort to root
Primitive Methodism in Shoreditch ill-fated, but Leeds circuit itself was
starting to lose impetus. Late in 1823 a Wesleyan itinerant stationed in
Birstall claimed that the sect was "dying out" around Leeds. "We are
gaining ground upon the Ranters," he boasted. "One of their main camps
[Churwell] . . . is just broken up, and Mr. Nelson received their travelling preacher and seventeen members into our society."[41] This prognosis
was extreme. The episode at Churwell was not the beginning of a mass
exodus into the Wesleyan Connexion, nor did the declining vigor of the
Leeds Primitive Methodist circuit point to an imminent demise. Even
after the creation of Bradford circuit in 1823, Leeds had 1,127 members.
When Dewsbury and Otley became circuits the following year, the total

in Leeds was reduced to 729. In fact, these figures represented gains: in 1824 there were 1,620 members in the area originally included in the Leeds mission.[42]

Because the West Riding was one of the strongholds of Methodism in England, it is useful to measure Primitive Methodist gains against the membership statistics reported from Wesleyan and New Connexion circuits. By 1823 Primitive Methodist totals in the southern West Riding surpassed those of the four New Connexion circuits in the region; there were about four Wesleyans (in ten circuits) to each Ranter. Strongest in Halifax, Primitive Methodism counted three members for every ten Wesleyans. In Barnsley and Wakefield the ratio was slightly better than one to four. The Ranters won fewer adherents in the more strictly agricultural part of the West Riding than they did in the west and south. Marshland, Tadcaster, Brotherton, Ripon, and Doncaster together accounted for only about 2,000 members in 1823.[43] The remaining West Riding circuits claimed more than three times that number. The obvious explanation is that the latter region had a higher population density. It is also probable, though, that social and economic conditions favored revivalism in certain of the textile districts. In general, the years between 1821 and 1825 were a time of increased prosperity; this was not, however, shared by everyone. Around Bradford, Halifax, and Huddersfield (where the Primitive Methodist cause finally began to thrive late in 1822) the putting-out system was becoming entrenched, and the weavers were being hurt by wage reductions and the warehousing of cut-price goods. These were circuits in which Primitive Methodism flourished during the 1820s. The economic situation of the small clothiers around Leeds deteriorated more slowly, and after the early years of enthusiasm there, growth in the circuit stagnated. As the economy improved, membership in Sheffield circuit dropped significantly.

The precise relationship between political agitation and Ranter revivalism is difficult to determine. Sheffield, Barnsley, Huddersfield, and Halifax were all centers of working-class radicalism, but, in the short term, reactions appear to have been contradictory. In Sheffield revivalism caught fire only after the Six Acts were passed; Barnsley was evangelized three months after the fiasco at Grange Moor and a positive response was immediate; Huddersfield, by contrast, did not embrace Primitive Methodism for two years, even though missionaries arrived soon after the ill-starred rising in March 1820.[44] If a longer view is taken, it may be true that during the early 1820s Primitive Methodism absorbed energies that for the previous nine years had been directed into Luddism or radicalism. If so, the pattern set in the manufacturing districts of the West Riding did not conform to that followed in Nottinghamshire. Nor did enthusiasm in the West Riding approach the scale of the revival in the East Midlands.

Cheshire and Lancashire

Macclesfield, Congleton, and Stockport each responded differently to the introduction of Primitive Methodism, but all displayed character-istics which, at one time or another, were typical of Ranter evangelism in mill towns. A center of silk manufacturing, Macclesfield exemplified the potency as well as the ephemerality that revivalism could manifest among laborers making their initial adjustment to urban life. Congleton, another silk-manufacturing town, was one of those places in which the Ranters failed to gain much headway, because Wesleyan Methodism was providing an acceptable outlet for religious fervor. Once established, the Primitive Methodist societies in both Macclesfield and Congleton suf-fered from schism, a recurring problem that also plagued the sect else-where. This tendency toward fissiparousness was a natural adjunct of the Ranter emphasis on democracy and lay participation. In Stockport, where an active Political Union, its auxiliary Female Union, and a radical Sunday-school movement were absorbing working-class energies, Primi-tive Methodism was largely ignored until the late 1820s.

Opened early in 1819, Macclesfield blazed with religious excitement. By the next winter there were 181 members, a dozen classes, and a thriv-ing Sunday school in the town. "There is a great work at Macclesfield," rejoiced Ann Brownsword; "they are joining classes almost every meet-ing." Between March and June societies were formed in seven neighbor-ing villages. Missionaries from Macclesfield also spread Primitive Meth-odism north to Stockport and Manchester, east into the High Peak of Derbyshire, and south to Congleton. Within three years, however, the flame of enthusiasm had almost burned out, and the short-lived Maccles-field circuit was reabsorbed by Tunstall.[45]

By 1820 the transformation of Congleton from an agricultural to a textile town was well under way. Poor rates had increased tenfold since 1750, as the population swelled with mill workers hired at inadequate wages. Methodism had made great strides during the late eighteenth century, partly because the vicar, who held two other benefices, was unpopular, negligent, and disliked his cure. In 1811 his successor had just 140 communicants in the parish church, the only Anglican place of worship thereabouts. Ten years later, there were an estimated 4,000 Nonconformists in a population of not quite 6,500.[46] The Ranters arrived in 1820 only to discover that the Wesleyan grip on Congleton was secure.

Their coming coincided with a revival which inaugurated a period of significant growth in the Wesleyan circuit. Although the Primitive Methodists did form a small society, Ranter efforts were eclipsed by Wesleyan dynamism.[47]

When evangelists from Macclesfield entered Stockport in July 1820, the working classes there were evincing little interest in any form of Methodism. Only six weeks before, a Wesleyan itinerant had observed, "I fear they are sad radicals." James Mort, the New Connexion preacher who had earlier engineered the dismissal of three colleagues suspected of radicalism, had also remarked on the "political disaffection" so "unfavourable to the interest of religion" in Stockport. The next New Connexion preacher, appointed to the circuit in 1818, had found it "in a state of spiritual declension"; in 1820 membership fell to 104, the lowest total recorded up to that time.[48] Between 1817 and 1820 radical organizations led by the sometime Methodist preacher Joseph Harrison seem to have acted as a counterattraction for people who might otherwise have retained a loyalty to Methodism. But if this was so, supporters of the Union did not gravitate into Methodist societies immediately after Harrison's imprisonment in 1820. Not until they re-evangelized Stockport ten years later did the Ranters win many converts in the town.[49]

Class conflict facilitated the early progress of Primitive Methodism in Manchester. As in the Black Country, an enterprising society member rather than a missionary deputed by the circuit committee undertook to open "Cottonopolis." The self-chosen evangelist was Eleazar Hathorn, the wooden-legged veteran who had once been John Benton's preaching partner in Derbyshire. Hathorn organized two classes, one of which met in a cottage, the other in a loft over a stable. Tunstall began supplying the new mission in March 1820, after which time Primitive Methodism made "abnormal progress" both in Manchester and in neighboring places. Bourne came in June, preached at Manchester and at Ashton-under-Lyne, and led a class at Salford. On a second visit in August he observed, the "society is going well, but is much opposed by ———."[50] The identity of "———" remains a mystery. Among the possible candidates might be the Wesleyan ministers in Manchester circuit, their New Connexion counterparts, or some of the more rabid Tories in the district.[51] Methodism was a significant force in southeastern Lancashire, but the tensions of the post-Waterloo period sundered their ranks. Most propertied Wesleyans and Kilhamites, whose antiradical sentiments were plainly voiced by the itinerants, were set over against working-class Methodists and their sympathizers, some of whom were local preachers.

Trouble between the Wesleyan ministers and some members of their flock at Manchester was nothing new, but it was exacerbated by political differences after Waterloo. Antagonism on the part of local preachers and leaders toward the authority of conference as represented by the "modern" Wesleyan itinerancy dated from at least as early as 1808. In 1815 Jabez Bunting had advised appointing a "firm superintendent" to subdue Manchester's "quite mutinous" local preachers, and in 1819 it was evident to at least one local preacher in the circuit that the "high Church party are very powerful and very desirous to crush us." John Stephens, the superintendent at the time of Peterloo and afterwards, detailed a plan to purge the society of "unsound elements." This scheme was "likely to succeed," he thought, as "they are completely at our mercy. We have no long speaches [*sic*]; no moving and seconding wild and absurd resolutions; not a soul of them ventures to propose anything without first consulting me and obtaining my consent. A few of the ringleaders have taken the sulks and seldom attend our meetings; but for this we are not sorry. . . . They are down and we intend to keep them down." Even Stephens was unable to annihilate all lay initiative in Manchester. Bitter because the conference of 1823 overrode local wishes and assigned an itinerant not of their own choosing, thirty leaders and trustees signed a compact agreeing "to render [his] way as rough as possible." The appointee found his new charge "extremely unpleasant, as it as the first time . . . [he] had been openly opposed."[52]

Added to this underlying conflict among Manchester Wesleyans was hostility between the "respectable people," vigorously championed by Stephens, and "the poor," who had espoused "that daring spirit of insubordination which threatens at once to subvert the religion and government of the country." After Peterloo, Stephens made such a "very extraordinary bustle" about politics that a local critic accused him of alienating popular opinion by urging his own loyal views "to a pernicious extreme."[53] Stephens's colleague at Manchester, Thomas Jackson, recalled that before August 1819 the laboring classes had been in a state of "incipient rebellion," while well-to-do members of the society had lost concern for things of the spirit and worried about protecting their material interests. At the time of the "massacre," Jackson, "knowing the hostility that existed there towards Methodist preachers and Methodist chapels," was "concerned for the welfare of my family and for our places of worship." After Peterloo, he remembered, the "disaffected masses" merely "brooded in silence." At least one man in his congregation did more than brood. During Jackson's sermon he "walked up the aisle to the middle of the chapel, there took his stand, looked me in the face, and held up his white hat." Jackson "immediately accepted his challenge" and switched to a discourse on Christian obedience to civil authority. In 1821 Wesleyan Methodism stood "high among the respectable people" in Manchester.[54]

Given the alienation of many poor Wesleyan and New Connexion

Methodists from most of their "betters," Primitive Methodism ought to have triumphed in the Lancashire cotton towns. By 1820, when the formal mission to Manchester and the surrounding area was opened, commercial distress and its attendant hardships were beginning to give way to some measure of prosperity. In February 1821 Stephens judged that formerly disaffected Methodists were "growing tired of radicalism, and as that dies, religion will revive." This renewal of interest in religion, however, was channeled primarily into Primitive Methodism. In July 1820 there were "great pentecostal showers," and by September the cause was in a "flourishing state." One local preacher addressed a crowd of 2,000 in the rain at Astley Bridge, another 2,000 on Bolton Moor, 4,000 at the stocks in Bolton, and 3,000 at Hay Brow, all in the space of two days during the summer of 1821. He claimed that 12,000 people thronged to a camp meeting at Bolton in July. According to a traveling preacher then working in Manchester, the evening love feast that followed this camp meeting attracted an audience large enough to fill the Cloth Hall at Bolton. A month later Bolton had nine classes and 160 members. An itinerant who sought contributions to pay for furnishing a preaching room met with "amazing success"; at one place some workmen donated the 16s. they had collected for a "footing" (a drinking bout initiating a newcomer) to "what they called the poor Ranters." By the end of the year there were 211 members at Manchester and another 321 at Bolton, and missionaries had been sent to the neighborhoods of Rochdale, Oldham, and Bury.[55]

Although the early converts to Primitive Methodism were mostly working-class, the sect won a degree of goodwill and a little financial support from some members of the gentry and middle class. In at least one such case, self-interest was clearly the motive: the overseers of a parish gave £5 toward a chapel because the Primitive Methodists were saving them money. Exposure to the gospel had caused formerly "extravagant and indolent" recipients of poor relief to become "sober, orderly, industrious, [and] virtuous."[56] Several "respectable persons" even joined the society. Among them were two self-made cotton manufacturers, Ralph and Samuel Waller, both of whom had been Wesleyans. Convinced that Ranter zeal, plainness of dress, and missionary tactics were "calculated to do good in turning sinners," and urged by a sense of duty to the "thousands who have no desire to go to church or chapel," Samuel Waller became a local preacher. While he was delivering a roadside sermon near Ashton-under-Lyne, Waller was observed by a cotton dealer who recognized him as a business acquaintance and summoned the constabulary. The presiding judge at his subsequent trial was W. R. Hay, the vicar of Rochdale, who had ordered the yeomanry to charge at

St. Peter's Fields. Waller's overt support of the Ranters was almost certainly seen as class betrayal. Found guilty of having unlawfully assembled a crowd, of having obstructed the king's highway, and of having made "a noise, riot, tumult, and disturbance . . . by shouting and singing," he was sentenced to three months in Manchester New Bailey. Waller, of course, became a popular hero among Primitive Methodists, and the connexional magazine printed a set of hymns to commemorate his release from prison.[57]

The advent of Primitive Methodism did apparently help to stifle growth in both the Old and New Connexions. Two of the New Connexion circuits in the region, Manchester and Ashton, together gained only 106 adherents between 1820 and 1823. A third, Stockport, lost ground. Numbers in the Wesleyan Stockport circuit also shrank, but these decreases cannot be attributed to the Primitive Methodists, who were equally stymied in Stockport during the same period. In terms of percentages Wesleyan Methodism fared even worse than the New Connexion in southeastern Lancashire. In 1819 there were 10,839 Wesleyans in eight circuits—Manchester, Salford, Stockport, Oldham, Bury, Ashton-under-Lyne, Rochdale, and Bolton. In 1823 their combined total was 11,084, an average increase of fewer than eight converts per year in each circuit. The Bolton circuit had actually lost members and would continue to do so until 1827. Here Primitive Methodist evangelism, at least during the early years of the decade, almost certainly had a negative impact on Wesleyan numbers. Bolton and Primitive Methodism "gripped each other"; the people there "eagerly, almost fiercely welcomed it."[58]

In the Black Country, in the villages of the Yorkshire textile districts, and in mill towns such as Leeds and Manchester the clientele of Primitive Methodism was almost entirely working-class. There was no consistent relationship between Ranter evangelism, radical agitation, and repression, but economic distress and social dislocation generally worked to the advantage of Primitive Methodism. Where Wesleyan Methodism was deeply rooted and the Wesleyan itinerants both encouraged revivalism and permitted a greater than usual degree of lay involvement, Primitive Methodism prospered least. In circuits like Manchester and Bolton, however, whose Wesleyan and New Connexion preachers aligned themselves with the middle class and stifled lay initiative, disenchanted Methodists were eager to embrace the sectarian alternative of Ranterism.

This and the preceding chapter have followed the progress of Primitive Methodism in those areas that had been evangelized by the end of 1819. It was also in 1819 that a dozen delegates assembled at Nottingham to draw up regulations for the connexion and to make plans for its first annual meeting. This preparatory gathering marked the coming of age of Primitive Methodism. It was now evident that yearly conferences and consistent policies were needed to preserve the unity of the connexion. Between 1816 and the close of 1819 missionaries had carried the sect across the Midlands from the Irish Sea to the North Sea and into the East and West Ridings of Yorkshire. Its most dramatic successes had come during the "great revival" among the miners and stocking knitters of eastern Derbyshire, southern Nottinghamshire, and northern Leicestershire. But Hull would prove the most potent and most prolific of the four circuits already in existence in 1819. In such areas as the textile and manufacturing parts of the West Riding, the Black Country, southeastern Lancashire, and the Potteries, the great majority of converts were coming from the "lower orders." In western Cheshire, eastern Staffordshire, sections of Derbyshire, the East Riding, and northern Lincolnshire, the Ranters were also gaining some adherents among tenant farmers and small landowners. Essentially, however, Primitive Methodism was projecting itself as a working-class religion, and that image would persist throughout the century.

Although during the mid-1820s the connexion would suffer temporary but significant decreases in some circuits, in the course of the decade it would spread through most of England as well as into southern Scotland and South Wales. In the triennium after 1819 alone, Primitive Methodism was to travel throughout the northern counties, there to be especially well received in Weardale and Allendale, and to strike deep roots among the colliers of Tyneside and southeastern Durham. Evangelists sent into the remaining parts of the West Riding and Lancashire would also meet with success, except in Liverpool, which, like London, would be slow to embrace the sect. After troubled beginnings, Primitive Methodism would become a significant force in the rural life of East Anglia. Missionaries arriving in the aftermath of the Cinderhill riots were to lay the basis for a strong circuit in Shropshire, one which would itself introduce the connexion into remote corners of southern Herefordshire and into the mining villages of South Wales and Gloucestershire west of the Severn. Except in perennially revivalistic Cornwall, regions opened later in the 1820s—and these were mainly in the southern counties—proved on the whole to be less congenial soil for Ranterism than the Midlands and the North.

Six

The Primitive
Methodist Experience

Like Wesley, the laymen who founded the Primitive
Methodist Connexion meant simply to revitalize religion from within the
existing ecclesiastical structure, not to establish a separate denomination.
As early as 1811, however, it was evident to them that the Wesleyan authorities were not prepared to tolerate either their evangelistic tactics or
their ethos, and they formed the Society of the Primitive Methodists. It
was not yet equally clear that the new body would last. "The connexion,
in its beginning, was small; its prospects were low and discouraging; . . .
no one, humanly speaking, would have supposed it could possibly have
risen to its present height," Bourne wrote after delegates to the planning
session at Nottingham in 1819 inquired about their sectarian origins. To
Bourne, as author of the first connexional history, the spurt of growth
which began with the revival in the East Midlands seemed amazing but
"providential." In fact, the rapid progress of Primitive Methodism during
its Ranter phase occurred because a complex of social and economic
factors had created a demand among the poor for exactly what the
connexion was able to offer—membership and fellowship in a community that esteemed the worth of individuals, that gave them purpose, and
that provided an alternative structure of values. These were precisely the
commodities which the Wesleyan and New Connexions had chosen not
to market at the time. Until 1819 the course of Primitive Methodist
expansion was left to private conscience, to individual initiative, and
above all to "the openings of Divine Providence." There was no coherent
system of government, no methodical record-keeping, no uniformly enforced discipline. Beginning with the meeting at Nottingham, however,
Primitive Methodism developed both a connexional polity and connexional policies.[1]

People and Preachers

A spirit of jealousy, with respect to the influence of preachers, pervades the whole [Primitive Methodist] system.

　　　　　　　　　　—A New Connexion Methodist, 1834[2]

Connexional Polity and Finances

As was so often the case among the lay-dominated Primitive Methodists, it was the "friends" in Nottingham circuit, not Bourne or Clowes, who set in motion the summoning of representatives to the "preparatory meeting" in 1819. The circuit committees in Tunstall, Loughborough, and Hull agreed with the Nottingham assessment: increased numbers and expanding frontiers required greater cohesiveness and more cooperation, objectives that they hoped to gain by establishing annual conferences and by formulating uniform rules for the connexion. Because "to send more would be too expensive," only three delegates were chosen from each circuit, one of whom was a traveling preacher. Even this much ministerial representation was challenged at first on the grounds that the laity would have less voice there than they did at other meetings. When they assembled at Nottingham in mid-August, the delegates concluded that the same system should be used in the future for annual meetings, but they also specified that itinerants might not vote on questions concerning their salaries. The quarter-day board in each circuit was to elect its own representatives, a measure that assigned much more weight to lay and local opinion than was permitted in the Wesleyan or even the New Connexion. Hull was designated as the site for the first annual meeting.[3]

　　　The minutes of the preparatory meeting were incorporated with those of the Hull assembly and published in the *Primitive Methodist Magazine* in 1820 along with "A Treatise on Discipline, Chiefly as It Respects Meetings for Business." This article on parliamentary procedure was officially adopted at the annual meeting and so became a part of the Primitive Methodist "constitution."[4] Although the name "conference" was laden with authoritarian overtones and was therefore avoided for a time, the question-and-answer form of the minutes was styled on the Wesleyan model. The first person to preside over a Primitive Methodist annual meeting was a layman, George Hanford. Hugh Bourne was appointed to edit the connexional magazine and James Bourne to act as book steward. The delegates legislated on a variety of matters concerning the admission, stationing, and salaries of traveling preachers.

Except for a maximum age limit of forty-five years, the only prerequisite for the itinerancy was acceptable "views of the ministry." A traveling preacher was forbidden to carry on private business for personal gain while itinerating and was required to keep a journal which had to be submitted periodically to his circuit committee. While the people might not request a specific itinerant, their quarter-day board had the right to reject one assigned by the annual meeting. The circuit committee (which administered the circuit between quarterly meetings) had the power to suspend a traveling preacher until his or her case was heard by the quarter-day board; the itinerant in turn could appeal the decision to the annual meeting, at which voting was done by ballot. Dress regulations for preachers and other "members in office" specified single-breasted coats and waistcoats, and no "pantaloons, fashionable trowsers, nor white hats."[5]

The governing bodies at the circuit level were composed chiefly of lay persons, and they retained a good deal of local autonomy. In addition to the itinerants working in the circuit, the quarter-day board included local preachers, class leaders, stewards, and delegates from the societies. The circuit committee was made up of the traveling preachers and seven lay appointees named by the quarterly meeting. Only two of the itinerants were allowed to vote at any one session of the circuit committee. The quarter-day board was empowered to make whatever regulations its members thought desirable so long as these did not contravene the general rules of the connexion, and it could grant anyone permission to administer the sacrament. The minutes also laid down guidelines for admitting new members, conducting class meetings, visiting sick members, and expelling habitual absentees. Nonmembers were not to attend more than three love feasts prior to joining a class unless they belonged to "other communities." Members were asked to pay a penny weekly "if they can afford it, and more if they choose," plus what they were able to contribute at the quarterly ticket renewal. All enjoyed "equal rights, according to the station they fill in the church." Among the "shalt nots" enjoined were buying smuggled goods, dealing dishonestly, and committing "other acts of immorality."[6]

The lay delegates at the first annual meeting were jealous of their prerogatives. Clowes was one of the itinerants present, but he had not been "regularly elected." The majority refused to seat him until a recess was called during which the Hull circuit committee properly appointed him. Bourne was not even chosen as a delegate to the annual meeting at Tunstall in 1821, and "like Achilles," he "retired sulking to his tent." He appeared by invitation after the meeting broke down because of wrangles over the stationing of traveling preachers. Bourne proposed a modification, which was adopted by the members: thereafter the circuits—now twelve in number—were to be grouped into four districts, each of which would assign its own itinerants within the district. The circuits would send representatives to district meetings; these in turn would select delegates to the annual conference. The proportion of laity to preachers remained unchanged. At the Tunstall meeting Bourne also took it upon himself to have a "speeching radical" expelled from the assembly and to offer unheeded advice on how the Hull circuit ought to dispose of its surplus funds. Bourne wanted the money to be used for the relief of "distressed" chapels; Hull's quarter-day board chose instead to open new missions. [7]

Financial worries plagued Primitive Methodism during the Ranter period. There were several reasons for this. Fundamental, of course, was the fact that the sect did recruit from the class which it had set out to evangelize—the poor. Giving class and ticket money was a real sacrifice for most, and those who did pay were demonstrating an allegiance to the cause that was both voluntary and genuine. Especially during times of severe distress, however, compassion dictated that money not be made the only measure of commitment. It was therefore possible for those who could not contribute to be members in good standing. On the other hand, preachers eager to report swelling membership figures sometimes failed to urge payment at all. Also, the free-gospel tradition present at the birth of the connexion persisted into its third decade. Several of the most successful apostles of Ranterism—Benton and Wedgwood, for example—were wedded to free-gospel beliefs. Finally, there existed a popular antagonism toward Methodist collections in general. "Bacon preacher" was perhaps the epithet most frequently hurled at the first generation of Primitive Methodist itinerants, and some of them were overly anxious to prove that their quest was for converts, not free board and lodging. Rapid expansion in the absence of any central authority compounded the financial problems, and these in turn played a key role in the troubles of the mid-1820s.

As early as 1818 Bourne was so perturbed by disputes over free gospelism in the East Midlands and by debts in Tunstall circuit that he "expected . . . [the connexion] must break up." During the following winter and spring he personally renewed nearly all of the tickets, and collections rose. [8] He was apparently regarded as something of a Cassandra about money matters. When the 1823 annual meeting convened, one circuit in Derbyshire, some in Lancashire, and "a number" in Yorkshire were "considerably embarrassed; and some of them [were] grievously embarrassed." Bourne requested a closer watch on budgets and asked the itinerants to subscribe £1 each, as "they had been the chief cause" of the deficits. When less than £4 was contributed, he circulated a "private communication" that stressed the critical level of the debts and named various guilty preachers. A majority at the conference of 1824 opposed "several sweeping resolutions" moved by Bourne, who then "poured out a volley of hard speeches and painted such a picture of delinquencies that is not often seen or heard of in the Christian ministry; and . . . warned the conference of the consequences that would follow if the circuits were suffered to be further embarrassed." For his pains he received a "torrent of abuse." Bourne's concern in 1824 was not only about debts but also about the failure of some itinerants to do family visiting and the resultant loss of contact between preachers and people.[9] During 1825–1826 several preachers and societies broke with Primitive Methodism, and membership seems to have declined throughout the connexion.[10] Six circuits in East Anglia were "shattered" by the actions of "improper" itinerants. All the components of this crisis have never been satisfactorily identified. Bourne blamed what he called "running out" preachers—those who failed to collect money and to minister adequately to their people. Others attributed the troubles to "commercial distress in the manufacturing districts," indiscriminate selection of traveling preachers occasioned by rapid expansion during the preceding years, and the admission of "questionable characters" into the societies.[11] Whatever the causes, their consequences startled the leadership into tightening discipline and regulating finances. The conference of 1826 ruled that each circuit must pay its own itinerants or be deprived of their labors, and that no circuit might accumulate a debt. Although this decision resulted in the exodus of thirty more itinerants and a further loss of members, it ultimately proved to be beneficial.[12] In 1829 numbers in the connexion surpassed the total of 1824, and membership grew steadily throughout the subsequent decade.

Bourne's frustrating experience with recalcitrant lay-dominated conferences during the early 1820s typified a weakness of the Primitive Methodist polity which was also manifested at the society and circuit levels. Not only were the perhaps wiser counsels of itinerants sometimes ignored—and traveling preachers often did have the advantage of a broader experience—but also disputes among the laity brought schisms and occasionally threatened to turn democracy into anarchy. Lay leaders did not always have as accurate a perception of majority sentiment as the itinerants did. Despite protests from Bourne, a series of annual meetings elaborated and extended the dress code until finally in 1828 the delegates realized its unpopularity and substituted a general recommendation in favor of "plainness." Even then the traveling preachers were subject to regulations on dress. Because the quarter-day board was "the seat of authority, the source whence all power was drawn," some circuits continued to impose the strictures, and in 1830 the conference had specifically to forbid their reenactment by quarterly meetings.[13] An attempt in 1825 to consolidate all evangelistic efforts under a general missionary committee appointed by the conference collapsed within a year because the various circuits preferred to open new territory independently. A nineteenth-century English variant on a famous French cartoon depicts a Wesleyan layman struggling under the burden of three stylish and well-fed ministers seated on his back. A New Connexion layman stands arm in arm with a traveling preacher under the superscription "We be brethren." Wesleyan "priestly tyranny" is inverted to show Primitive Methodist "lay despotism," and two shabby laymen, one of whom wields a stick, are astride a dowdy and pained-looking preacher.[14]

The advantage of according so great a role to the laity more than compensated for mistaken judgments, fissiparousness, and inefficiency. Men who were not even enfranchised until 1867 or, in many cases, until 1884, received an early opportunity to influence decision-making and to undertake responsibilities. Though they usually occupied less important public positions, female members were even further in advance of most of their sisters. Both men and women functioned as itinerants, local preachers, class leaders, exhorters, Sunday-school teachers, and "praying labourers," but the posts of steward, trustee, and delegate to conference were a male preserve. Even if Bourne sometimes resented being balked by lay opinion, he understood the value of lay participation. As early as 1811 he had objected to "lording" over the people. "This lording is dreadful work," he had written in his journal, "and while the preachers live who are now at the head of our society, I believe we shall have no mastering. O Lord Jesus, preserve us."[15] The title given to the minutes of the preparatory meeting at Nottingham exemplified the delegates' perception of their sect: it styled Primitive Methodism a "Society of People."

The Call to Preach

In 1819 illness forced an itinerant working in Cheshire to retire before he could finish his round of appointments. The innkeeper's son sent to convey the message that a replacement was wanted instead enlisted a friend who was harvesting grain. The second youth threw down his sickle, changed his clothes, and completed the preacher's circuit. In this fashion Thomas Brownsword, one of several Primitive Methodist "boy-preachers," began his career as an itinerant. Brownsword was soon followed into the ministry by his sister Ann, who itinerated until she married, then settled in Burslem and became a local preacher. Thomas Webb left his plow to become a traveling preacher, and William Newton did not let blindness prevent him from itinerating for the connexion. Such stories were not unusual in the early history of Primitive Methodism. What distinguishes these four is that all were inhabitants of a single village, Englesea Brook.[16] The call to preach could be heard and accepted by virtually anyone.

There were four kinds of preachers: paid itinerants, paid local preachers, self-financed missionaries, and—the great majority—unpaid local preachers. Movement from one category to another was common, especially the transition from local to traveling preacher and back. Local preachers were often recruited even when they thought their talents inadequate to the task. In 1881 an old man who had preached in the Black Country for fifty-three years recollected that, as soon as his initial nervousness and objections had been overcome, he had been filled with pride at the "honour" of having been chosen, and on his own initiative he had visited hamlets where there were no societies. He had preached, he recalled, to "godless villagers, who often severely persecuted [ministers] . . . but who rarely molested me, I having lived among them."[17] The local preachers and exhorters in Belper circuit were reminded that "it is upon your faithfulness, zeal, and united efforts that the prosperity of God's cause in this circuit in very great measure depends." Reprinted in the connexional magazine for all literate local preachers to read, this "address" also warned against tardiness and neglect of assignments.[18] The quarter-day board at Hull did not hesitate to reprove even "Praying Johnny" Oxtoby when he failed to keep his preaching appointments.[19]

Itinerants were ill paid. In 1820 the maximum annual salary for an unmarried male preacher was £15. A man with a wife and two children could not earn more than £37 14s. each year, and then only if both children were under the age of eight and had been born after their father began to itinerate. A woman was paid £2 per quarter.[20] The son of a Lincolnshire man who had begun to preach in 1819 claimed that his father had resigned from the Primitive Methodist itinerancy chiefly because the "small stipend" allowed was "altogether inadequate to the support of his large family."[21] A positive consequence of this parsimony was that it tended to discourage the half-committed from entering the ministry. Another result was a fairly rapid turnover in the itinerancy. Bachelors, for example, often gave up traveling and became local preachers when marriage brought a need for more remunerative employment. Their places were readily taken by others who needed a "call" but no formal training. So much shifting into and out of the full-time ministry helped to blur the distinction between itinerant and lay preachers, and therefore retarded the growth of that "black-coat" professionalism which was then provoking criticism in the Wesleyan Connexion. Unless they were among the few fortunate enough to have other income, men who persisted in their vocations after marrying faced real hardship. A New Connexion writer faulted the Primitive Methodists for not paying salaries sufficient even to meet the basic wants of their itinerants. The preachers' families, he declared, were "almost dependent on charity for the daily supplies of life."[22] If, however, inadequate salaries imposed a severe economic strain on the traveling preachers, they also facilitated the spread of Primitive Methodism among the poorer sections of English society. A preacher who earned less than a skilled worker was easily identified as "us" rather than "them," and a cheap ministry let the connexion expand without overtaxing the financial resources of its members.

Within specified limits traveling preachers were allowed to accept hospitality from society members, and this tempted some nonmembers to pose as itinerants in order to gain free meals and lodging. In June 1821 the cover of the *Primitive Methodist Magazine* cautioned against an imposter in Hull circuit. A similar warning during the next summer told of a fraudulent preacher operating in the vicinity of Sleaford. By 1823 the deceivers were more numerous and their schemes more sophisticated. Some of the "shameless imposters" who were "swarming about the connexion" solicited contributions to nonexistent funds for ailing or aged preachers. Many strangers who were not Primitive Methodists passed themselves off as impoverished members of societies elsewhere in the kingdom. They told hard-luck stories, accepted alms, and then decamped. "We have received an abundance of complaints of this kind," warned Bourne. He also observed that, especially in "trading towns," there was so much immigration and emigration that it was difficult to distinguish the pretenders from those who deserved charity at the hands of fellow society members.[23] The imposters who masqueraded as itinerants seemed, of course, to confirm the widespread notion that Primitive Methodist ministers were merely "bacon-preachers."

An early Victorian "theological dictionary" noted four identifying characteristics of the Ranters: they were generally illiterate, they were extremely noisy, they relied mostly on local preachers, and they allowed "females to preach in promiscuous assemblies."[24] In 1818 one of every five Primitive Methodist preachers was a woman. Local preachers of both sexes outnumbered itinerants, but proportionately fewer females than males became traveling preachers. Although Primitive Methodist women were given many more opportunities to exercise their talents than were women in the Wesleyan or New Connexion, their status was not yet on a par with that of men. Circuit plans of the period designated male itinerants by name, women by initials. A ruling of 1824 banned female superintendents and denied voting privileges to female members of quarter-day boards. Nor were women permitted to speak at quarterly meetings "unless specifically called upon." They were, however, highly esteemed as missionaries and revivalists, roles in which many performed more successfully than did their male colleagues.[25]

The aborted career of George Eliot's heroine Dinah Morris illustrates the shift in Wesleyan views of female preaching. Wesleyans soon came to regard women preachers as aberrations. In the course of a funeral sermon one Wesleyan preacher observed, "Balaam was converted by the braying of an ass, and Peter by the crowing of a cock, and our lamented brother by the preaching of a woman; God often uses strange instruments."[26] This had not been the usual attitude of Methodists at the end of the eighteenth century. Though preaching by females had not been customary, women had, nevertheless, been among the most popular and prominent speakers during the revivals of the 1790s. According to John Wesley, "the work of God termed Methodism" was an "*extraordinary* dispensation" of divine providence; consequently, "several things occur therein which do not fall under ordinary rules of discipline." He had argued that Methodist use of unordained preachers was allowable under this "extraordinary dispensation," and that, while women were less likely than men to receive "extraordinary" vocations to preach, both might legitimately respond to such calls.[27]

Women in the ministry constituted one point of difference in the early nineteenth-century controversy between "primitive" and "modern" Methodists. The Wesleyan conference could not bring itself to bestow on women the "virtual ordination" that set itinerants apart from nonprofessional preachers. This was a natural attitude at the time; females might be servants or mill girls or prostitutes, but they were not career women. For schismatic groups like the Bible Christians, the Independent Methodists, and the Primitive Methodists, all of whom rejected the "high" Wesleyan view of the ministry, this was simply a nonissue. The real crux of the matter, however, was that the Wesleyan conference saw preaching women, refractory laymen, and "wildfire" revivals as bound together in an unholy alliance that would thwart the speedy realization of its current aims. There was indeed a link between female preaching and successful revivalism, and this was precisely why Hugh Bourne encouraged it. Kilhamite indifference toward revivalism goes far to explain why the otherwise liberal New Connexion cast women as "lovely examples of domestic piety" but did not want them in "stations of authority and publicity."[28] The Bible Christians, who *were* revivalistic, not only employed young females as traveling preachers but also sought to prevent their early retirement into marriage by offering higher salaries to couples who itinerated together.[29] Lorenzo Dow, the American preacher anathematized by the Wesleyan conference, was likewise convinced that women were superior revivalists. The Wesleyan ruling of 1803 did not absolutely forbid preaching by females, but it might as well have done so.[30] Some members of conference did not want to silence the women. At its meeting of 1802 only a slim majority favored denying tickets to females who persisted in exhorting or preaching in public. Bunting believed that the subsequent conference had equivocated on the matter; the minute of 1803 reflected its "cowardice" in not meeting the question with an explicit rejection of the "evil" and unscriptural practice of preaching by women. A few Wesleyan itinerants like William Bramwell were champions of female revivalists. Others shared the opinion of John Pawson: "I have been no great friend to women preaching among us; but when I evidently see what good is done, I dare not forbid them." Still others were aware that the ban was forcing, not following rank-and-file sentiment. In 1809 Zacharias Taft maintained that, while there was opposition among the itinerants to preaching by women, there was "very little (comparatively) among the people."[31] Conference fiat and Wesleyan popular opinion were antipathetic. For Primitive Methodism this situation served both as rationale and as opportunity.

The Primitive Methodist Connexion adopted Bourne's positive views on female preaching, and these were validated by success. Bourne's thinking was in no way shaped by advanced ideas concerning the place of women in society. If by his actions he contributed to the liberation of nineteenth-century women, this was only incidental to his purpose. Bourne was driven by a single concern—the salvation of souls. Whatever facilitated this crusade was good; whatever frustrated it was bad. If novelty attracted the curious to hear Sarah Kirkland preach in a Nottingham slum and a revival ensued, if Hannah Woolhouse was able to raise up two classes in Hull, if the factory workers of Bolton were awakened by the sermons of Ann Brownsword, then women should be allowed to evangelize. These women were only three among many who demonstrated the utility of female preachers. For Bourne and for the Primitive Methodist Connexion that was argument enough.

During the early 1820s the connexion's frontiers were expanding rapidly into uncharted territory, newcomers were joining the itinerancy, and veterans were periodically being restationed. In December 1821 a notice on the cover of the *Primitive Methodist Magazine* requested traveling preachers to make maps indicating mileage, the meeting places of their societies, and the location of market towns and villages. To assist novice itinerants and to encourage uniform practices among the experienced, the conference of 1822 ordered the *Magazine* to publish a preachers' manual in serial form. Although various itinerants contributed to it, the handbook was written mainly by Nathaniel West. Among the seven great preachers held up as models were Luther, Wesley, and Bramwell. Unmarried itinerants were cautioned to "beware of wicked women lest you lose your character." Preaching should not be lengthy, hurried, or done from "skeletons." While he ought not to seem "covetous," neither should the itinerant neglect his duty to make quarterly collections. The primary message of "Advice to Travelling Preachers," however, was the necessity of cementing close ties with and among the people. Rural members were to receive as much attention as those in the towns; cottage visits were imperative; the preacher should always allow time for conversation both before and after his sermon. When giving tickets, he ought to "inquire with personal concern after each individual" and "shew gratitude for whatever the people give." One bit of advice in the handbook epitomized the entire thrust of Ranterism: "Be humble and you will not be ashamed to traverse through the most wretched garrets, alleys, lanes, and cottages in search of souls . . . , to endure insults, hunger, cold, and hardships."[32]

Conversion

> Stop, poor sinner, stop and think
>   Before you further go,
> Can you sport upon the brink,
>   Of everlasting woe?

> When we had got a house to preach in, we went round the town to let the people know. Had a good congregation; some tears were shed.

> . . . and in the prayer meeting, after preaching, brother John Shaw rose up, full of joy, saying: "My burden's gone! My burden's gone!" He now walked in the liberty of the sons of God.

> When I'm imprisoned here below,
>   In anguish, pain, and smart;
> Oft time those troubles I forego,
>   When love surrounds my heart.[33]

The four epigraphs that head this section summarize the manner in which Primitive Methodism won many of its early converts; they also suggest what conversion meant for the individuals who experienced it. The first is the initial stanza of a hymn habitually sung in the street by preachers upon entering a new village or town. The second, an extract from an itinerant's journal, describes what happened if the missionary found an opening. The third, taken from the obituary of a farm servant in Cheshire, points not only to a deeply felt sense of release from bondage into freedom but also to the fact that Primitive Methodists judged the conversion and death of a laborer worth recording. The quatrain at the end can, of course, be read as another dose of opiate for the people; opiate or not, the popularity of the hymn of which it forms a part suggests that Primitive Methodism did make life more bearable for those who joined. How did the Ranters reach their potential members? What prompted conversions? Who were the converted?

The Tactics

If "the word went 'round that the Ranters were coming," people flocked to hear, to jeer, to satisfy their curiosity. Numbers in the East Midlands came merely because they hoped to be told "something new"—a symptom of discontent with an unsatisfactory or disintegrating old order. The very name "Ranter" provoked interest. So did the novelty of such practices as "walking prayer meetings," singing in the streets, and open-air preaching by women and adolescents. Events like outdoors love feasts and camp meetings were social occasions from which no one was barred. Ranter preachers knew the value of keeping in the public eye, of exploiting opportunities, of always being accessible. Clothing, speech, and demeanor all signaled that theirs was a mission of the poor to the poor, not a well-meant but condescending work of charity aimed at improving morals and manners. Articles in newspapers, even derogatory ones, helped to publicize the sect. The *Primitive Methodist Magazine* sometimes fell into the hands of people like Elizabeth Shaw of Honley, for whom the Wesleyan services were "as dry breasts." Jeremiah Gilbert read extracts from his journals to stir enthusiasm among the throngs that gathered in West Riding streets and marketplaces. The chief means of communication, however, was word of mouth. In dozens of obituaries the details of conversion included phrases like "she heard the Ranters were in town," or "a friend related his experience." News was frequently carried by travelers. Abraham Dixon went to buy wool in Lincolnshire and returned to Silsden "telling that Ranters were converting sinners by the thousands." The Primitive Methodists were summoned to Silsden, and, little more than a year later, the village headed a missionary branch with over 600 members.[34] Even an argument could further the cause. During a heated debate with another Wesleyan about "wildfire, disorder, and confusion," Joseph Peart was chided with the words, "You should have been a RANTER!" Peart construed this rejoinder as a prompting from God, wrote to Clowes asking for a missionary, and so introduced Primitive Methodism into North Shields.[35] In the opinion of Hugh Bourne, properly conducted camp meetings were the single most important means of converting people. John Benton relied on singing to draw crowds and to awaken sinners. Camp meetings and hymns, as well as the content and style of Primitive Methodist preaching, need closer scrutiny.

At the heart of Primitive Methodist theology were two key teachings —assurance and perfection. Assurance brought a "new birth." By the direct working of the Holy Spirit a person "convicted" of his sins gained experiential knowledge of divine forgiveness and, through the merits of the Atonement, was personally reconciled to God. The "new man" so born was justified by saving faith and freely bestowed grace. He was then able to strive for sanctification—holiness made possible by a further access of grace, informing and inspiriting his own efforts to lead a sinless life. Though progress toward this state of perfection was usually gradual, it could be gained instantaneously. Perfection might also be lost, and the outward sign of this was backsliding. Four distinct things were experienced at Primitive Methodist meetings or through the agency of sermons, exhortations, and hymns: (1) a person might be convinced of sin and become a mourner; (2) a mourner might be prayed with and encouraged until he was "liberated" (justification); (3) the "new man" might undergo sudden sanctification; and (4) a backslider might be reconverted to the quest for holiness. Apart from its function of publicizing the availability of salvation, the camp meeting served primarily to bring about conviction of sin and restoration from backsliding. Justification and sanctification did occur at camp meetings, but they were more likely to happen at such services as love feasts and prayer meetings. The doctrine of assurance was inherently leveling: both the mighty and the lowly were sinners; the lowly as well as the mighty could experience the "new birth." In fact, the poor were better situated to do so, the entry of the rich into the kingdom of heaven being more difficult than the passage of a camel through the eye of a needle. Because assurance was experiential, ignorance of theology (or, by extension, the lack of any formal education) was no obstacle. Primitive Methodist preachers consciously avoided highflown language and allusions to topics outside the ken of their hearers.

The well-run camp meeting was like a three-ring circus. The simile is not meant to be derogatory. Bourne intended camp meetings to be counterattractions to traditional festivities; if they were to draw and hold an audience, they had to be fast-paced, vibrant, and sociable. Many activities took place simultaneously, thus multiplying opportunities for participation. Timekeepers cut off sermons, prayers, and exhortations promptly so that interest would not flag. The Primitive Methodist conference directed that five minutes before a preacher's time expired, a conductor should signal him "by pressing the point of an umbrella or something else against his foot." The preacher was then to end his discourse by strongly urging "a present faith and a present salvation." He was also admonished to "avoid all senseless talk about literature and college education."[36] Although there was a flavor of condescension about it, the description of a camp meeting recorded by a country gentleman in the 1830s captured something of its warmth and exuberance:

> A crowd of rustic people is assembled; a wagon is drawn thither for a stage, and in it stand men with . . . coloured handkerchiefs tied upon their heads to prevent taking cold after their violent exertions; . . . In their addresses you are continually catching the most picturesque expressions, the most unlooked-for illustrations,—often the most irresistibly amusing. [But] . . . with much ignorance and outrageous cant, there is often mixed up a rude intellectual strength, and a freshness of thought that never knew the process of taming and trammeling called education, and that fears no criticism; . . . and, suddenly the crowd will divide itself into several companies, and go singing to different parts of the field . . . ; they kneel down, each company in a circle; the leaders pray; and it is curious to see what looks of holy jealousy are cast from one circle to another, as the voice of one leader predominates over those of the others by its vehemence, its loudness, or its eloquence; drawing speedily away all the audience of the less gifted.[37]

Unlike a circus, the camp meeting was not for spectators; it was designed to engage the whole person actively. If one did not undergo conviction or justification, he could sing, pray for himself or others, tell his own religious experience, counsel mourners, move from one preaching station to another seeking inspiration, or just chat and picnic with acquaintances. Nothing that might further salvation was forbidden. If people occasionally were moved to leap, fall, dance, or "go into vision," the customary attitude was that indicated by one itinerant's retort to critics in Manchester: "If you don't like this sort of work, you can take your hats and leave us."[38]

A contrast to the more staid hymns sung in Wesleyan chapels and to the drone of "Anglican chant," Ranter hymns belonged to a world of ballads and street songs, of drinking songs, colliers' rants, and costermongers' cries. The hymnal was compiled for use at "camp meetings, revivals, &c.," and the selections in it were chosen with that end in view. A few of the sort written by Charles Wesley and Isaac Watts were admitted, but the favorites, sung to popular tunes, were verses turned out by revivalists like Dow, Benton, and Bourne. A Primitive Methodist from Manchester remembered that around 1820 "it was very common to hear lewd or ribald songs sung in the streets" and that the Ranters set their own words to the "most effective" of these tunes. "At our camp meetings," he recalled, "people, chiefly young ones, used to run up to hear us, thinking we were singing a favourite song. But they were disappointed therein; nevertheless, they were arrested and often charmed by the hymn, which at times went with power to their hearts." With their "wild vivacity" and "metaphoric boldness," Ranter hymns earned "many a bright shilling" for street singers. One of these singers reported that "children stand to listen to us, and they get hold of a few lines or of the chorus, and with the tune, or as much of it as they can think of, they run home, and for days they sing it in their homes, and their mothers and sisters get hold of it."[39] John Coulson heard the hostess in a Nottinghamshire public house beg a sweep to "sing that hymn with the hallelujahs . . . , for the children will not go to school until they hear it."[40] Many who became Primitive Methodists were initially attracted by their hymns. Some like Thomas Taylor of Sleaford joined because they wanted to participate. An irreligious habitué of taverns before his conversion, Taylor "had a peculiar talent for singing, which in his early days often proved a snare."[41]

Besides being set to lively tunes, Primitive Methodist hymns had other qualities that appealed to an audience of ordinary folk. Some of these assets were structural; others had to do with content. A majority of hymns were written either in the first person plural ("Our conflicts here, though great they be, / Shall not prevent our victory") or were directly addressed to the congregation ("Is there anybody here that wants salvation?"). Several had choruses that allowed variety, such as "save backsliders," "save our children," "save our parents," and "save our neighbours." Others were designed to be sung in dialogue form.[42] A few celebrated Ranter victories ("Camp meetings with success are crown'd") or honored heroes like Samuel Waller. Some hymns rang with defiance, such as the one recounting Wedgwood's imprisonment in Lincolnshire and the one which "scorned to fear" the "wicked men" who let bulls loose, threw filth, and arrested preachers. Enemies guilty of "perse-

cuting" or "hindering" the "work of God" were depicted in one hymn as
having "deep horror painted" on their features as devils dragged them
"into the gulf of burning woe!" Threats of punishment and lurid descriptions of hell were much less usual, however, than were promises of beatitude. Primitive Methodist hymns about paradise employed traditional
imagery—gold crowns, jewels, sweet perfumes—but the dominant
theme was food. While the heavenly banquet was at least as old as the
biblical "feast of fat things," the great frequency with which auditors
were invited to "come, the rich provision taste" was significant. The
rural bias of the sect was reflected in songs using agricultural figures of
speech ("You'll with the reapers come . . . to shout the harvest home").
The "we" in other hymns were oppressed people who would ultimately
be rewarded. The Primitive Methodists saw themselves as persons of
"low estate" whom God had chosen "to spread" the "truth around."
They, not "the rich and great," had been elected to bring about the deliverance of England. Meanwhile, a "dreadful curse hath overspread / the
land, both far and wide," and people "mourn for lack of bread." Finally,
there were two other recurrent motifs, each of which pointed to an
important feature of Primitive Methodism. One of these was a strong
sense of community that derived from shared experience: "Our souls, by
love together knit, / Cemented, mixt in one, / One hope, one heart, one
mind, one joy, / 'Tis heaven on earth begun; / Our hearts have burn'd
while Jesus spake, / And glowed with sacred fire, / He stopt, and talk'd,
and fed, and blest, / And fill'd th'enlarged desire." The other theme,
although it related specifically to spiritual worth, might also be understood as a suggestion that the "new man" would be fit to make his way
without deference or dependency in the new society of the nineteenth
century: "Let not conscience make you linger, / Nor of fitness fondly
dream; / All the fitness he requires, / Is to feel your need of him."[43]

The message urged in Primitive Methodist sermons was "free, full,
and present salvation through and by faith." Clowes was sure that true
religion "consist[ed] . . . in the soul taking hold of God and realizing a
PRESENT SALVATION." Although his sins had weighed on his conscience for
some time before he was liberated, Clowes's own conversion had been
sudden: "The power of Heaven came down upon me, and I cried for help
to Him who is mighty to save. It was towards the close of the meeting,
when I felt my bonds breaking; and when this change was taking place, I
thought within myself, What is this? This, I said, is what the Methodists
mean by being converted: yes, this is it—God is converting my soul. In
an agony of prayer, I believed God would save me,—then I believed he
was saving me,—then I believed he had saved me, and it was so."[44]
Bourne, who had not undergone "quick conversion," reproached himself

for doubting its genuineness: "Such things do not depend on length of time, but on faith," he wrote in his diary. According to Bourne, a "converting preacher" was like "a skilful general," who "warns by setting forth the terrors of hell and encourages by preaching the glories of heaven," and then relies on the assistance of "pious, praying labourers" to pray souls into liberty. Bourne noted a phenomenon that Bateman also observed during the Cheshire revival in 1819—the "conversation-words of the common people" stirred enthusiasm "almost without the aid of regular preaching."[45] Bateman, who spoke from a layman's point of view, recalled that in the 1820s a preacher was "not so much looked to for a fine and florid address as for bringing down the converting power."[46] This was the sentiment of a Yorkshireman who, unimpressed by a digression on stars, called out, "They'll go reet; and thee come down and talk to us a bit."[47]

Preachers sometimes recorded which verses of Scripture they had used as texts for their sermons. A convert often remembered exactly which was the text and sermon that had awakened him, and, because personal testimonies were customary, he was likely to share this information. Journals and obituaries, therefore, as well as more general comments provide clues as to the content of Ranter preaching. Wedgwood's favorite theme appears to have been the impending day of judgment, a motif that Bourne also employed at times. Bourne, however, was likely to choose a text that stressed the felicity to be enjoyed by the faithful when that day of wrath and mourning came. Undiluted millenarianism could halt the "converting and liberating work." When a millenarian spoke at a love feast at Stockton-on-Tees, the "power" went out of the meeting.[48] Bourne was convinced that a balance should be struck between the "sorrowful part of religion" and the "joyful part." If people were taught to expect only "happy feelings" after conversion, they would be badly prepared to combat "strong temptations."[49] Many sermons, however, did convey a positive message: among these were one based on the much-used text, "Behold, I stand at the door and knock," and another expounding the vision of lifegiving waters from Ezekiel. A popular text that must have struck many hearers as thoroughly appropriate to their circumstances was, "By faith Noah, being warned of God . . . prepared an ark to the saving of his house; by the which he condemned the world and became heir of the righteousness which is by faith" (Hebrews 11:7). The transitoriness of life ("all flesh is grass") was the usual text for funerals, and there were many to be solemnized among the poor in the second and third decades of the century.

The flames of a revival might be fed by contagion, but conversion was a private experience. Just as Clowes understood this, so he knew that fear was an effective way to goad loiterers on the way to salvation. More than any other preacher, it was he who "terrorized" his listeners. Sometimes this was owing to his choice of text; sometimes his anecdotes frightened the unconverted; most often it was his manner that compelled sinners to "flee immediately from the wrath to come."[50] Even when addressing a group, Clowes was able to convince each listener that his or her salvation was at that moment of paramount importance. George Herod once watched him bring a wheelwright to conviction of sin. Clowes "fixed his eye on him" and said "with a very shrill voice, 'Thou art looking at him! I know Thou wilt do him good!'" After the wheelwright, who "was all the time trembling," suddenly raced out of the chapel, Clowes rested "his elbow on the pulpit bannister, placed his head in his hand, and waited in silence. It struck me he was following the individual, and we concluded we would watch and see the result." About ten hushed minutes passed before the "runaway" returned, looking "very wild," and "dropped on his knees beside Clowes and loudly cried out for mercy."[51]

The salvation tactics of Primitive Methodism were exemplified in the practices of Robert Key, a layman who had retired from the itinerancy and was the leader of a class in Oldham: "He sang lively tunes, prayed short, spoke to his members short and pointed, and exhorted them to look for free, full, and present salvation." It was assumed that, "if Robert Key was in a meeting, all went on lively and well."[52]

The Saved

During its first decade the Primitive Methodist Connexion recruited a majority of its members from the adult population. For several reasons it is impossible to know exactly what prompted these men and women to be convinced of sin, to "get liberty," or to be certain of sanctification. The very nature of their experience was private and not easily communicated. Not many wrote about the intimate details of their own spiritual odysseys. Such confidences were, of course, shared verbally with fellow society members, but what was recorded in the obituary when someone died were the remembered bits. Although the *Primitive Methodist Magazine* carried many obituaries, not all the deceased were memorialized. Some traveling preachers were more conscientious than others about submitting obituaries; some wrote at length, while others were very terse. Also, because the budget of the *Magazine* was meager, space was limited. If an issue included a long article or considerable news, its obituary section might be abbreviated. A few diaries, then, and numerous obituaries written at second hand are the only information available about conversion from the perspective of those who underwent it.

Mary Bowman, Catherine Worrall, and Mary Hopkinson all recorded their experiences. Mary Bowman spent much of her life in loneliness. Orphaned at the age of ten, she "was put out [as a] town's apprentice to a very bad place" where, in order to avoid beatings, she stopped attending chapel. Although she often wanted to commit suicide, she dared not, because she would "certainly go to hell." At nineteen she married, but her husband enlisted in the navy and left soon after the birth of their child. Nine years later, he sent for her, and they embarked on a voyage that ended in shipwreck. During a second attempt to emigrate he died and was buried at sea. Widowed, friendless, "left to the wide world," Bowman returned to the West Riding, where she encountered the Primitive Methodists and regained her faith. In retrospect it seemed to her that "the Lord was my husband, the Lord was my friend . . . [who] brought me back to Sheffield, where I began afresh to serve him for his goodness and mercy to me."[53] Only twenty when she died, Catherine Worrall was a mill girl in Macclesfield. Childhood exposure to Wesleyan Methodism had convinced her of sin, but it was the Primitive Methodists who "prayed her into liberty." An "improper timidity" kept Worrall from testifying freely at meetings; instead she poured out her feelings in a diary. Her spiritual life was characterized by surges of exaltation followed by troughs of despair. The last entry, dated sixteen days before her death, hailed "my King and God of Love—my desire and joy!"[54] Mary Hopkinson, it seems, desperately wanted attention. The mother of several children, she lived in "comfortable circumstances" and was indifferent toward religion until she thought her health was beginning to fail. When she heard about the Primitive Methodists' mission in Lincolnshire, Hopkinson told a friend, "I believe the Ranters are the people who will be instrumental . . . to the conversion of my soul." Although she had dreams and visions about hell and her own need for repentance, it was only after individual counseling that she entered the penitents' square during a meeting and was prayed into conviction of sin. During the subsequent months preachers and society members regularly visited her at home. Through their colloquies and supplications she finally gained pardon shortly before her death.[55]

The specter of death often spurred a "change of heart." Obituaries of persons in whom this change lasted suggest that fears occasioned by illness and death frequently coincided with conversion. Such instances included an outbreak of typhus in Lincolnshire, pit accidents in Staffordshire and Derbyshire, an attack of consumption, the drowning of a brother, a miscarriage, the death of an only child, a disabling injury, the death of a spouse, a paralytic stroke, and the loss of both parents.[56] In several of these cases the subjects were Wesleyans who had lapsed. Ann Wilson, for example, had been awakened shortly after her marriage by the "praying colliers" but had later lost interest. After her husband died leaving her with eight children to support, she again yearned for society membership. By then the Wesleyans had withdrawn from her village, but the Primitive Methodists had just arrived.[57]

Conversions prompted by the fear of death were not peculiar to the first decade of Primitive Methodism. An "awful visitation of the cholera" in 1832 swelled numbers in Leeds circuit and added 250 new members during a single quarter in both Hull and North Shields. Even "hard" Liverpool had a revival. Though traveling preachers observed that such gains were apt to be ephemeral, Manchester retained the converts won during the epidemic.[58] Membership throughout the connexion grew by 7,120 during 1832–1833. Mortality rates from cholera were even greater at the end of the 1840s, and the gain of 9,205 in 1849–1850 was the largest annual increase in the history of Primitive Methodism.

It was also very common for conversion or recovery of zeal to occur when individuals felt despair or were in straitened circumstances. An alcoholic who thought himself "lost" was prevented from taking his own life. A farm laborer and his wife joined the society after habitual drunkenness cost the man his job. Some converts were farmers whom the postwar collapse of agricultural prices had "reduced from abundance to poverty." William Bateson's father, a farmer and lead miner in Cumberland, had been able to provide his son with a "liberal education" during the 1790s. About 1818 the mining concern for which William worked as an agent went bankrupt. Unemployed and sure that death was imminent, he moved to York, where he was converted. In the early 1820s he served as class leader, local preacher, and circuit steward. William Goodrich, a former Wesleyan, was once a hosier in Leicester. About 1814 he had lost both his property and his friends and had applied for parish relief. While living at St. Martin's workhouse, he joined the Primitive Methodists, and according to his son, "among them he found that consolation and assistance which he needed." James Robinson had lost touch with the Wesleyans as he traveled from Yorkshire to Lancashire and Cheshire searching for work. The prelude to Samuel Barber's conversion, while typical in some ways, was unusual in other respects. Accustomed to comfort as a youth, he was later obliged to hire out as a servant because his parents had squandered a sizable inheritance by trying to "make a figure in the world." Barber's mother was English, his father an ex-slave from Jamaica, the "faithful black servant" of Samuel Johnson. Barber believed that "there was no mercy for him because he was of African extraction and was of the coloured tribe." Clowes convinced him that he was neither an "outcast" nor a "reprobate."[59]

The decision to join the Primitive Methodists was not always related to their message of free and full salvation. One elderly Yorkshireman built them a chapel because he was lame and wanted a place of worship nearby; another had been cast out of the Wesleyan society for drunkenness fourteen years before, and though readmitted, apparently still harbored a grudge. A deaf man in the High Peak district joined the Ranters because, being deaf, "these [he] could hear better." A Nottingham framework knitter was ashamed to go elsewhere because "his coat was so bad." People received a good deal of personal attention from the itinerants. Ann Armstrong habitually questioned the not quite converted about their spiritual progress. Bourne wrote out a doctrinal statement for a deaf woman who disliked Methodists. Clowes visited many cottages to converse with potential members. He was particularly adroit at handling sticky situations: a servant in Derbyshire complained that "the members looked upon her but indifferently, therefore did not receive her." Though her abilities "were not of a superior kind," Clowes secured her allegiance by putting her to work as a local preacher.[60]

Certain conclusions can be drawn about the first generation of Primitive Methodists even though their obituaries did not always include all the information that might be wanted.[61] Of one hundred converts memorialized, fifty-five were female. It was stated in forty-one of these obituaries that the new member had had a premonition of death, had died within a year of joining, or had been in very poor health.[62] Of the seventy-nine people whose age at the time of conversion was supplied, six were under fifteen, while ten were fifty-five or older. Slightly more than half were between the ages of fifteen and thirty-four, and twenty-eight of these were under twenty-five. Occupation or status was mentioned in only forty obituaries.[63] Over half were servants or farm laborers, or were described as poor or "in deep poverty." One-fifth were artisans; five were unskilled workers outside of agriculture; two were farmers; three were called "respectable." Of the fifty-two persons whose religious backgrounds were specified, twenty had been Wesleyan or under Wesleyan influence; ten had been Anglican; ten were "irreligious"; eight came from Primitive Methodist families; three had been non-Methodist Nonconformists; and one had been a Roman Catholic.

A somewhat different perspective can be had by looking at the converts won in each of two different counties during the connexion's first decade. Obituaries appeared for forty-four such Primitive Methodists from Derbyshire, twenty-five of whom were female. Thirty-seven percent of those whose age at conversion was given were twenty or younger. Occupations were unmentioned in twenty obituaries; among the remainder, seven were described as "prosperous" farmers or "gentlemen"; eleven were servants, agricultural laborers, poor, or "impoverished"; four were mill workers, one was a collier, and one a joiner. Thirty-three obituaries of the earliest Leicestershire converts were published between 1820 and 1844. Two-thirds of them were males. One-third of these men were in their twenties when they joined the sect, and six others were forty-five or older. Half the females were between fifteen and twenty, and another third were in their forties. Of the twenty-one whose previous religious affiliations were stated, twelve had Wesleyan ties. In only half of these obituaries was occupation indicated, and in all but two cases the converts were servants, laborers, cottagers, or unemployed, or they were described as poor. Although there were several important similarities, the counties differed in two significant respects: Leicestershire had many more male converts and very few members who could be called well-off. In terms of occupations it appears that Lincolnshire, the East Riding, and Cheshire tended toward the Derbyshire pattern, while Nottinghamshire, the West Riding, Lancashire, and the Black Country were more like Leicestershire. North Staffordshire seems to have varied from one part to another.[64]

What did conversion bring to those who experienced it? For an eighteen-year-old girl at York, being a Primitive Methodist meant estrangement from a wealthy family, loss of friends, and marriage to a traveling preacher. A widow from Derby, driven by poverty "into the fields, with her children by the hand, to partake of such fruits as the hedges produced," was enabled to "fall down and return God thanks." An aged farmer learned to experience "some of his best times" while meditating and praying in his Staffordshire fields. Another old man, who died at age sixty-five was simply proud to have been one of the first Primitive Methodists in Leicestershire and to have accumulated the sixty-four quarterly tickets that proved him so. The Lancashire owner of property in the West Indies immediately freed her "several" slaves because she had been liberated from the "slavery of the devil." An orphan at Newark, who was a lapsed Wesleyan, recovered her zeal, gained full sanctification, became a traveling preacher, and was instrumental in bringing about the delayed revival of religion in Huddersfield. Deprived of his knitting frame, a young stockinger in Nottinghamshire joined the itinerancy, learned Greek and Hebrew, studied philosophy and theology, and wrote books on history and biography.[65]

Curiosity and word of mouth might attract crowds; preaching, camp meetings, and popular hymns might provoke conversions; and "getting liberty" might help individuals to cope with anxieties and problems. Yet, if members were to be retained, Primitive Methodism had to provide something more. What it offered was a sense of community and set of values.

Community

A very great strictness grew up among the people,
and none were willingly allowed to exercise in public
who were not correct in their conduct and diligent in
the duties of their callings.

—Hugh Bourne, 1821[66]

In 1821 the "Society of People Called Primitive Methodists" directly affected the lives of less than 1 percent of the adult population in Great Britain, and only about one-third of those influenced by the sect were actually members of it. If a typical Methodist congregation included two "hearers" to each member, even at its peak Primitive Methodism touched perhaps no more than three out of every hundred people over the age of fourteen.[67] Nevertheless, in certain regions and especially in certain locales within these regions the connexion made an impact. In such places it offered the poor a viable form of community and played a significant role in shaping attitudes. A village society or one whose members had been transplanted into the alien soil of a growing mill town provided fellowship and a sense of "place" in a shifting environment. The society was not an abstract concept; it was an immediate presence and could be experienced in a variety of ways. Active participation in the affairs of the society meant that traditional rural pastimes were replaced by pursuits better suited to the dawning modern age. Membership entailed adherence to a structure of values that facilitated the break with an older, more dependent way of life. Within the society the worth of individuals was affirmed: each person's spiritual progress was a matter of consequence; men and women with initiative had multiple opportunities to undertake responsibility, to organize, to budget monies and keep records, to make decisions affecting others; those who merited praise for a task done competently received that recognition. Anyone might climb upward into a position of leadership within the circuit, or, through the publicity given by the *Primitive Methodist Magazine*, earn connexionwide fame as an evangelist. Above all, the sect belonged to the people who had created it—small farmers, servants, mill workers, colliers, agricultural laborers, weavers, and framework knitters. As such, it stood as both a reprimand and an alternative to the Church of

England and to the social order, the economic system, the government, and the set of attitudes represented by the established church.

A convert who became a Primitive Methodist did more than add his name to a membership roll. The society was less an organization than an extended family in which shared values were substituted for blood ties. To join was to be adopted into that family. Instead of traveling the way of holiness alone, the spiritual pilgrim gained the support and counsel of fellow members and was expected to reciprocate. A newcomer who asked to join, if "accounted eligible," was given a probationary ticket and a copy of the rules. If he could read, he was to study the rules; if he was illiterate, the preacher was supposed to read and explain the regulations to him. After a quarter spent in attending meetings and endeavoring to live according to Primitive Methodist precepts, the probationary member was given a "complete" ticket and took his full place in society.[68] A society bound together all the Primitive Methodists in a single village or town, and its members gathered for preaching, prayer meetings, and love feasts. Unless a society was very small, it was divided into classes of twelve to twenty people, and each class was put in the charge of a leader. In addition to starting class meetings promptly and conducting them efficiently, the leader was supposed to check on absent members, visit the homebound, and rally those in danger of backsliding. During the Ranter period, when new places were being opened almost daily, a potential member might be designated a leader and asked to "raise up" a class. In 1820 a Wesleyan woman who went to hear a missionary preach in the street was handed a class paper and told to "go to Horton and seek out souls." The preacher then departed, "saying she might do as she was pleased, but she must remember the eye of God was upon her." Though "agitated" about "how to bear the name RANTER," the new class leader did as she had been bidden.[69]

The formal meetings of the society were structured to allow for considerable lay participation. More than 80 percent of the preaching was done by lay persons, and sermons were always followed by extemporaneous prayer and often by testimonies. Even the preacher was encouraged to "tell his experience." Prayer meetings were limited to forty-five minutes or an hour in length. Every activity was intentionally kept short: singing, exhortations, prayers by the leader and by every member followed one another in quick succession. Only the need to pray with mourners in distress justified breaking the prescribed timetable. Hymns were sung and prayers offered at a love feast, and the preacher might make a few remarks, but the raison d'être of the event was the blessing and sharing of bread and water, followed by the sharing of personal experiences. As at prayer services, none were "allowed to run into useless exhortation, drag out to tedious lengths, or to speak unprofitably of others." The main purpose of the class meeting was to give and gain support in the battle against sin. The leader inquired into the spiritual health of every class member; each person spoke for a minute or two; each prayed briefly. More time was devoted to a class member who was struggling to overcome severe temptation or who had received some special access of grace. As a novice, Clowes had quickly learned that effective class leading "did not consist so much in talking to the members, as in getting into the faith, and bringing down the cloud of God's glory, that the people might be truly blessed in their souls as well as instructed in divine things." "Telling your experience" at preaching services, testifying during love feasts, sharing insights, trials, and victories at class meetings were all ways in which people could learn to articulate publicly their private feelings in a systematic and socially acceptable manner. The singing of hymns helped common folk develop a literary consciousness to complement the ballad tradition that was already theirs. Most important, the mutuality of the exercises contributed to the cohesiveness of the society.[70]

Special occasions such as a baptism or the opening of a chapel were marked, but none was observed more elaborately than the funeral of a member who had died triumphant. Often, funeral sermons for those whose deaths had been exemplary were preached at various places throughout the circuit. The congregation that assembled for one of these at Loughborough could not be accommodated in the chapel, and "many had to return home." When Richard Ward of Countesthorpe, a man from the "lower walks of life" who became an exhorter and a class leader, died, "hundreds" attended his "street-funeral" in the village. "Numbers" came from the adjacent villages to the funeral of a woman in County Durham, and the "service was powerful." Four people who attended the prayer meeting that followed the funeral "were brought into glorious liberty."[71]

Pastoral duties were incumbent on preachers and class leaders, but all members were expected to make cottage visits and to engage in the "conversation ministry." This was especially urged in cases of illness, and no deathbed was to be left unattended. In Loughborough circuit the itinerant alone called eight times on a consumptive girl, and a Lincolnshire layman visited a dying member eight times within the space of two weeks.[72] That numerous Primitive Methodists were ready to assist fellow members materially was shown by the fact that so many imposters tried to exploit their generosity by falsely claiming to belong to societies elsewhere.

Apart from their proven effectiveness as revivalists and exhorters, women escaped being thrust into the background partly because the society necessarily functioned as a surrogate family. During the early years of the connexion most people joined as individuals, not in family units. Husbands and wives might later follow their spouses into the society and bring up their children in Primitive Methodist households, but this pattern was more characteristic of a later period. In Bourne's mind the idea of women as "mothers in Israel" seems to have antedated the conviction that they were highly useful as missionaries.[73] Casting females in the symbolic role of mothers may partially explain why male members were willing to allow them a larger public field of activity than was permitted in English society in general at that time. In any case, for economic reasons a poor woman was not very likely to find herself imprisoned in a "doll's house." If a Primitive Methodist woman could labor in a factory, she could also be accepted as a class leader, a preacher, or a member of a quarter-day board.

Young people were valued members of the community. Adolescents who joined the connexion were treated as adults and were expected to participate fully in all meetings. Thomas Brownsword and John Skevington were only two among many "boy-preachers," and Sarah Kirkland took her place on the plan at nineteen. Kendall, who began his own preaching career at the age of eleven, commented that a youth was never told to "wait until his beard was grown" before "exercising" in public.[74] Although at first there were not many preadolescent converts and only a few families, children were not neglected. Bourne customarily preached short, simple sermons to children, and he insisted that others follow his example. He sometimes held meetings especially for youngsters, and in 1816 he started to write a commentary on the Scriptures for their use.[75] The earliest volume of the *Primitive Methodist Magazine* included a hymn for children, a letter stressing the need to chastise them in a "loving" way, a series recommending colloquy between parents and children as a means of "pious education," and an obituary in which the deceased was eulogized at length because he had a gift for conversing with children. Later volumes also printed such articles as "A Treatise on the Duty of Parents" and "On the Instruction of the Rising Generation."[76] If adult members preferred rough eloquence in their sermons, they nevertheless wanted some formal education for the "rising generation." Sunday schools were established as early as 1814, and the teaching of writing, often discouraged in Anglican and Wesleyan Sunday schools, was allowed a place in their curricula. The connexion also launched a *Primitive Methodist Children's Magazine*, one of the first periodicals of its kind in the world. In October 1824 this publication introduced itself to its young readers with the words, "We are now entering on a new work, a work designed for you." Demand for the magazine so far exceeded expectation that several printings of the October issue had to be made, and monthly circulation reached 6,000.[77]

To a great extent adult readers of Primitive Methodist publications had their literary diets chosen by Hugh Bourne. Because books had been the medium of his own conversion, Bourne attached considerable importance to reading, and he also wrote extensively. He judged literature as he judged all else—worth and usefulness in promoting salvation were synonymous. Although a committee determined what should be published by the connexion, for various reasons Bourne's opinion usually prevailed. He was editor of the *Primitive Methodist Magazine;* his brother was the book steward for the sect; all publications emanated from the Book Room, a barn with a printing press located on the Bourne farm at Bemersley. Some publications earned a profit. The revival hymnbook of 1809 brought in "hundreds of pounds," despite its having been pirated several times before a copyright was obtained in 1821.[78] Profits were used to defray the expense of evangelizing new places, but losses were absorbed by the Bournes. This financial arrangement naturally lent weight to their views when the book committee met. The *Primitive Methodist Magazine* was sold at the lowest possible price. At 3d. an issue it cost only half as much as either its New Connexion counterpart or the abridged "sixpenny" edition of the Wesleyan *Methodist Magazine.* Mostly given over to connexional news, extracts from journals, articles about personal piety, obituaries, reports from the conferences, and tips on ways to maintain fervor at meetings, the *Magazine* also occasionally included poems, descriptions of exotic peoples, places, and customs, moralizing anecdotes, and accounts of "providential" happenings. One educated layman confessed that he had once had "very low and mean views" of the *Magazine* and had tried to keep his wife from reading it because she was already opposed to the Ranters. She read it anyway and was converted by the obituaries. He changed his mind about its value.[79] Bourne considered some secular literature to be pernicious, some frivolous, and much of the rest distracting. Even theological writings could sometimes hinder progress toward holiness; he was pleased when Thomas Woodnorth "left off a variety of books and sold some of them; and now he looks more to God to open the scriptures."[80] When, as frequently happened, this narrowness was absorbed by local leaders, it caused some converts to drop out of the societies. The Chartist Thomas Cooper was not the only erstwhile member who refused to feed solely on the Bible and religious books.

In part Primitive Methodism defined itself by rejecting practices and attitudes accepted in the world around it. Although members disliked picayune regulations about clothing, the general counsel to unite plainness and cheapness in dress was welcomed because it sanctified what was

for most people an economic necessity. Smoking was forbidden to itinerants and discouraged among the laity chiefly because tobacco was
"believed to induce sloth."[81] The annual meeting of 1822 enjoined members not to marry anyone whose life and conversation failed to conform
to gospel teachings—presumably as this ideal was understood by Primitive Methodists. They were urged not to use public bakehouses nor, bar-
ring emergencies, to purchase beer on the Sabbath. While the conferences of the 1820s did not legislate on the use of alcohol, both drunkenness and wasting time in public houses were declared unacceptable. So
were attending public or "worldly" amusements and following the "fashions of the world."[82] When the connexion did take a negative stand on
alcohol at the beginning of the next decade, this was less a way of asserting a separate identity than it was an expression of working-class concern
about the social and economic effects of drinking. Alcohol had come to
be as suspect as theaters, lotteries, and grog shops, and for the same reasons: these evils were the "purse-draining and demoralizing" causes of a
"very large share of the miseries existing among the labouring classes."[83]
The conference endorsement of temperance societies in 1832 was the first
official step in a process that soon transformed Primitive Methodism into
a temperance sect. While they were not the very first to formally pledge
total abstinence, Primitive Methodists were among the earliest to champion teetotalism. It was a member of the society at Preston who allegedly
coined the word "tee-total," and abstinence was increasingly favored
over moderation. So caught up in the movement did Bourne become that
he "almost got to believe that he was the father of teetotalism as well as
of English camp meetings."[84] In fact, during the 1830s and 1840s temperance and teetotalism provided Primitive Methodism with a rallying
cause, much as the issue of camp meetings had done for the Ranters a
generation before.

Setting themselves apart as a "peculiar people"—something the
Primitive Methodists thought that most Wesleyans were no longer doing
—implied a criticism of contemporary English society. As early as 1807,
when he had traveled to Lichfield to get Mow Cop licensed as a site for
worship, Bourne had been convinced of the iniquity in both the church
and the nation. He greatly admired George Fox, and perhaps being in
that "bloody city" whose wickedness the Quaker had once denounced
had unconsciously provoked a parallel response:

> I went into the minster. After the service began, it ran through
> my mind, "Get thee out of this place, and beware of the woman
> that has the golden cup in her hand, and those that are with her;
> their ways are death:" . . . I saw much lightness and sin among
> the parsons. . . . It then struck me, "These people draweth nigh

unto me with their lips," &c. . . . I then thought to go out, and a voice came, "Escape for thy life." . . . I took my hat as soon as they had done the *Te Deum*, and went out, and the burden was removed. It looked as if judgments hung over that place. I stopped all afternoon in Lichfield, and such a travail of soul came upon me as I never before experienced—it was for the city; I mourned greatly; it seemed as if the people had almost sinned out the day of their visitation.[85]

Although, fifteen years later, this message would probably have been conveyed through a different medium, its content would have remained unchanged.

Opposition to some aspects of popular culture was not unique to Primitive Methodism. Wesleyan and New Connexion Methodists as well as Anglican evangelicals regarded such events as wakes and fairs with a jaundiced eye because they were opportunities for the "lower orders" to shake off the "bridle of restraint."[86] Borough councils, members of Parliament, and voluntary associations sought to suppress cruel sports like bullbaiting and cockfighting. What the Primitive Methodists did earlier and better than most was to provide counterattractions to the tippling, gambling, fighting, and promiscuity that characterized traditional celebrations. Leisure time and festivities came infrequently enough in the lives of laboring men and women, and older forms of entertainment were not easily relinquished. To sermonize and rule against wakes and brutal sports was one thing; to challenge them by offering alternatives was another. The Primitive Methodists habitually timed their own activities to coincide with "occasions of sin." To preserve members from the "vanities of the racecourse," a parade of children from the Sunday school and a "frugal feast" were scheduled during race week at Preston. A camp meeting near Alton aroused "much complaint" from the "wake-folk, [who] say there has been no mirth, and that they could not go on with the wake." Ranter interference with time-honored practices was sometimes frustrated by local authorities. A missionary was imprisoned for street preaching at a hiring fair in Shrewsbury, and an outdoor service held during a back-swording contest resulted in the arrest of another evangelist, who was charged with interrupting the "due order and observances of the fair."[87] For those who were diverted to them, Primitive Methodist camp meetings, revivals, open-air love feasts, and "walking prayer meetings" helped to serve as a bridge between customary kinds of recreation and the music hall, football match, and "telly" of later eras.

Spurning some habits, attitudes, and fashions of the world while confronting others head-on was the negative side, the sect as a counterculture. Primitive Methodism also had a positive side. In addition to the numerous opportunities within the society for developing independence and initiative, a sense of responsibility and self-worth, and organizational and decision-making abilities, there was also a set of values to be learned and put into practice. In promoting sobriety, perseverance, thrift, honesty, promptitude, trustworthiness, and diligence, Primitive Methodism inculcated nothing new. The difference lay in the fact that these virtues were taught by working-class people to their peers, and they were communicated in a homely way. Among the "rules for holy living" printed in a handbill were these:

No. 4. If you are able, read a chapter or part of a chapter every day. . . . You have time—you have all the time that comes, for when you live with a single eye to God, you serve him in all things, even in your bodily labours.
No. 7. On the Sabbath be diligent and attend public worship as often as possible. . . . Be sure to shave and clean the shoes before Sunday; and be at all times as fearful of sin as you would of burning your finger off, for that will not be so painful as hell.
No. 8. If the Lord call you to any public exercise or to assist in a Sunday school, he will give you wisdom and patience.[88]

There are very few local histories of Primitive Methodist societies founded as early as 1821. The society at Silsden is an exception. Fortunately, it was typical enough so that a description of it can also depict life in other Primitive Methodist communities of the period. Situated between Airedale and Rombalds Moor in the West Riding, Silsden had about 1,300 inhabitants, most of whom made their living from agriculture, nailmaking, and woolcombing. Word of Ranter successes in Lincolnshire and in Leeds reached Silsden about the same time that two Wesleyan local preachers resigned because they had been chastised for preaching in lanes, on greens, and from doorsteps. One of them, twenty-year-old John Flesher, wrote to Hull asking for a Ranter missionary. John Hewson and his wife arrived on Easter Sunday, 1821, and preached in a barn owned by Flesher's father, a grocer and schoolmaster. After the sermon "showers of blessing fell," and the many "wounded" had to be carried from the barn into a house "to be prayed with and fully healed." A society was formed, and the people dug the foundations and hauled stone for a chapel, which was opened at Christmas. As many of the people in Silsden were illiterate, once the chapel was completed, the barn was turned into a school. One of those who "resolved to improve his mind" was Joshua Fletcher. Fletcher's childhood had been spent working first in a coalpit and then in a mill, so he was twenty when he "took his seat among [the children] . . . and there learned his ABC." In 1822 he became a local preacher; later, with a "second-rate engine" and almost no capital, he and two others set up Beck's Mill. The mill ultimately prospered, and Joshua Fletcher became a "mainstay" in the Silsden circuit. Another of the pupils was Thomas Bradley, who at the age of eight was already working as a nailmaker. The lessons that he learned in the barn equipped him to serve as secretary to the local Oddfellows for thirty years. Flesher eventually became editor of the *Primitive Methodist Magazine* and took charge of the connexion's Book Room when it was moved to London in 1843. Most members of the society were poor. The collection when "the Ranters' chapel opened," commented a Wesleyan from nearby Keighley, "only amounted to about £6." Their sense of shared mission, however, was strong. Together, they evangelized the surrounding moors and dales, and by the summer of 1822 there were more than 600 members in Silsden branch and forty places provided for by its preaching plan. A quarter-century later Silsden Primitive Methodists remembered the barn as a "birth-place for souls" where forty-four had been "pricked" and nine converted on a single night. They recalled their "mighty processionings" from village to village. They took pride in having maintained their solidarity "in the face of the hottest persecutions" from constables, magistrates, and mobs.[89]

Silsden was one example of the early experience of community in a Primitive Methodist society. For that minority of English men and women who were its members, this strong sense of identification with Primitive Methodism persisted as the connexion passed from sect to denomination later in the nineteenth century. In 1932 the Primitive Methodist Church ceased to have a separate existence within English Methodism.[90] Even so, several decades later, many who had been its members before 1932 thought of themselves first as "Prims" and then as Methodists.

Ranters and Radicals

Joseph W—— was a very wicked man and usually spent the Lord's Day in wandering from one publichouse to another. One day he heard a person say that the "Ranters" were come to ——— Hill. "Oh!" said Joseph, "it is only the Radicals under a feigned name. I will go and hear them."
—Nottinghamshire, ca. 1817[91]

The relationships between Primitive Methodism, revivalism, and political agitation are not easy to determine. The political posture of Clowes is a matter for speculation; Bourne's stance can be ascertained partly from his diaries, mostly from his actions. The views of the Ranters themselves are not often discoverable, though there are indications that not all of them saw the pursuit of holiness and opposition to the established political and social order as mutually exclusive. Comparing the degree of receptivity shown toward Primitive Methodist missionaries in various locales or the incidence of revivals with the ebb and flow of revolutionary or reform activity yields a few tentative conclusions. Finally, it is possible to demonstrate that under certain external circumstances revivalism usually functioned according to an inner dynamic of its own.

The journals of both Clowes and Bourne are of limited use. Clowes disliked writing and wrote infrequently. What he sketchily recorded was done in late middle age and from memory. What he remembered—not always accurately—were the circumstances of his own conversion and events related to the spread of Primitive Methodism. Bourne's diaries, which have never been published in their entirety, were methodical, voluminous, and, above all, religious. Rarely did Bourne allude directly to contemporary affairs, and, even when he did, he seemed aloof and unconcerned. Typical of the handful of such entries were two made in 1810: in January "Clowes was exercised about the nation. Mourning and lamentation and woe are at hand"; four months later, Bourne "heard the dreadful news that there were riots in London. Well, the Most High ruleth; and the Lord is still a hiding-place."[92] John Walford, Bourne's brother-in-law and the author of his *Memoirs*, believed him to be in favor of reform in church and state but absolutely convinced that Primitive Methodists should "steer clear of all parties disaffected toward the government."[93] That Bourne did not want the leveling implications of the "new birth" pushed to their conclusions in the secular sphere is intimated in a pamphlet that he published in 1827 countering a Baptist attempt to proselytize among Primitive Methodists in the North of England. Arguing against total immersion, a "fangle" invented by Thomas Münzer, Bourne also attacked the man as "a mover of sedition, who set himself up for a prophet."[94] Occasionally Bourne referred in his journals to "improper persons" causing "confusion" in a society. Some of these entries are explicit. In December 1819 he investigated and substantiated a charge "that ——— had preached politics." Usually such comments are vague and could refer to anything from free gospelism to factiousness to immorality. For example, there was, wrote Bourne, "a very good work" at Northwich but "some things unpleasant among the society"; troubles at Nantwich were "aris[ing] from T. W."; John Gorman's "conduct has lately been such that it would be very improper to put him on any plan."

It is suggestive, however, that Gorman was conducting himself improperly in the industrial villages around Nottingham during 1817, while the misbehavior of T. W. and the unpleasantness at Northwich occurred in 1819 in a county then designated by the government as disturbed.[95]

Bourne justified obedience to the government and acceptance of the political status quo on scriptural grounds, but his reasons for opposing involvement with "disaffected parties" were practical, a corollary of his passion for saving souls. The individual would be distracted from his quest for salvation; societies would be rent by political differences. To Bourne's mind no Primitive Methodist could serve two masters: a member's loyalty and energies had to be wholly committed to that movement which God had raised up as the instrument of England's conversion. As avidly as he later crusaded for total abstinence, Bourne yet warned against "non-religious" teetotalism.[96] When he secured the expulsion of a "speeching radical" from the annual meeting at Tunstall, part of his rationale was pragmatic: "I told them . . . that the king was favourable to liberty of conscience and had conferred favour on us, for when prince regent, in June 1812, he signed the act which opened our way to hold camp meetings . . . ; that up to the present time we stood well with the government; and that if the conference set up against government, as government had an eye upon us, measures might be taken to stop our camp meetings, and the Connexion might receive an injury from which it would never recover."[97]

Bourne's phrase, "if the conference set up against government," raises a pair of related questions. To what extent were his views shared by the membership? How effective was his control over what Primitive Methodists did and said, especially at the local level? From Bourne's own account it is clear that the malcontent "employed in speaking against the government" at the annual meeting of 1821 had a receptive audience. When Bourne demanded expulsion, "They opened out against me, against the king, and against the government." During the ensuing argument Bourne "got into strong and peremptory language," and, though a majority finally agreed to eject the offending delegate, "the proceedings of this conference were strange."[98] That the acrimonious debates at the annual meeting in 1824 concerned circuit debts and free gospelism is indisputable. Bateman anticipated a "sharp and long" struggle and wrote in his journal, "I trow the pruning-knife will have to be used with an unsparing hand. Many dead branches will have to be lopped off if the tree must live and thrive."[99] Irresponsible preachers certainly were "lopped off" within the next few years, but political agitators may also have been among the "dead branches." Were the "sweeping resolutions" proposed by Bourne and resisted by the Halifax conference only about money matters? The question can be put but not satisfactorily answered. Primitive Methodist conferences did not automatically assent to all of Bourne's recommendations. Nor, given the structure of the connexion, could all the itinerants acting together at an annual meeting outvote the lay majority. Although representatives elected during the 1820s were not reticent to speak out against smoking, dawdling in pubs, and worldly fashions, apart from proscribing white hats, they left it to the delegates of the next decade to legislate against the involvement of itinerants in politics.[100]

In 1819 a clerical magistrate complained that there were too "many Parson Harrisons" traveling about, "exercising their vocation out of their proper sphere."[101] Some among these "religious as well as political itinerants" may well have been Ranter preachers. The blacksmith Joseph Capper joined the Primitive Methodists after the first Mow Cop meeting in 1807. For years a respected local preacher in Tunstall circuit, he was arrested for Chartist activities in 1842. John Skevington claimed that "from early life" he had "advocated the rights of the many." Still in his teens when he became a local preacher, the future Chartist began to itinerate at the age of twenty. Between 1822 and 1824 Skevington worked successively in Halifax, Barnsley, and Bradwell circuits before retiring to Loughborough, where he served as a class leader and local preacher until 1836. Described in 1839 as a "veteran in the radical cause," Skevington was convinced that "a man cannot be a Christian and not a Chartist unless through ignorance."[102] "Parson Harrison" of the Stockport Union Society may himself have been a Primitive Methodist preacher. The name is a common one, but the Joseph Harrison memorialized in the Primitive Methodist Magazine in 1870 was described as a man of sometimes "weak judgment" who had stopped itinerating in 1849 because he felt unable "to preach to so fashionable a people as resorted" to the Primitive Methodist chapels in Brighton circuit, his last assignment. This Harrison was born near Nantwich, was converted by the Wesleyans in 1812, and in 1824 became a Primitive Methodist traveling preacher in Tunstall. It was "not known" when he had joined the connexion, nor, according to the obituary, did anyone know about his early career. Most of his itinerancy was spent in the Midlands, and there was "not a station in the Nottingham district but was prepared to receive Joseph Harrison."[103]

Outsiders frequently regarded Primitive Methodism as likely to harbor political dissidents. During the post-Waterloo years this perception on the part of Tory magistrates was probably founded less on knowledge of the sect than on distrust of its revival tactics. Those among the poor who supposed that Ranters were radicals "under a feigned name" were not yet acquainted with the connexion. On the other hand, this public image persisted, and it lingered in places evangelized many years earlier. As late as 1836 a gentleman in Yorkshire was told that the Primitive Methodist break with the Wesleyans had occurred "because of something of a political nature." Only after he was shown a copy of the conference minutes forbidding itinerants to engage in politics was he willing to contribute £5 toward the building of a Primitive Methodist chapel in Wakefield.[104] The idea that Ranters might also be radicals likewise existed in the minds of the well informed. In 1819 a Wesleyan itinerant stationed at North Shields asked the current president of conference how to deal with a local preacher who had taken to the hustings during a meeting and denounced the "Manchester murders." The traveling preacher feared that the Wesleyan name would be blackened if the layman were not expelled, but knew that, if he were, "a general ferment" was probable, as "three-quarters of our people are radical reformers." The president advised moderation, because "if you expel such men, . . . the Ranters will greedily gather them up." The Ranters soon did.[105]

Some contemporaries, however, saw and valued Primitive Methodism as a "taming" influence. This was the reading that George Herod gave to the revival in the East Midlands. Herod was one of those converted, and he testified that the "missionaries brought a counteractive influence to bear upon the masses, and in multitudes of instances destroyed the baneful virus of infidelity and insubordination." Of a camp meeting held in Nottingham Forest in 1816, he claimed, "Many to our knowledge became sobered down and were brought into the enjoyment of religion, and became as zealous . . . for Christianity as they had been for Luddism or the levelling system."[106] An East Anglian farmer commented on the impact of Primitive Methodism in the aftermath of the Swing riots: "It cost me two shillings a night all through the winter to have my house watched, . . . and then we went to bed full of anxiety lest we should be burnt out before morning. But you came here and sung and prayed about the streets—for you can never get these 'varmints' into a church or chapel. But your people brought the red-hot gospel to bear upon them in the street, and it laid hold of their guilty hearts, and now these people are good members of your church."[107]

In practice the political temper of Ranterism must have depended to a great extent on the predilections of local leaders. Until the preparatory meeting in 1819, when Bourne stepped down as superintendent, he was able to exert a good deal of control. After 1819 several factors limited his influence. Circuits were virtually autonomous, and their quarter-day boards and administrative committees were dominated by lay persons. Missions were opened by individuals or by circuits, not under the aegis of the connexion as such. Between 1819 and 1824 the sect grew very rapidly, both in numbers and in area. Bourne's position as editor of the *Primitive Methodist Magazine* did enable him to shape opinion indirectly and he seems to have closely supervised the itinerants in the Midlands. Also, well into old age, he continued to tour on foot and to visit societies, but these were mainly in the Tunstall district. Hull, its progeny, and its dependencies, however, were Clowes's domain, and Clowes was chiefly concerned with evangelizing new territory and with efficiently deploying his army of traveling preachers. Given these circumstances, the degree of freedom for engaging in radical political action would have varied widely from society to society and from circuit to circuit.

Bourne was convinced that the mixing of politics and religion worked to the detriment of religion. Wesleyan itinerants often coupled the words "infidelity" and "radical" or referred to the "low state of religion" in the same breath as they did to the "evil influence of Tom Paine." In the autumn of 1816, for example, William France expressed his belief that the Wesleyans had a "good prospect" at Oldham "if these fair blossoms are not blasted this winter by the nipping frost of politics."[108] Diagnosing the Primitive Methodist crisis of the mid-1820s, John Petty noted that unemployment and social unrest "naturally operated prejudicially" among the societies in the manufacturing towns.[109] Similarly, the absence of political dissent was often seen as promoting religious vitality. Gratified by an increase of one hundred new members in the Wesleyan Bradford circuit during a single quarter, Joseph Entwisle declared, "In town and country attentive crowds flock to hear the Word —and many receive it." Preaching was "like running downhill" because "we are exempted here from political noise and animosity." Like Petty, Entwisle introduced an economic factor: "good trade" was acting as an "antidote to disaffection."[110] All but one of these writers had the advantage of being eyewitnesses to the interplay of political agitation, economic conditions, and Methodism during the decade following the defeat of Napoleon. Was their assessment accurate, or were they just echoing an unexamined commonplace? The early progress of Primitive Methodism suggests that privation often contributed to a climate favorable for revivals or stimulated conversions in new territory, but that it affected existing societies adversely or with mixed results. The relationship between political agitation and receptivity toward Ranterism varied from one district to another as the sect opened new missions.

A brief look ahead to a time when Primitive Methodism was already established shows that depression and unemployment, such as occurred during the economic downturn in the mid-1820s, might or might not be offset by gains. The society in Great Horton suffered when an abortive weavers' strike following a period of good trade threw people out of work, and many members emigrated. Stockton and Sunderland circuits increased their numbers by 291 during one quarter in 1825, but others were "expelled or left of themselves." At Oldham the years 1825 and 1826 were "as . . . elsewhere, a time of waste."[111] While these reverses were complicated by problems within the connexion, the same pattern also emerged during the next decade. In 1832 hardship resulting from strikes followed by reprisals in the northern coalfields had a uniformly negative impact. The societies in Sunderland had "great difficulties through the untoward misunderstanding between the coal-owners and their workmen." South Shields also experienced "great difficulties owing to the disturbances and movings in the collieries." Some of the societies in Newcastle were "kept in a fluctuating state by reason of the unsettledness of the pitmen," and "many of our members and friends in the coal interest have been out of employment during the year." Membership in these three circuits had surged from 2,208 in 1831 to 3,360 in 1832, but then fell to 2,900 in 1833. The significant increase before and during the strikes suggests that Primitive Methodist classes may have been used as a ready vehicle for organizing labor action. To the losses blamed on unemployment when mine owners retaliated, however, must be added deaths from pit accidents (especially high in 1832–1833) and from cholera.[112] Depression at the end of the 1830s brought a revival of enthusiasm in Tunstall circuit, while during the same year fifty-two members left Birmingham "in consequence of the great embarrassment in trade." Belper, which had lacked vitality "in recent years," was stirred by a revival during the first six months of 1838, but thirty-five members were cast out "for not walking according to the Gospel." In Mansfield, where trade was severely depressed and "nearly the whole" of the society were stockingers, eighty were lost and ninety gained.[113] It was presumably such phenomena as these, features characteristic of Methodism after its initial missionary phase had ended, to which nineteenth-century Wesleyan itinerants alluded when they ascribed decreases or fluctuations in membership to economic adversity.

Before reviewing the interaction of politics and economic conditions with the spread of Ranterism in the Midlands, Yorkshire, and Lancashire, it is necessary to draw some distinctions and to recall some qualifying factors. First, the term *revival* was sometimes used by Wesleyan and New Connexion Methodists to mean merely the renewal of vitality in a society or the acquisition of members. To the Ranters a revival was what the Wesleyans of the 1790s had regarded as unprecedented and what their conferences in the next decade had suppressed because of the disorder and indiscipline entailed. There was an important difference between participating in this kind of revival and joining a society. The former involved the wider population, was often stimulated by external circumstances, and gained momentum through the mechanism of contagion. The latter implied personal commitment and life in a community on the part of members, and pastoral duties in addition to the use of conversion tactics on the part of preachers. Benton and Wedgwood were only two of many who stirred tremendous enthusiasm but were impatient with the pedestrian task of organizing their converts into classes. Of the thousand or so caught up in the drama of a revival meeting, perhaps a dozen or two would actually become lasting members of the connexion. Events such as camp meetings were social occasions open to the public. The early ones on the Yorkshire Wolds, for example, were anticipated with pleasure and attended by great numbers who never went to either church or chapel.[114] By definition, novelty does not last and could not forever attract. The vast majority of those who hastened to hear what new message the missionaries might be bringing did not become Primitive Methodists. The seasonal element that affected the timing of outdoor meetings—and these were the ones that commanded the attention of both people and magistrates—impedes any attempt to correlate Ranter success with the rise and fall of overt political activity. The tightening of discipline with regard to free gospelism as well as the variations that existed from place to place concerning what was acceptable Primitive Methodist behavior also raise problems. Finally, almost none of the people concerned, whether as members, regular "hearers," or casual partakers of revival excitement, wrote about their experience of Ranterism.

A depression in the 1830s could render Primitive Methodists in an established society "incapable of assisting" and thereby "damp [their] spirit," so that it became "almost impossible to keep up" the cause,[115] but this had not been the case when Ranterism had burst out of the Potteries to overspread the Midlands and the North. The "great revival" in and around Nottingham coincided almost exactly with a period of acute distress from the autumn of 1816 through the end of 1817 and began to wane during the short-lived economic upturn of 1818. Loughborough responded enthusiastically just after Heathcote and Boden had caused considerable unemployment there by transferring their operations to Somerset. Hungry times returned in 1819, and this depression lasted until 1821. During this triennium the connexion triumphed in northern Lincolnshire and in the East Riding. Especially hard hit were the manufacturing districts, and during 1819 and 1820 Primitive Methodism began to flourish in the areas that later became Leeds, Bradford, Sheffield, Darlaston, Barnsley, Manchester, and Bolton circuits. Tunstall circuit reawoke and began to expand into unmissioned parts of Cheshire; Belper and the surrounding region also experienced a vigorous revival.

No very clear picture emerges when political agitation and reform activities are set alongside Ranter revivals and missioning efforts. In the East Midlands the revival in the neighborhood of Nottingham preceded and outlasted the Pentridge rising; in northern Leicestershire the timing substantiates a "chiliasm of despair" interpretation. In Belper Primitive Methodism, vital before Pentridge, waned during the ensuing months, and the renewal of fervor preceded the Six Acts. The reformist Political Protestants won a following simultaneously with the very successful evangelizing of Hull. The "amazing progress" in Leeds began in the autumn of 1819; Sheffield delayed its positive response until after repression began at the end of the year. Barnsley caught the revival spirit soon after the fiasco at Grange Moor, but Huddersfield did not awaken until long after the doomed rising that was centered there. Stockport shunned all Methodists both before and after Peterloo, while Manchester embraced Ranterism in its wake, and Bolton followed suit the next summer. Both in the Black Country and at Macclesfield the cause began to prosper during the spring of 1819; Darlaston circuit continued to thrive, but at Macclesfield the blaze of enthusiasm was snuffed out within three years.

Two firm conclusions can be drawn from this array of seeming contradictions: (1) political aspirations did not have to be stymied before Ranter revivals could flourish; and (2) people did not consistently turn to Primitive Methodism in the immediate aftermath of an abortive rising or when the government instituted repressive measures. Some conjectures can also be offered. (1) Political alternatives may sometimes have diverted interest from religion, as appears to have been the case at Stockport. (2) Between 1816 and 1820 the same conditions that bred disaffection also seem to have worked in the interests of Ranterism—such conditions as social dislocation, privation, awareness of the widening gap between country gentlemen and the rural poor, the textile workers' consciousness that their status and their independence were rapidly eroding. (3) There is no reason to suppose that all levelers or Political Protestants absented themselves from camp meetings and outdoor love feasts. (4) Whether Ranters were also radicals is quite a different question. Certainly, Bourne and those who shared his biases prevented this whenever they could, but discipline was not uniform throughout the connexion, and it was often extremely loose in newly opened territory. It is possible that in some locales Primitive Methodist classes—or at least the bonds formed between members—furthered organized political discussion and activity. Much later in the century, a significant number of labor leaders were men who had practiced public speaking and administrative skills in Primitive Methodist societies.[116] There may have been members during the Ranter generation who also put to secular uses their discovery that being inarticulate, dependent, and deferential were not necessarily synonymous with being poor.

The social, economic, and political tensions of the years just after Waterloo created a climate that was highly conducive to revivals, but they were infrequent among Wesleyan and New Connexion Methodists. Primitive Methodist revivalism did flourish during the period, and this can be ascribed to the fact that Ranterism fulfilled all the conditions that had generated the "wildfire" awakenings of the 1790s. For the inner dynamic of revivalism to function well, four prerequisites had to be met: there had to be a corps of effective revival preachers, a desire for an outpouring of the spirit, a willingness to let decorum fall by the wayside, and some means of communicating revival experiences from one place to another. The Ranters measured the worth of a preacher according to the number of souls won. Women, local preachers, and self-appointed missionaries were all welcome to participate so long as they furthered the "converting work." Maximum use of lay exhorters and "praying laborers" expanded the ranks of available revivalists. That so many early Primitive Methodists had once been Wesleyans showed that the yearning for revivals was not dead. These were the people who so often hailed Ranterism as a return to the "good old ways of Bramwell." Many who had been converted by the "praying colliers," the "village blacksmith," or "Praying Nanny" rejoiced when the Ranters arrived. Throwing open revival sessions to all comers assured that no unticketed seeker after a "new birth" was denied admission. Noise, disorder, and the various physical manifestations of spiritual awakening were all tolerated. Traveling preachers were frequently restationed; the transition from local preacher to itinerant and back was commonly made. Lay workers and travelers carried word of revivals from one district to another; the *Magazine* circulated the same kind of news; and missionaries read aloud from their journals. When the inner dynamic was not allowed to operate freely, both revivals and conversions languished. The copying of the Wesleyan model in Tunstall circuit between 1816 and 1819 had precisely this effect. So too, according to Bourne, did neglecting to stress "free, full, and present salvation, through and by faith." "Indeed," he wrote, "the welfare of the Connexion depended on it; when it was promoted, the work rose; but when it was not promoted, the work declined."[117] It is hardly surprising that Bourne urged itinerants to use Bramwell's *Salvation Preacher* as their handbook or that the Book Room at Bemersley printed a threepenny sketch of Bramwell's life.

The publications of the Book Room yield another insight into Primitive Methodist revivalism. Bourne learned by trial and error what generated awakenings. He was quick to adopt Benton's cheap hymnal and to print and sell Bramwell's *Life* of Ann Cutler. These books were typical of the early phase of Primitive Methodism when "providence" made "openings" for the Ranters to exploit. The consequences that followed first the imposition and then the abandonment of the "non-missioning law" suggest that, as long as the Ranters were penetrating new territory, evangelism itself became a kind of crusade that caught the people's imagination and acted to stimulate conversions. By the late 1830s the closing of the Primitive Methodist frontier was accomplished in England. Bourne looked for ways to instigate revivals, and he discovered Charles Grandison Finney's *Lectures on Revivals of Religion.* Not only did he keep a copy of the *Lectures* near his desk, but also in 1839 the connexional magazine carried extracts from it, and the Book Room printed an abridged version for the use of itinerants. Finney asserted that when a "conspiring of events . . . open[ed] the way," a revival could be expected if certain conditions were met. Although Finney thought that the idea of inducing religious awakenings was new, the conditions which he enumerated had characterized the Wesleyan revivals of the 1790s as well as those of the Ranter missioning era.[118] The inner dynamic perceived by Finney and quite successfully encouraged by the Primitive Methodists during the 1840s was virtually identical to what the Ranters had promoted less scientifically a generation before.

Despite the strong convictions of Hugh Bourne, Ranterism was apparently not immune to political dissent. The Ranters, however, were not numerous enough, even if their "hearers" were to be included, to exert an appreciable influence on lower-class sentiment. Nor was there a constant negative correlation between their revivals and the waxing and waning of radical activity between 1816 and 1821. What does emerge clearly is that the sect expanded rapidly because the Primitive Methodists gave free rein to the inner dynamic of revivalism at a time when external circumstances were optimal.

Not many people shared directly in the early Primitive Methodist experience. Most of those who did were poor men and women living in villages or in towns that had been little more than villages a quarter-century earlier. They were people caught between a passing traditional order and a developing society; Primitive Methodism helped them to make the transition from the old world to the new. Becoming a Primitive Methodist meant affirming that one's soul was important, not only in the divine scheme for mankind, but also to other members of the society.

Ordinary working-class people were bound together in a fellowship in which each was given responsibilities and opportunities. A person's opinions counted, his health and his material welfare mattered, his labors on behalf of the society made a difference, his spiritual odyssey during life and his triumph at death would be recorded. Intimate love feasts as well as giant camp meetings brought spiritual drama and song and color into lives that were otherwise drab. The challenge of carrying the Primitive Methodist gospel throughout England expanded horizons and lent importance to one's own small efforts in a local society. Above all, the Primitive Methodist experience was one of participation in a community of the people's own making, not something bestowed or imposed by their betters.

Conclusion:
An Opportunity
Missed, an
Opening Exploited

In 1821, as Primitive Methodism completed its first decade, 16,394 English people were members of the sect. The total belonging to the Wesleyan body in 1821 was 188,668. Thirty years later, membership in the Primitive Methodist Connexion was almost 38 percent as large as the Wesleyan figure. Throughout the period Primitive Methodist growth had surpassed that of the Wesleyan Connexion. The Wesleyan annual rate of growth, which had stood at 5.5 in 1816, slipped steadily during the subsequent four years and was actually negative (−2.4) in 1820. These were the same years during which Primitive Methodism advanced across the Midlands and the East and West Ridings of Yorkshire. If between 1816 and 1820 the Ranters could win 7,000 members while the Wesleyans lost more than 1,700, it would seem that the Old Connexion missed an opportunity.[1] The Ranters demonstrated that conversion to Methodism as well as to Hampden Clubs and Union Societies was possible during the time of unrest and privation that followed the war against France. Wesleyan recruitment gathered some momentum after the returns for 1820 had jarred conference into a self-scrutiny that resulted in the issuing of new pastoral guidelines and a relaxing of its policy on revivalism. But as membership statistics for the next thirty years show, the Primitive Methodists had already preempted the Methodist mission to a sizable segment of the working-class population.

The opening exploited by the Ranters was the product of change. A man born in 1780 typically began life in a not very heavily populated kingdom that was still rural and traditional. If he died at the age of seventy, his last years were spent in an urban, industrial nation. Only a year after his passing, like a coda, the Great Exhibition would crown "progress" as the reigning monarch. During his lifetime old social ties were sacrificed to the pursuit of profit; market towns and villages were transformed into the crowded factory towns whose smoke seemed so beautiful to a newly powerful and affluent class of Bounderbys; ideas and institutions that had endured for generations came under attack; and traditional sources of authority were shown to be fallible. For all who experienced it, but especially for the laboring classes, living through a period of so much flux must have been perplexing and unsettling. Even while such changes bewildered, however, they also promised advantages to those able to benefit from new opportunities. For the men and women who were its adherents, Primitive Methodism provided a structure of values, a viable community, schooling in social and organizational skills, and, not least, hope.[2] The Ranters achieved their most impressive victories in agricultural districts like northern Lincolnshire and the East Riding of Yorkshire and in mining regions like Tyneside. Their appeal was likewise great in "really rural and retired" places such as the dales of the North and the hill country of Derbyshire and Staffordshire.[3] But they were also well received in textile and industrial villages and by newcomers in burgeoning mill towns. The progress of Primitive Methodism was made easier where people were not so dependent on the squirearchy—among the framework knitters of the East Midlands, for example; where social control was lacking, as in the new factory towns; or where, like Cheshire, the hold of the established church was weak and provision was inadequate. For people like the weavers of the West Riding, the fellowship, opportunities, and values of Primitive Methodism could help to compensate for reduced substance, diminished status, and loss of independence. The factory workers of Bolton or Manchester could find both a fixed point of reference that gave stability to a dislocated existence and a community in which they were more than "hands." In remote places like Weardale, revivals and participation in Primitive Methodist societies became a way of village life.

There were also special social and economic factors peculiar to the farming and mining districts where the Ranters made their greatest impact. The practical application of capitalistic ideas to farming was, of course, not new in the late eighteenth century. The pace of agricultural improvement, however, quickened during the wars, and large tracts in the midland counties and Yorkshire were enclosed between 1793 and

1815. During the same period extensive drainage was effected in the Lincolnshire fens and in the Humber region. The demand for labor caused by both the enclosures and the drainage projects, the commandeering of rural workers by the military, and high prices for agricultural products all combined to raise the wages of farm workers.[4] After Waterloo, discharged soldiers and sailors swelled the available labor force, while the corn laws kept the price of bread high. The enclosures, which had been especially numerous between 1805 and 1815, deprived cottagers of all means of support apart from their wages and thrust small farmers into a losing battle against larger landowners. At the same time, real wages fell because of inflated prices. According to one who witnessed its consequences, enclosing wastes and commons wrought an "enormous" negative change in the attitudes of the rural poor: "They have a sense of injustice, if they have not the power to resist it; and when they see a system of this kind, they say—'much will have more,' and their spirits are none the better for the feeling that accompanies the melancholy truth."[5]

While the gentry and aristocracy increasingly pursued profits to the neglect of paternalism and of their customary tasks of social control, a newly enriched body of clergy not only pushed upward to become country gentlemen but also filled half the magistracies.[6] Along with their new pretensions—country houses, genteel manners, fashionable pastimes— they now appointed parish constables and administered the poor law. Important as it is that enclosures widened the gap between classes generally, it is even more significant that the poor parson of former times was now a member of the governing gentry. This stigmatized the established church in the eyes of those whom enclosures had proletarianized. Alienated from the church, in which even the pattern of seating underscored class distinctions, the rural poor were enabled to express both independence and disdain by choosing instead to worship with the Ranters in cottages and barns. It is hardly surprising that squires and clergymen so often sought to prevent Primitive Methodism from gaining a foothold in the villages. What commands attention, however, is that both were so often defied. In the Vale of Belvoir, one of the richest farming districts in the Midlands, the laborer was impoverished in the midst of plenty, and this as a direct consequence of agricultural capitalism. Here village rowdies, well plied with drink and urged on by clergymen, hurled filth at Benton, Wedgwood, and Harrison, while supporters of the Ranters were evicted from their stud-and-mud dwellings. Nevertheless, the missionaries found openings. Their job was less difficult, of course, in places where at least some of the people were not under clerical or aristocratic influence or in need of parish relief. These could pro-

vide a refuge, and once a society was established, some of the more dependent would join. If the commercialization of agriculture brought
great financial rewards to the Church of England, it also entailed the
loss of many souls no longer content to remain in its pastoral charge.
This was the situation that the Ranters exploited, and nowhere did they
do so more successfully than in northern Lincolnshire and the East
Riding.[7]

Mining communities were likewise congenial territory for Primitive
Methodism. The sect made remarkable progress among the pitmen in
Durham and Northumberland as well as in the Black Country. Strong
societies were also formed in east central Shropshire, the Erewash
Valley, the Forest of Dean, and parts of South Wales. The numerous
obituaries of colliers who died in pit accidents provide one clue as to
why miners embraced Primitive Methodism. The Davy lamp, which
ought to have reduced the number of accidents, instead tempted owners
to work deeper and more dangerous seams. Young children were sometimes given the task of running lift cages or of closing trapdoors, duties
which, when not properly carried out, could and did result in fatalities.[8]
Colliers quite literally lived in the valley of the shadow of death.
Secondly, apart from the pub, there was virtually no form of recreation
available in mining villages. The imagery of Ranter hymns and the
drama of "soul-shaking" revivalism brought color into the lives of men
who daily worked in underground gloom. Finally, mining was practi-
cally a hereditary occupation, and mining settlements were closed and
homogeneous societies, often culturally isolated from currents in the
outside world. This meant that, once the missionaries earned the
approval of community leaders, most of the village would take up Primitive Methodism, and the cause would endure.

As a Ranter evangelist would have put it, these parts of England
were a "field ripe unto the harvest." That the Primitive and not the Wesleyan Methodists reaped it was owing to trends that developed within
the Wesleyan Connexion between 1800 and 1820. In addition to stifling
revivalism, for which there was clearly a demand, the Wesleyan conference ignored local opinion, frustrated lay initiative, encouraged social
stratification, and burdened poor members with frequent requests for
money. Mainly to tighten discipline and so protect the Wesleyan image,
the conference increasingly stressed its own authority. This connexionalism forced sometimes trivial local disputes to the center and pushed
central policy out to the periphery, where on occasion it clashed with
local points of view. The extreme localism and lay dominance of Primitive Methodism stood in sharp contrast to Wesleyan connexionalism
and clericalism. Bourne never chaired an annual meeting. The layman

Thomas Bateman, who did so, noted that "no change of any moment took place [in the connexion] without my being consulted."[9] A critic described the lay-controlled quarterly meetings of Primitive Methodism as having "almost unlimited powers" and "more than apostolic authority."[10] The antithesis of this situation appears in a letter complaining about the high-handed action of the Wesleyan conference of 1820, which had appointed a preacher unacceptable to "the Birstall friends." The irate writer suggested that "a little attention paid" to the wishes of Methodists in their circuit "might prevent" conflict and ill will.[11] Wesleyan laymen also resented the claims of their "virtually ordained" ministers. Not only did this seem a reversion to the Anglican system they had rejected, but it also implied that an education in theology was somehow better than simple faith and piety. There were Wesleyan itinerants too who disliked the new professionalism and its corporate ladder. Thomas Stanley, not one of the all-powerful Legal Hundred, was disappointed with his assigned circuit and wondered if he might have fared better had he gone to the conference "to take care of himself," as others did. Stanley thought that the "system of jockyship [sic] in use amongst us" reflected "no honour to a body of Christian ministers."[12] For the Primitive Methodists none of these tensions existed. Annual meetings appointed traveling preachers, but circuit committees reserved the power to veto the choice. In any case, both bodies were composed primarily of lay persons. Similarly, because of the ease and frequency with which people moved into and out of the itinerancy, the line between lay preachers and traveling preachers was so blurred as to be almost nonexistent. Survival of the fittest determined whether or not a Primitive Methodist itinerant would "make his way." If he failed to fulfill the expectations of the people, they withheld both contributions and hospitality. A traveling preacher either preached well or perished in the "rude college of circuit life."[13]

The problems that beset the Wesleyan purse also worked in the interests of Primitive Methodism, especially in times of economic distress. A Wesleyan itinerant stationed in the North Riding warned that abandoning small societies in order to cut costs would be "exceedingly painful" to loyal Wesleyans, "however [much] this might please the Ranters who preach in every place in this circuit."[14] The Wesleyan litany of requests for contributions supplied the Ranters around Hull "with texts and matter, which they do not fail to make use of," and the "consequences" of this were "begin[ning] to be alarming."[15] In 1819 a Primitive Methodist traveling preacher with a wife and two children earned about half the minimum salary of a Wesleyan itinerant with a comparable family. When in 1821 expenditures in the Primitive Methodist Hull circuit exceeded income, the quarter-day board agreed that, "if money did not come up to pay the preachers' salaries, according to the stated allowance, then each preacher should be paid short." There were to be "no more meat bills" submitted to the quarterly meeting, and itinerants would have "to throw [themselves] upon the Lord fully."[16] It was not at all unusual for a Primitive Methodist evangelist to sleep in fields and hedges, particularly if he was opening new territory. A young missionary working near Cambridge in 1821 reported, "I have been obliged to suffer much hunger. One day I traveled near thirty miles with a penny cake and preached to near 2,000 people till I was scarcely able to stand, and when I had done, I made my supper of cold cabbage; and as I did not like to expose my poverty, I was driven to seek my lodgings in the fields and slept under a hay stack till about four o'clock in the morning, when I was awoke by the little birds."[17] Bourne once walked thirty miles to preach at an anniversary service. When asked the amount of his expenses, he replied, "Twopence half-penny, . . . a pennyworth of bread, a pennyworth of cheese, and a half-pennyworth of treacle-beer."[18] Wesleyan itinerants at this time were commonly given extra allowances for servants and for horses. Poor Wesleyans felt out of place among their fashionably clad brethren, who rented pews in the new and pretentious chapels being built in the early nineteenth century. The Ranters prayed and preached in barns, warehouses, and cottages, or they erected stark pewless chapels on undesirable but inexpensive sites. They made a virtue of simplicity and cheapness in dress, and the great majority of them were poor.

The desired image of decorum in Wesleyan worship was sometimes achieved at the cost of vitality. Sermons embellished with literary allusions and delivered in highflown language impressed part of the congregation but left others unmoved. Worried about the effects of this new style, a Wesleyan itinerant commented on the "considerable success" that the Ranters were enjoying among the common people, an achievement he attributed to their using "the language of the first preachers."[19] The members at Wakefield "preferred power to ornament" in preaching, and they wanted to sing "unsuitable" hymns. The superintendent dealt with the latter easily; he boarded up the door to the singers' gallery and curtailed the singing at love feasts.[20] One writer claimed that the Ranters tried to lure members away from the Wesleyan fold by singing the "devil's music." But, he gloated, they were paid in their own coin because "profane persons" attended Ranter services and put "obscene" words to their tunes.[21] With revival "excesses" forbidden and Wesleyan worship dominated by eloquent preaching and sedate hymns, there was little left to thrill the soul.

One of the most serious errors that the Wesleyans made before 1820 was to neglect rural areas. The Primitive Methodists, on the other hand, excelled at village evangelism and followed up their field and street preaching with cottage prayer meetings and the "conversation ministry." Not only did the Ranters have more itinerants per capita,[22] but they also made more extensive use of lay workers to carry out pastoral tasks. This practice brought a double reward: country folk did not feel slighted, while the members who were engaged in the lay apostolate recognized that they were sharing important responsibilities, a realization which enhanced their self-esteem.

In *The Methodist Revolution* Bernard Semmel suggested that Bunting and his coterie discovered in overseas missions a means of diverting the attention of lower-class Wesleyans from their own wretchedness to the worse plight of the heathen abroad. This maneuver, launched in 1813, exploited an interest that was shared by English evangelicals generally. By choosing to redirect Methodist energies into missions overseas, Wesleyan leaders went a considerable distance toward resolving a paradox: "how to reconcile the Enthusiasm inherent in Methodist evangelism, with its revolutionary, Antinomian tendencies, with an obsession with order in both Church and state." As Semmel pointed out, the alternative to a missionary crusade in distant lands was "to accept the revolutionary risks inherent in releasing the evangelistic energies of a Methodism, seemingly near the zenith of its powers, upon the ancient preserves of the Establishment. The result of such a choice might be repression and the necessity of a loyal Methodism invoking the right of resistance."[23] In 1813 the struggle to block Sidmouth's proposed restrictions on the licensing of preachers was still a fresh and frightening memory. The New Toleration Act was but a year old. Certainly, the half-decade after Waterloo was a period in which the Wesleyan conference would have wanted to encourage the poor to apply their imaginations and their energies to worrying about the miseries of people other than themselves. Semmel's assertions about Bunting and those who backed his scheme are supported with cogent arguments. It is necessary to emphasize, however, that, while missions abroad remained a lasting concern, recent neglect of home missions, whether intentional or not, was the central problem that occupied the Liverpool conference of 1820. Jabez Bunting prepared an abridged version of these discussions on pastoral work, and the conference of 1821 mandated their annual reading at all district meetings. Beginning in 1853 these guidelines had to be read and discussed at the yearly meeting of itinerants in each circuit, and, as of 1885, all candidates for the Wesleyan ministry had to be versed in their content.[24]

It can be demonstrated that the conference of 1820 did try to remedy past negligence and that the delegates did modify their views. Itinerants may have suspected that the connexion was losing members (they certainly knew this to be the case in many of their own circuits), but, when the figures were added up, they discovered that Wesleyan Methodism as a whole had suffered its first reverse since 1801. For six hours the members of the conference discussed "means of promoting . . . the work of God." They sanctioned camp meetings, "but gave them a different name."[25] They urged itinerants to establish cottage prayer meetings, to distribute tracts systematically among the row houses of the poor, to enlist the assistance of local preachers and leaders in spreading the gospel, and to be especially diligent in their attentions to rural societies.[26] At the next conference Bunting reiterated the cardinal points of the "Resolutions on Pastoral Work" and rejoiced that putting them into effect had generated many revivals "in the *gradual* and regular way."[27] During 1820–1821 several itinerants sent letters to the *Methodist Magazine* alluding to the "remarks made at the last conference upon the state of religion in our connexion" and describing how they had achieved gratifying results by using the tactics recommended at Liverpool. In Bradford circuit, for example, lay missionaries went "from house to house, to those that need such visits, to distribute tracts, hold prayer meetings, invite the people to the preaching, &c." At a watch night conducted by an itinerant who was accompanied by "several pious, lively local preachers and leaders," there was a "*short* sermon, a short exhortation, and ten or twelve short prayers, lively, and for a *present* blessing; with now and then a verse of a hymn." The "object kept in view" when preachers prepared their sermons was "a present salvation from sin by faith."[28] At the time of his last appointment to Leeds, William Bramwell's colleague in the circuit had preached from the text, "I have seen an end to all perfection." Bramwell did not live to witness the changes brought about by the conference of 1820, but doubtless some among the multitude who had thronged to his funeral at Leeds in 1818 also attended the numerous open-air services that were held throughout the circuit in 1822.[29]

The newly adopted pastoral techniques did result in revivals during 1821 and 1822. These, however, were often described by such phrases as not "carried on with noise, confusion, or disorder, but with deep solemnity."[30] The *Methodist Magazine* printed a series of articles entitled "On the Character of the Early Methodists," which praised their "plain dress," their "simplicity of manners," and their "non-worldliness."[31] This was evidently an effort subtly to reprimand "sleek grocers" while commending the poor. The connexion did make good its losses in 1821, and in

1822 over a thousand new converts were won. But this momentum soon slowed. The real opportunity to carry on a significant work among the majority of laboring men and women had already passed from Wesleyan hands and had been seized by the Ranters. A Wesleyan Connexion that perceived the role of government as standing *"in loco parentis"*[32] had less appeal to the working people than a Primitive Methodism that recognized their aspirations to govern themselves.

Primitive Methodism emerged at a critical time, as traditional culture was fading, but before a new working-class culture had taken clear shape. It appeared just when the effects of economic depression, enclosures, factories, and the putting-out system had convinced many that something serious was wrong with the old social and political order. Ranterism harnessed and transformed into positive action the sterile frustrations with contemporary Wesleyanism felt by numerous Methodists. Although the name which they adopted was "Primitive," a hearkening back to the past, for those men and women who found their place in it, this "Society of People" effectively served as a bridge to the future.

Notes

Select Bibliography

Index

Notes

Introduction

1 Petty later revised and enlarged his book, a new edition of which was issued in 1864. A third edition, revised and further expanded by James Macpherson, was published in 1880.
2 According to *The British Library General Catalogue of Printed Books to 1975*, the first edition of Kendall's history was published "c. 1905."
3 Elissa S. Itzkin, "The Halévy Thesis—A Working Hypothesis? English Revivalism: Antidote for Revolution and Radicalism, 1789–1815," *Church History* 44 (1975): 47–56.
4 Bernard Semmel, *The Methodist Revolution* (New York, 1973), p. vii.
5 Elie Halévy, *The Liberal Awakening, 1815–1830*, trans. E. I. Watkin (2d ed. rev., New York, 1949), p. 105.
6 Eric J. Hobsbawm, *Primitive Rebels: Studies in Archaic Forms of Social Movement in the 19th and 20th Centuries* (Manchester, 1959), pp. 134, 138.

1 / The Anxious Years, 1791–1820

1 By ordaining superintendents for America (who called themselves bishops) and by creating, through a Chancery Deed, the Legal Hundred—itinerants who were to inherit authority after his death—Wesley had in 1784 made eventual separation almost certain.
2 *Strictures on the Expedience of the Addingtonian Extinguisher with Satirical Observations on the Influence of Methodism on Civilized Society in All Its Gradations* (London, 1811), p. 26.
3 Thomas Coke to Joseph Benton, 15 July 1791, in John Vickers, *Thomas Coke, Apostle of Methodism* (London, 1969), pp. 196–197.
4 George Smith, *History of Wesleyan Methodism* (London, 1858), vol. 2, *The Middle Age*, 13; Richard Terry to Joseph Benson, 15 July 1791, Methodist Archives and Research Centre, John Rylands University Library of Manchester, Preachers' Letters and Portraits Collection. When I used it, this collection was partially alphabetized, and was housed at 25–35 City Road, London. Now the correspondence has been cataloged, and access to it is through the in-

formation provided in the catalog. Letters from this closed-access collection are hereafter designated by the abbreviation M.A.

5 Thomas Wray, "Facts Connected with the History of Methodism in Leeds and Its Vicinity," Notebook, p. 79, Methodist Archives.

6 A parallel development took place in regard to the scheduling of Methodist meetings during church hours. Wesley had always discouraged this practice. In 1786, however, he had ruled that concurrent services might be held in exceptional circumstances—where, for example, the parson was morally or doctrinally unfit to minister, or where church accommodation had not kept pace with growth in population. Such exceptions became more and more numerous as many societies pressed toward denominationalism. Finally, in 1795 conference submitted to a mounting tide of lay opinion and permitted Wesleyan services to rival those of the established church wherever a majority of the local authorities had agreed that this would not divide their society (*Minutes of the Methodist Conferences, from the First Held in London by the Late Reverend John Wesley, A.M., in the Year 1744* [London, 1862–1864], 1: 189; 2: 322–324 [hereafter cited as *Wesleyan Conference Minutes*]).

7 William Bramwell to Mrs. Thomas Tatham, 19 January 1802, in Samuel Dunn, *Memoirs of Mr. Thomas Tatham and of Wesleyan Methodism in Nottingham* (London, 1847), p. 167.

8 For a succinct account of Wesleyan separation from the Church of England see W. R. Ward, *Religion and Society in England, 1790–1850* (London, 1972), pp. 27–39. Ward has convincingly argued that "popular backing for 'Church' Methodism was being destroyed by the same complex of political and social forces as destroyed popular complaisance toward the establishment and made Church-and-King mobs impossible to raise" (p. 32).

9 George Isaac Huntingford, *A Charge Delivered to the Clergy of the Diocese of Gloucester* (London, 1807), pp. 29–30. Huntingford was a personal friend of Lord Sidmouth. See also *Truth and Error Contrasted in a Letter to a Young Gentleman, in Answer to His Apology for Joining the People Called Methodists* (London, 1808), p. 24.

10 *A Letter to a Country Gentleman on the Subject of Methodism, Confined Chiefly to Its Causes, Progress, and Consequences in His Own Neighbourhood* (Ipswich, 1805), p. 21.

11 James Byron, *Thoughts on the Evil of Persecution Occasioned by the Rioting at Newent* (Gloucester, 1806), pp. 6–11.

12 *Resolutions of a Meeting of the General Committee of the Societies of the Late Reverend John Wesley Convened for the Purpose of Taking into Consideration a Bill Brought into the House of Lords by the Right Honourable Lord Viscount Sidmouth* (London, 1811), Resolution X. Statements of this sort occurred frequently in Methodist propaganda. The belief that Methodism played a decisive role in habituating the lower orders to a modern work-discipline owes a considerable debt to the Methodists themselves.

13 For example, John Stephens, *Christian Patriotism: A Sermon Preached at Rotherham, February 28, 1810, the Day Appointed for a National Fast* (Rotherham, 1810) and Thomas Rutherford, *The Voice of the Rod* (London, 1803).

14 *Methodist Magazine, Being a Continuation of the Arminian Magazine* 44 (1821): 511–512 (hereafter cited as *Methodist Magazine*); *The Patriot: A Tale Illustrating the Pernicious Effects of Bad Principles on the Lower Orders of Society* (London, 1821).

15 Thomas Coke to Joseph Benson, 21 December 1795; Coke to Benson, 6 February 1796, in Vickers, *Thomas Coke*, p. 218.

16 *Report from the Clergy of a District in the Diocese of Lincoln Convened for the Purpose of Considering the State of Religion in the Several Parishes in the Said District As Well As the Best Mode of Promoting the Belief and Practice of It, and of Guarding, As Much As Possible against the Dangers Arising to the Church and Government of This Kingdom from the Alarming Increase of Profaneness and Irreligion on the One Hand, and from the False Doctrines and Evil Designs of Fanatic and Seditious Teachers on the Other* (2d ed., London, 1800).

17 Smith, *History* 2: 334. The Methodists had also enlisted the support of a powerful ally in Parliament—Pitt's friend William Wilberforce.

18 *Resolutions of the Methodist Ministers of the Manchester District, Assembled at Liverpool, May 23, 1811, on the Subject of a Bill Introduced into Parliament by the Right Honourable Lord Viscount Sidmouth, to Which Is Added an Abstract of the Debate in the House of Lords on Tuesday, May 21, 1811, When the Said Bill Was Rejected* (Liverpool, 1811), pp. 10–12.

19 *Wesleyan Conference Minutes* 2: 54–55, 187, 290, 404–405.

20 William Leach to Jabez Bunting, 5 November 1817 (M.A.). According to Leach, the condemned man, Isaac Ludlam, had been expelled from the Wesleyan society eighteen months before the rising. Two persons who had known him since boyhood said that they "never heard of his being a preacher."

21 Robert Pilter to Jabez Bunting, 23 October 1819, in W. R. Ward, ed., *The Early Correspondence of Jabez Bunting 1820–1829* (Camden 4th ser., London, 1972), pp. 21–24.

22 *A Letter to the Reverend John Stephens Occasioned by Some Recent Transactions and Occurrences in the Methodist Society in Manchester* (Manchester, 1820), p. 8.

23 Jonathan Edmundson to Jonathan Crowther, 16 November 1819 (M.A.).

24 John Beaumont to Mr. Dutton, 16 September 1803 (M.A.).

25 Thomas Shaw, *The Bible Christians, 1815–1907* (London, 1965), p. 6; *Minutes of the Yearly Meeting of the Independent Methodists* (Sheffield, 1815), pp. iii–iv; Stephen Rothwell, *Memorials of the Independent Methodist Chapel, Folds Road, Bolton* (Bolton, 1887), p. 81. The Tent Methodists likewise relied on voluntary contributions to finance their mission to the "poor and profligate" (*Tent Methodists' Magazine and Register of Events Connected with the Spread of the Gospel at Home* [Bristol], 1 [1823]: 31–32, 153 [hereafter cited as *Tent Methodists' Magazine*]).

26 James Douglas, *Methodism Condemned, or Priestcraft Detected* (Newcastle-on-Tyne, 1814), pp. 12–14.

27 For example, *Methodism in 1821, with Recollections of Primitive Methodism* (London, 1821), pp. 10–11, and Douglas, *Methodism Condemned*, p. 14. On the financial strains imposed by supporting preachers' families see William

Midgley to William McKittrick, 28 April 1813; William Myles to John Stamp, 27 November 1817; Myles to Jabez Bunting, 5 June 1819 (all M.A.).

28 Jonathan Crowther, *A Portraiture of Methodism* (London, 1815), p. 195.

29 W. Greenwood, *Memoir of the Life, Ministry, and Correspondence of the Late Rev. George Sykes of Rillington* (Malton, 1827), pp. 193–194.

30 William Myles to Jabez Bunting, 5 June 1819 (M.A.). See also John Beaumont to Mr. Dutton, 26 September 1803 (M.A.).

31 William Jenkins to John Broadhurst, 17 June 1803 (M.A.).

32 Thomas Jackson, *Recollections of My Own Life and Times*, ed. B. Frankland (London, 1878), p. 135.

33 John Uriah Walker, *A History of Wesleyan Methodism in Halifax and Its Vicinity* (Halifax, 1836), pp. 156–157; Thomas Percival Bunting, *The Life of Jabez Bunting, D.D., with Notices of Contemporary Persons and Events* (2 vols., London, 1859, 1887), 2: 33–34.

34 *Founded on the Rock: A Chronology of Wesleyan Methodism in Berry Brow to 1897* (Edinburgh, n.d.), p. 21. For rural opposition to class and ticket money see also John Beaumont to Mr. Dutton, 26 September 1803; Joseph Entwisle to Jabez Bunting, 1 October 1803; David Stoner to Entwisle, 11 December 1823 (all M.A.).

35 William Myles to John North, 5 October 1819 (M.A.). For example, Hull was paying 9d. out of every shilling spent to maintain a horse for the circuit as well as half the cost of keeping horses for its local preachers.

36 Douglas, *Methodism Condemned*, p. 14.

37 Jackson, *Recollections*, p. 176; John Stephens to Jabez Bunting, 1 February 1821, in Ward, ed., *Early Correspondence*, pp. 61–62.

38 *Methodism in 1821*, p. 26; Benjamin Smith, *Methodism in Macclesfield* (London, 1875), p. 232.

39 James Everett to James Sigston, 14 August 1820; Mark Dawes to Jabez Bunting, 7 July 1819; Isaac Turton to William Marriot, 12 March 1822; Richard Waddy to Bunting, 11 October 1820; Zechariah Taft to George Marsden, 15 March 1821; William Leach to Everett, 22 February 1817 (all M.A.).

40 *Wesleyan Conference Minutes* 4: 336–337, 452; 5: 44–45.

41 William Myles to Jabez Bunting, 5 June 1819 (M.A.); Myles to Bunting, 18 August 1820 (M.A.).

42 Robert Currie, Alan Gilbert, and Lee Horsley, *Churches and Churchgoers: Patterns of Church Growth in the British Isles since 1700* (Oxford, 1977), p. 140. The greatest increase was 11,526 in 1813–1814; the slightest was 876 in 1818–1819.

43 James Everett to James Sigston, 14 August 1820 (M.A.); James Holroyd to Jabez Bunting, 23 December 1819, in Ward, ed., *Early Correspondence*, pp. 24–26. Everett also commented that "several have ceased to meet . . . under the mistaken notion that they *must pay* if they attend class," an idea presumably inculcated by his more exacting predecessors in Sheffield circuit. It is of course impossible to calculate the impact of all these factors on membership. Their existence, however, does diminish the useful of membership statistics as primary data for drawing conclusions about the relationship between Methodism and radicalism before and after Peterloo.

44 In 1819 a Primitive Methodist traveling preacher with two children under the age of eight earned at best about half the *minimum* allowance of a Wesleyan minister with a comparable family.

45 Joseph Sutcliffe to Joseph Entwisle, 30 October 1830 (M.A.).

46 "Begging," ca. 1815. The handwriting is that of Robert Melson, himself a Wesleyan preacher (M.A.).

47 James Williams to Jabez Bunting, 5 April 1808 (M.A.).

48 Joseph Sutcliffe to John Simpson, 10 August 1810 (M.A.); George Tindale to John North, 17 September 1811 (M.A.). See also Joseph Sutcliffe, *A Review of Methodism* (York, 1805), p. 35. Joseph Entwisle had voiced similar anxieties as early as 1797 ([W. Entwisle], *Memoir of the Reverend Joseph Entwisle, Fifty-four Years a Wesleyan Minister* [Bristol, 1848], pp. 184–186).

49 John Hill, *A Vindication of the Methodists in the Societies of the Late Reverend John Wesley from Several Popular Accusations of the Present Day, Especially Those Contained in the "Annual Review" of Mr. Arthur Aikin* (London, 1806), p. 33; *Methodism in 1821*, p. 10; Richard Burdekin, *Memoir of the Life and Character of Mr. Robert Spence of York* (York and London, 1827), p. 135.

50 James Williams to Jabez Bunting, 28 December 1812 (M.A.); David Stoner to Joseph Entwisle, 11 December 1823 (M.A.).

51 *Letter to a Country Gentleman*, pp. 23–24. See also Huntingford, *Charge*, pp. 29–30.

52 *Truth and Error Contrasted*, p. 18. See also *An Address to the Lower Class of His Parishioners on the Subject of Methodism* (Ipswich, 1806), p. 10.

53 *Letter to a Country Gentleman*, p. 20.

54 *Wesleyan Conference Minutes* 2: 140; Adam Clarke, 14 July 1806, in *Observations on the Importance of Adopting a Plan of Instruction for Those Preachers Who Are Admitted upon Trial in the Methodist Connexion* (London, 1807), p. 3; George Tindale to Robert Pilter, 23 March 1815 (M.A.).

55 John Pawson, "A Serious and Affectionate Address to the Junior Preachers in the Connexion," in James Sigston, *A Memoir of the Life and Ministry of Mr. William Bramwell* (2 vols., London, 1821–1822), 2: 288; William Bramwell, ed., *The Salvation Preacher, Recommended to the Serious Perusal of Preachers and People of All Denominations* (Nottingham, 1800), p. 1; William Hatton, *Methodist Remembrances, Comprising a Contrast between the Original and Present State of Methodism and the Methodists* (Birmingham, 1823), p. 17; David Stoner to John Hanwell, 31 August 1821 (M.A.).

56 Robert Pilter to Maximilian Wilson, 9 June 1820 (M.A.); John Maggs to Jabez Bunting, 22 February 1821 (M.A.); *Lay Preaching Defended: A Few Plain Remarks for the Consideration of the People Called Methodists* (London, 1820), pp. 6–16. See also *Thoughts on the Case of the Local Preachers in the Methodist Connexion* (Bristol, 1820), pp. 16–18.

57 [Mary Ann Clark], *An Account of the Religious and Literary Life of Adam Clarke by a Member of His Family*, ed. J. B. B. Clark (London, 1833), 2: 72; Richard Allen, *History of Methodism in Preston and Its Vicinity* (Preston, 1866), p. 32; Bunting, *Life* 1: 63–67. Joseph Entwisle, for example, founded an extensive home-mission program which employed lay volunteers to "reclaim

. . . wanderers" in Macclesfield circuit. Entwisle's project was an imaginative response to an awkward dilemma. He was reluctant to violate the conference minute of 1803; on the other hand, virtually all of Macclesfield's leaders and local preachers were active in irregular meetings. Energetic and tactful, Entwisle merely improved their organization and made himself and his colleagues responsible for the entire network. "The people are much more free and open in a house than a large chapel," he told Bunting. "There is less *appearance* of formality, and more of power" (Entwisle to Bunting, 9 September and 1 October 1803 [M.A.]).

58 See Robert F. Wearmouth, *Methodism and the Trade Unions* (London, 1959), p. 38.

59 *Wesleyan Conference Minutes* 2: 289; William Myles to Jabez Bunting, 5 June 1819 (M.A.). See also Myles to John North, 5 October 1819 (M.A.); Myles to John Stamp, 27 November 1817 (M.A.).

60 *Methodist Magazine* 44 (1821): 461; *Wesleyan Conference Minutes* 5: 146–152.

61 Jabez Bunting to Richard Reece, 15 July 1803 (M.A.).

62 William O'Bryan to Hugh Bourne, 15 February 1821, in *Primitive Methodist Magazine* 2 (1821): 16 (hereafter cited as *P.M.M.*). See also *P.M.M.* 2 (1821): 7, 112–113, 138, 162–167. A Primitive Methodist local preacher serving in the army was stationed in Cornwall in 1820. After he told local Bible Christians about camp meetings, the sect began holding outdoor meetings similar to those of the Ranters.

63 *Tent Methodists' Magazine* 1 (1823): 155.

64 William Thom, who presided over the first New Connexion conference, was the Wesleyan superintendent at Halifax in 1797. Prior to the schism he cultivated dissent in the neighborhood; afterwards he remained there to consolidate its fruits (Walker, *History*, p. 215). Similarly, William Bramwell, Henry Taylor, and Michael Emmett gave momentum to the cause of Methodist reform in Sheffield circuit. Much to the chagrin of New Connexion stalwarts, all three later reneged, Taylor and Emmett at the eleventh hour (*Minutes of the Conversations between Preachers and Delegates in the Methodist New Connexion* [Leeds, 1798], pp. 11–12 [hereafter cited as *New Connexion Minutes*]).

65 Jabez Bunting to Walter Griffeth, 12 April 1810 (M.A.); Rowland C. Swift, Typescript of notes compiled from the files of Nottingham newspapers, Methodist Archives. These societies were at Basford, Hucknall Torkard, and Arnold, all industrial villages later notorious for Luddism. During the Luddite period Hucknall Torkard Kilhamites met with "active opposition" from other villagers. About 1815 "the church at Hucknall Torkard began to be received with some favour by the working population" (*A Jubilee Memorial of the Local Preachers' Conferences, Biographical and Historical Sketches* [Nottingham, 1876], pp. 71–73).

66 Hatton, *Methodist Remembrances*, p. 7.

67 Stephens, *Christian Patriotism*, p. iv.

68 *New Connexion Minutes* (Hanley, 1820), pp. 35–36; (Leeds, 1801), pp. 9–10; (Manchester, 1813), pp. 27–28; W. H. Lockley, *The Story of Stockport Circuit of the United Methodist Church* (Stockport, 1909), pp. 37–38.

69 Greenwood, *Memoir of George Sykes*, p. 194.

70 The delegates are named in Smith, *History* 2: 694.

71 Frederick Hunter, *Methodism in Stockport and District* (Stockport, n.d.), n.p.; E. V. Chapman, *John Wesley & Co. (Halifax)* (Halifax, 1952), p. 48. See also T. D. Crothers et al., *The Centenary of the Methodist New Connexion, 1797–1897* (London, 1897), pp. 94–96.

72 *Methodist Magazine, or Evangelical Repository* 10 (1807): 455, 291–293; 12 (1809): 418–421; 11 (1808): 71–72. To avoid confusion with the Wesleyan *Methodist Magazine* this will be cited hereafter as the *New Connexion Magazine*.

73 *New Connexion Minutes* (Hanley, 1808), pp. 24–25; ibid., 1813, p. 15.

74 [George Beaumont], *The Helmet; or, An Answer to the Eighth Resolution of the Minutes of Conference . . . 1813* (Sheffield, n.d.), p. 51; Edward Oakes to Jabez Bunting, 17 September 1814 (M.A.); MS. Private Minutes of the Methodist New Connexion Conferences, 1814 and 1815, Methodist Archives; Local Preachers' Minute Book, in Chapman, *John Wesley & Co.*, p. 64; "Address of the Methodists of the New Connexion to the British Public," in William Salt, *A Memorial of the Wesleyan Methodist New Connexion from Its Formation in 1797 to the Present Time* (Nottingham, 1822), p. 255.

75 The course steered by the New Connexion is epitomized in the career of George Beaumont, a Stockport layman turned preacher. In 1808 he published *The Warrior's Looking Glass*, a radical antiwar tract which conference seems to have received with equanimity. Beaumont's next pamphlet, *The Helmet* (1809), excited no alarm until his colleagues learned that it had reputedly kindled the Luddite disturbances around Huddersfield. Their response was the ban on political writing enacted in 1813. Refusing to surrender his freedom of expression, Beaumont wrote a second *Helmet* which inveighed against the war, economic dislocation, press-gangs, rack rents, land monopolies, placemen, and pensioners, but what most aroused the wrath of conference and assured its author's dismissal was the allegation that several Kilhamite preachers—he named them—were erstwhile or practicing democrats. Thrust out of the ministry in 1814, Beaumont instigated a schism at Norwich, then applied for and was denied readmission as a preacher. The contrast between these events and his subsequent life well illustrates New Connexion history. After moving to Halifax Beaumont opened a drapery business, set up a cloth mill using power looms, advanced sizable sums to the circuit, and contributed generously to the Kilhamite Paternal Fund; he won a seat on the town council, developed a suburb, and worked tirelessly for sanitary reform. George Beaumont died a devout member of the Church of England, having reared two sons for its clergy ([Beaumont], *Helmet* [1813]; Private Minutes of the Methodist New Connexion, 1821; *New Connexion Minutes*, 1812–1815, 1818–1823; Chapman, *John Wesley & Co.*, pp. 42–43).

76 Delegates at this conference came from Manchester, Warrington, Stockport, Oldham, Wilmslow, Preston, and Sheffield (*Minutes of the Yearly Meeting of the Independent Methodists,* 1814 [Stockport, n.d.]).

77 Wray, "Methodism in Leeds," pp. 85–86; Jabez Bunting to Richard Reece, 15 July 1803 (M.A.); Lorenzo Dow, *The Dealings of God, Man, and the Devil, As Exemplified in the Life, Experience, and Travels of Lorenzo Dow . . . Together with His Polemic and Miscellaneous Writings Complete, to Which Is Added "The Vicissitudes of Life" by Peggy Dow,* ed. John Dowling (Cincinnati, 1860), p. 124.

78 Bunting, *Life* 1: 97; William Jenkins to John Broadhurst, 17 June 1803 (M.A.); *A Statement of Facts and Observations Relative to the Late Separation from the Methodist Society in Manchester, Affectionately Addressed to the Members of That Body by Their Preachers and Leaders* (Manchester, 1806), p. 8; Rothwell, *Memorials,* p. 23.

79 Hugh Bourne, in John Walford, *Memoirs of the Life and Labours of the Late Venerable Hugh Bourne,* ed. William Antliff (2 vols., London and Burslem, 1855–1856), 1: 228. The bulk of Walford's two-volume work was taken directly from Bourne's manuscript journals. Walford also included some of Bourne's published writings.

80 Rothwell, *Memorials,* pp. 13–14; Dow, *Life,* p. 124.

81 Jabez Bunting to James Wood, 21 January 1805 (M.A.). Immediately after they met the Stockport revivalists at a love feast at Congleton, Bourne and his friends experienced their first "extraordinary outpouring of the Spirit" (Hugh Bourne, *History of the Primitive Methodists, Giving an Account of Their Rise and Progress up to the Year 1823* [2d ed., Bemersley, 1835], p. 11). Contingents from Stockport attended both Mow Cop camp meetings in 1807.

82 Jabez Bunting to George Marsden, 10 June 1803 (M.A.); Bunting to Richard Reece, 11 June 1803 (M.A.); Joseph Nightingale, *A Portraiture of Methodism, Being an Impartial View of the Rise, Progress, Doctrines, Discipline, and Manners of the Wesleyan Methodists* (London, 1807), pp. 89–90; *Falsehood Exposed, or Truth Vindicated, Being a Critique of Mr. Nightingale's Portraiture of Methodism* (London, 1808), p. 16; Dow, *Life,* pp. 123, 130, 136; Bourne, *History,* p. 18; Walford, *Memoirs* 1: 149.

83 Walford, *Memoirs* 1: 149, 170, 172; "Primitive Methodist Preaching Plan, March 1810," ibid., p. 270.

84 James Vickers, *Independent Methodism: Origin, Constitution, Polity* (Wigan, 1910), p. 1; Arthur Mounfield, *The Quaker Methodists* (Nelson, 1924), pp. 8–10.

85 Walford, *Memoirs* 1: 154, 186, 376, 2: 9.

2 / Fire from Heaven

1 Hugh Bourne, comp., *A Collection of Hymns for Camp Meetings, Revivals, &c. for the Use of the Primitive Methodists* (Bemersley, 1832), no. 25. Part 1 of this hymnal duplicates the *Collection* of 1809, which was published at Newcastle.

2 John F. C. Harrison, *The Second Coming: Popular Millenarianism, 1780–1850* (New Brunswick, N.J., 1979), p. 218. In his final chapter Harrison discussed the adequacy of interpreting millenarianism in terms of its relationship to three factors—a time of crisis, feelings of anxiety and insecurity, and a deprived or oppressed class. He pointed out that millenarianism was basically an ideology of change, one response to a widely felt and fairly constant need for salvation from a variety of social and individual ills. See also Richard Allen Soloway, *Prelates and People: Ecclesiastical and Social Thought in England, 1783–1852* (London and Toronto, 1969), pp. 36–40; M. H. Abrams, "English Romanticism: The Spirit of the Age," in *Romanticism Reconsidered*, ed. Northrop Frye (New York and London, 1963), p. 37; Edward P. Thompson, *The Making of the English Working Class* (2d ed. rev., paperback, Harmondsworth, 1968), p. 127. In its revised form Thompson's influential study was published by Penguin Books in 1968 as "Pelicanbook no. A1000." This edition contains data and insights not included in the original hardcover version (London, 1963).

3 Norman Cohn characterized as millenarian "any religious movement inspired by the phantasy of salvation which is to be" terrestrial, collective, imminent, total, and "accomplished by agencies which are consciously regarded as supernatural" (Norman Cohn, "Medieval Millenarism: Its Bearing on the Comparative Study of Millenarian Movements," in *Millennial Dreams in Action: Essays in Comparative Study*, ed. Sylvia L. Thrupp [The Hague, 1962], p. 31).

The Methodists used a number of terms to describe the process of salvation. A *mourner* was one in whom the working of the Holy Spirit had produced *conviction of sin*. The person so convinced hoped first to *get liberty* and ultimately to gain *entire sanctification*. Knowing himself to be forgiven, a reconciliation made possible by Christ's atonement on the cross, the spiritual pilgrim experienced a *new birth*. *Justified* by faith, he endeavored to lead a holy life. The freely bestowed grace of God made sanctification possible, but progress towards the state of *perfection* required effort on the part of the *new man*. Usually perfection came gradually; however, it was possible for an individual to undergo instantaneous sanctification. A *professor* (someone who avowed his faith) had to be watchful lest he *backslide* from the quest for holiness.

4 John Moon to Thomas Coke, 22 August 1794, in Sigston, *Memoir* 2: 373.

5 *Methodist Magazine* 24 (1801): 452–453; *New Connexion Magazine* 8 (1805): 511–516, 523–525, 526–528; William Bramwell to Burnley, 20 March 1807 and Bramwell to James Sigston, 1 December 1807, in Sigston, *Memoir* 2: 77, 254. Even some New Connexion circuits were swept by revivalism in 1805, an atypical phenomenon that was construed as a preparation for the Second Coming.

6 Bourne, comp., *Hymns*, nos. 25, 15, 5.

7 In May 1810 Nancy Foden "saw" that Lorenzo Dow crowned the hierarchy of believers. Bourne and William Clowes were portrayed holding trumpets (the word of truth) and bearing cups of honey (salvation) (John T. Wilkinson, *Hugh Bourne, 1772–1852* [London, 1952], p. 79).

8 See the Editor's Introduction to Charles Grandison Finney, *Lectures on Re-*

vivals of Religion, ed. William G. McLoughlin (Cambridge, Mass., 1960), pp. xl–xli. *P.M.M.* 16 (1835): 192.

9 Robert Newton Barrett, "Extracts from the Unpublished Journal of One of John Wesley's Ministers, *viz.*, Reverend John Barritt," pp. 26–27, Methodist Archives.

10 [William Henshaw], *Copy of an Interesting Letter from Mr. William Henshaw, Methodist Preacher, Plymouth Dock, to Mr. William Bramwell, Methodist Preacher, Birstall* (London, 1814), pp. 3–4. See also *A Selection of Letters, etc., upon the Late Extraordinary Revival of the Work of God* (Manchester, 1800).

11 *Arminian Magazine, Consisting of Extracts and Original Treatises on Universal Redemption* 18 (1795): 476 (hereafter cited as *Arminian Magazine*). This periodical, the official organ of Wesleyan Methodism, became *Methodist Magazine* in 1798.

12 Beginning in the 1830s Finney's *Lectures* served as a methodological guide for Finney and other American evangelists. In 1839 Bourne urged Primitive Methodist preachers to use them as a handbook for inducing revivals.

13 See Gustave Le Bon, *The Crowd: A Study of the Popular Mind* (London, 1896), pp. 141–147. In this pioneering and influential analysis of crowd behavior, Le Bon maintained that collective action is often the result of contagion, a natural force which diffuses opinions and emotions in the way microbes spread disease. Contagion, or imitation, can exert its sway over considerable distances, override personal interests, and induce uniform patterns of behavior. It does not depend on rational persuasion, but is based on man's propensity to emulate others and so to be drawn into mass actions.

14 William Bramwell, *A Short Account of the Life and Death of Ann Cutler* (new ed., Whitby, 1819), pp. 20–21. See also Sigston, *Memoir* 1: 44–45.

15 *Memoir of the Life and Ministry of the Reverend William Bramwell, with Extracts from His Letters by Members of His Family* (London, 1848), p. 44; Sigston, *Memoir* 1: 82–83.

16 Charles Atmore to Thomas Coke, 20 June 1794, in *Arminian Magazine* 18 (1795): 520; Walker, *History*, pp. 194–195, 201.

17 "The Experience of Mr. Zechariah Yewdall," *Arminian Magazine* 18 (1795): 474–475. According to one witness, Mary Barritt "had a wonderful knack at inflaming the passions, but was *extraordinarily* defective in the art of informing the judgment" (Nightingale, *Portraiture*, p. 456).

18 James Wood to Thomas Coke, 7 June 1794, in *Arminian Magazine* 18 (1795): 519–520; Wray, "Methodism in Leeds," p. 85.

19 James Wood to Thomas Coke, 7 June 1794.

20 Alexander Mather, quoted in *Arminian Magazine* 17 (1794): 603, 649–650.

21 "The Experience of Mr. Robert Miller," *Methodist Magazine* 24 (1801): 197–198, 238.

22 Jabez Bunting to George Marsden, 28 March 1809 (M.A.); Thomas Cooper to Joseph Benson, 5 April 1797 (M.A.); Sigston, *Memoir* 1: 75; John Moon to Thomas Coke, 8 August 1794, in *Arminian Magazine* 18 (1795): 415–418. Several of the preceding details about Sheffield radicalism were drawn from Thompson, *Making of the English Working Class*, chapter 5, pp. 111–203.

23 *Memoir of Bramwell*, pp. 49–53; Alexander Seed, *Norfolk Street Wesleyan Chapel, Sheffield* (Sheffield, 1907), p. 63.

24 J. Blackner, *History of Nottingham* (Nottingham, 1815), pp. 245–247.

25 Malcolm I. Thomis, *Politics and Society in Nottingham, 1785–1835* (Oxford, 1969), pp. 15–16.

26 Much of this information was derived from "Say to the Wind: A Study of the Revival of Religion in Nottingham, 1780–1850," a privately reproduced shortened version of a thesis presented to the University of Nottingham in 1957 by John C. Weller.

27 Dunn, *Memoirs of Mr. Thomas Tatham*, pp. 33, 163; George H. Harwood, *The History of Wesleyan Methodism in Nottingham and Its Vicinity* (new ed., Nottingham, 1872), p. 132.

28 Joseph Beaumont, *Memoirs of Mrs. Mary Tatham* (London, 1838), p. 93.

29 In this context it is important to note that Nottingham Wesleyans were little involved in local politics. What influence they had "was believed to be exercised on the conservative side." To Francis Ward, a political activist, they were "'an accursed set,' proverbial among Dissenters for their loyalty" (Thomis, *Politics and Society*, p. 137).

30 Dunn, *Memoirs of Mr. Thomas Tatham*, p. 64.

31 Beaumont, *Memoirs of Mrs. Mary Tatham*, pp. 92–93; Dunn, *Memoirs of Mr. Thomas Tatham*, pp. 69, 78.

32 Beaumont, *Memoirs of Mrs. Mary Tatham*, p. 97.

33 Harwood, *History*, pp. 97, 143; *Memoir of Bramwell*, pp. 206–212. Every one of Nottingham's major revivals was somehow associated with William Bramwell. At the time of his visit in 1796 Henry Longden was Bramwell's junior colleague in Sheffield. Mary Barritt, the traveling evangelist who spent nine months stirring Nottingham revivalism in 1799–1800, was a Bramwell protégée. Miller, who had been converted during the Sheffield revival, discovered his preacher's calling under Bramwell's tutelage. As a young man, John Smith had studied with James Sigston, Bramwell's biographer and chief ally in Leeds. Even the first Primitive Methodist missionaries had links with Bramwell: Sarah Kirkland's childhood conviction of sin came while he was praying in her parents' house, and Robert Winfield urged female preaching because he owed his conversion to Mary Barritt.

34 Dunn, *Memoirs of Mr. Thomas Tatham*, pp. 156–158; William Bramwell to Henry Longden, 16 October 1800, in *Memoir of Bramwell*, p. 207.

35 Richard Treffry, *Memoirs of the Life, Character, and Labours of the Reverend John Smith* (London, 1832), pp. 38–40.

36 The Primitive Methodists recognized that Bramwell was the main agent of the "new" revivalism, a movement which both they and he saw as a return to "primitive" zeal. Bourne taught his missionaries to emulate Bramwell's methods, and he printed and sold Bramwell's *Life and Death of Ann Cutler* as a testimony to the effectiveness of female preaching. As late as 1863 Primitive Methodist itinerants were peddling a threepenny sketch of Bramwell's life.

37 With regard to long-term trends Eric Hobsbawm probably came nearest the truth when he wrote: "The periods when Wesleyanism recruited most rapidly . . . [were also the] periods of mounting popular agitation." Hobsbawm sug-

gested that this "peculiar parallelism" might be explained "either by saying that radical agitations drove other workers into Methodism as a reaction against them, or that they became Methodists and Radicals for the same reasons. Both are probably true" (Eric J. Hobsbawm, "Methodism and the Threat of Revolution," in *Labouring Men: Studies in the History of Labour* [London, 1964], p. 32). In the short run Hobsbawm's "peculiar parallelism" sometimes breaks down—in Nottingham in 1793-1794 and during the early years of Luddism, for example.

38 Quoted in Lorenzo Dow, *Travels and Providential Experiences, &c. of Lorenzo Dow* (Dublin, 1806), p. 155; Nicholas Snethen to "My Unknown Friend" in the Irish conference, 16 November 1805, in Dow, *Life,* p. 163.

39 Hugh Bourne, *Observations on Camp Meetings, with an Account of a Camp Meeting Held on Sunday, May the 31st, 1807 at Mow, near Harrisehead,* in Walford, *Memoirs* 1: 121 (Walford reprinted this penny tract in its entirety, pp. 119-125); "Analects upon Natural, Social, and Moral Philosophy," in Dow, *Life,* p. 69; Joseph Entwisle to George Marsden, 7 February 1814 (M.A.). Entwisle's letter also provides an insight into the democratic implications of revivalism. An English Methodist back from a journey to America reported that "the good American Methodists, *who were democrats,* would not believe" his accounts of revivalism in Cornwall. The Americans, it seemed, simply rejected out of hand the notion that "any good [could] be done" or a religious awakening accomplished under monarchical rule.

40 Dow, *Travels,* pp. 97, 125, 144.

41 Bernard A. Weisberger, *They Gathered at the River: The Story of the Great Revivalists and Their Impact upon Religion in America* (Boston and Toronto, 1958), p. 37; *Methodist Magazine* 25 (1802): 217, 423, 522; 26 (1803): 82-93, 269-272, 419.

42 Quoted in Charles Albert Johnson, *The Frontier Camp Meeting, Religion's Harvest Time* (Dallas, 1955), p. 99.

43 On the Kentucky revivals, see *Methodist Magazine* 26 (1803): 82-93.

44 Dow, *Life,* p. 251; George Herod, *Historical and Biographical Sketches, Forming a Compendium of the History of the Primitive Methodist Connexion up to the Year 1823* (2d ed., London, 1857), p. 185; Bourne, *Observations,* in Walford, *Memoirs* 1: 121.

45 Bourne, *History,* p. 4; Herod, *Biographical Sketches,* pp. 213, 215.

46 *Portraiture,* pp. 209-210.

47 Joseph Benson, quoted in [William Naylor], *A Friend of Many Years: A Memorial of Mr. Thomas Simpson of Armley near Leeds* (Wednesbury, 1864), p. 14; John Pawson, "An Account of Mr. Alexander Mather," *Methodist Magazine* 24 (1801): 114; [Entwisle], *Memoir of Entwisle,* p. 211.

48 William Jenkins to John Broadhurst, 17 June 1803 (M.A.).

49 Richard Reece to Robert Lomas, n.d., in Bunting, *Life* 1: 147.

50 Sigston, *Memoir* 2: 139; William Bramwell to Zacharias Taft, 30 November 1802, ibid. 1: 212; Bramwell to James Sigston, 23 April 1807, in *Memoir of Bramwell,* p. 221.

51 *Wesleyan Conference Minutes* 2: 54-55, 187, 404-405.

52 David Barker, *A Catechism of the Methodist New Connexion, Shewing the Origin of that Community, with the Great Principles on Which It Is Founded* (London and Ashton-under-Lyne, 1834), p. 35.

3 / The Formative Years

1 Bourne, *History*, pp. ii, 5–6.
2 Quoted in Wilkinson, *Hugh Bourne*, p. 32.
3 H. B. Kendall, *The Origin and History of the Primitive Methodist Church* (2 vols. in 1, London, [ca. 1906]), 1: 10.
4 Bourne, *History*, p. 9. Harriseahead was not the only village in the region badly served by the Church of England in 1800. Since the Reformation only seven places of worship had been erected in north Staffordshire; many churches were badly maintained; pluralism and nonresidence were common (L. W. Cowie, "The Church of England since the Reformation," *A History of the County of Stafford*, ed. M. W. Greenslade [London, 1970], 3: 69). Neither was Methodism particularly vigorous in the district. The New Connexion's Hanley circuit had 380 members in 1800, while the Wesleyan Burslem circuit, which Bourne described as "in a forlorn state," numbered 750.
5 Walford, *Memoirs* 1: 31, 54–63, 66. Shubotham advertised his conversion so enthusiastically that even his wife thought he had gone mad.
6 Bourne, quoted in Walford, *Memoirs* 1: 67; Bourne, *History*, p. 9.
7 Bourne, in Walford, *Memoirs* 1: 65, 77–78.
8 Walford, *Memoirs* 1: 85–86. See also Kendall, *History* 1: 33.
9 Bourne, in Walford, *Memoirs* 1: 88; Bourne, in *P.M.M.* 2 (1821): 9.
10 Joseph Sutcliffe to Thomas Jackson, 20 May 1813 (M.A.); *Wesleyan Conference Minutes* 2: 113.
11 The conference held its annual meetings during the summer. Preaching assignments, membership statistics, and financial reports were based, not on a calendar year, but on one that ran from 1 September to 31 August.
12 Bourne, *History*, p. 10; Bourne, in *P.M.M.* 2 (1821): 9, and in Walford, *Memoirs* 1: 94.
13 Bourne, *History*, p. 11; Bourne, in Walford, *Memoirs* 1: 99, 101, 105–106, 113.
14 Thomas Pinder to Jabez Bunting, 15 September 1806 (M.A.); *P.M.M.*, n.s. 23 (1900): 827.
15 Bourne, in Walford, *Memoirs* 1:114; William Edward Miller to Jabez Bunting, 1805 (M.A.); Bourne, *History*, p. 12. At the Wesleyan conference held in 1807, however, the circuit reported an increase of fifty members.
16 Bourne, *History*, p. 10; Bourne, in Walford, *Memoirs* 1: 90.
17 Bourne, *History*, p. 13.
18 What was called a wake in Staffordshire and Derbyshire was known as a feast in Yorkshire, a revel in the West Country, and rushbearing in Lancashire. It originated as a festival commemorating the dedication of the parish church.
19 Bourne, in Walford, *Memoirs* 1: 117–118; Bourne, *Observations*, ibid., pp. 119–125.

20 Bourne, *Observations*, in Walford, *Memoirs*, 1: 121–122; Bourne, in Walford, *Memoirs*, 1: 147. Clowes's account of the first camp meeting on Mow Hill appears in [William Clowes], *The Journals of William Clowes, a Primitive Methodist Preacher; Containing Chronicles of Events Relative to His Unregenerate State, His Conversion to God, His Call to the Ministry, the Commencement and Progress of the Primitive Methodist Connexion, and to His Itinerant Labours Therein from the Year 1810 to That of 1838* (London, 1844), pp. 68–71.

21 Bourne, *History*, pp. 16–17; Bourne, in Walford, *Memoirs* 1: 149–152.

22 Bourne, *History*, pp. 18–23; Walford, *Memoirs* 1: 157–163.

23 H. Thornhill Timmins, *Nooks and Corners of Shropshire* (London, 1899), pp. 150–151.

24 Bourne, *History*, p. 26.

25 Ibid., pp. 28–30; Bourne, in Kendall, *History* 1: 85.

26 [Clowes], *Journals*, pp. 1–10, 17. Samuel Clowes was "healed [of] his back-slidings" when poised "on the margin of the grave"; after her son's conversion Ann was blessed for a time with that understanding of the "way of salvation by faith" thought by William to be missing from religion as usually practiced in the established church (p. 2). During the period of near despair that preceded his conversion Clowes confided in his wife: "I told her, with tears in my eyes, that I was anxious to serve the Lord, and regularly to attend the Methodist chapel." Unimpressed by mere good intentions, his helpmate briskly "replied that if we became industrious as some around us were, there was no necessity for any thing more, especially of crying and going to chapels" (p. 14).

27 Ibid., pp. 72–75, 79–80, 83–86.

28 Bourne, in Walford, *Memoirs* 1: 165, 295.

29 [Clowes], *Journals*, pp. 87, 94–95; Bourne, *History*, p. 38; Thomas Church, *Popular Sketches of Primitive Methodism* (new ed., London, 1850), p. 25; Herod, *Biographical Sketches*, p. 405.

30 Bourne, *History*, pp. 40–41; [Clowes], *Journals*, pp. 93–94.

31 Bourne, in Walford, *Memoirs* 1: 154; Herod, *Biographical Sketches*, pp. 466–467. In 1808 the societies at Risley and Runcorn united with the Camp-Meeting Methodists. Bourne's *Remarks on the Ministry of Women* is reproduced in Walford, *Memoirs* 1: 173–177. According to Herod, the autobiography of Abbott "took well among the working classes."

32 [Clowes], *Journals*, p. 72; Bourne, in Herod, *Biographical Sketches*, p. 257; Bourne, in Walford, *Memoirs* 1: 141, 155. In 1808 Bourne himself "had an admonition from heaven to bring my manual labours to a close, to give myself wholly up to the work of the ministry" (Walford, *Memoirs* 1: 185).

33 [Clowes], *Journals*, pp. 43–44, 77–79; Bourne, in Walford, *Memoirs* 1: 179, 199, 281, 290–293, 296. Early in 1810 Bourne "almost" sensed an "opening for me" in the United States and for a time considered emigrating. A later "impression by the spirit" changed his mind (Walford, *Memoirs* 1: 242, 251). About one of his visions Bourne wrote, "I received evidence that I should be a pillar in the temple," and he added, "I was also sensible of being in Mount Zion, and the building was of fair colours. . . ." (ibid., p. 221).

34 [Hugh Bourne], "Experience of a Person in Regard to Acquiring a Knowledge of the Doctrine of a Present Salvation," *P.M.M.* 16 (1835): 34–35. Bourne's article appeared in four installments (ibid., pp. 32–36, 150–152, 376–380, 457–462).

35 Thomas Cotton was a poor collier with a large family to support. If a missionary journey to a distant place caused him to miss work, the Bournes made good whatever wages were lost. He did not receive a regular salary.

36 Bourne, in Walford, *Memoirs* 1: 281, 296–299; [Clowes], *Journals*, pp. 89–90.

37 Bourne, in Walford, *Memoirs* 1: 260, 307. Like Dinah Morris, Elizabeth Evans had her preaching career for the Wesleyans cut short by conference edict; unlike Dinah, she withdrew for a time from the Wesleyan society to join the Arminian Methodists. Bourne, who visited the Evans's home in March 1810, called her an "extraordinary woman" and likened her to Ann Cutler. The "Hayslope" of *Adam Bede* was Ellaston in Staffordshire where Bourne and Evans held a camp meeting in 1809.

38 Bourne, *History*, p. 35; Kendall, *History* 1: 96–97.

39 Bourne, in Walford, *Memoirs* 1: 267; Bourne, *History*, p. 34.

40 [Clowes], *Journals*, pp. 94–95. According to Clowes, the identity of the "actual founder" of Primitive Methodism was a "disputed question" among the delegates to a connexional meeting held at Nottingham in 1819. The issue was referred to the "Tunstall friends," who decided in his favor (ibid., pp. 162–163).

41 Herod, *Biographical Sketches*, p. 405; Bourne, *History*, pp. 42–43.

42 "Plan for June–September 1811," in Kendall, *History* 1: 113; [Clowes], *Journals*, p. 97.

43 Kendall, *History* 1: 130.

44 Bourne, *History*, p. 44; [Clowes], *Journals*, pp. 95–96; Bourne, in Kendall, *History* 1: 131.

45 Barker, *Catechism*, p. 35; Walford, *Memoirs* 1: 368.

46 Edward Langton, "James Crawfoot, the Forest Mystic," *Proceedings of the Wesley Historical Society* 30 (1955): 12–14.

47 "A Plan of the Preachers in the Society of the Primitive Methodists in Tunstall Circuit," reproduced in Kendall, *History* 1: 134. This plan for the spring quarter of 1812 was the first to be printed instead of handwritten. The contest over the societies in Derbyshire was enlivened by visionists propagandizing for both sides. Dunnel "saw" two Primitive Methodist preachers, Clowes and William Alcock, "quite on the back ground, their trumpets lying idle, and their heretofore overflowing cups nearly empty." A seer for the opposition promptly discerned that Clowes was in fact far above Dunnel on the spiritual ladder and that Bourne was close by (Walford, *Memoirs* 1: 330–332, 344).

48 Joseph Sutcliffe to Thomas Jackson, 13 July 1812 (M.A.).

49 [Clowes], *Journals*, pp. 98–100.

50 Beneath the formal charges of tardiness and neglect of appointments lay a quarrel with Bourne that was partly personal. After proclaiming the virtues of celibacy Crawfoot wedded a woman who had already rejected a marriage proposal from Bourne. Crawfoot also began to attack the existing leadership and to regard himself as the "generalissimo of the Primitive Methodist forces."

He formed a secret coterie to depose Steele and the Bournes and accused Hugh of seeking to replace the itinerants with local preachers. Hugh Bourne resented the discord Crawfoot was causing and blamed him for having introduced a Quaker-like "hat whim" that "injured the revival cause" (Bourne, in Walford, *Memoirs* 1: 355–362).

51 Bourne, *History*, pp. 49–50.
52 In March of that year Steele told Bourne that "the power is stronger now than it was when the revival [of 1805] was begun." A "great congregation" attended a camp meeting during wake week at Tunstall in July (Bourne, in Walford, *Memoirs* 1: 369, 392). Depression was still affecting the Potteries at the time of this revival. According to Joseph Sutcliffe, poverty was afflicting the Wesleyan circuit in May 1813. At the beginning of the year one of every seven people was receiving parish relief (Sutcliffe to Thomas Jackson, 20 May 1813 [M.A.]).
53 Bourne, *History*, p. 51.
54 Benton penned his sentiments on the back of the preaching plan and returned it to Tunstall. He wrote: "A plan from God I have in mind; / A better plan I cannot find; / If you can, pray let me know, / And round the circuit I will go" (quoted in Kendall, *History* 1: 190).
55 Herod, *Biographical Sketches*, p. 467; Bourne, in Walford, *Memoirs* 1: 396, 411. Benton gauged the market for his hymnal accurately. Six years later, when a slightly revised version of it was registered as the property of the connexion, the original had already gone through several editions. Benton's "circuit" included Alstonefield, a village in which his methods succeeded at about the same time as both the Wesleyans and the Baptists failed to establish societies. His society at Hulme End filled a void left when the Wesleyans vacated the place. The one at Warslow antedated the Wesleyan society there. A Wesleyan preacher assigned to the area in 1803 blamed the weather and the scattered population for his not very fruitful year there (see J. B. Dyson, *A Brief History of the Rise and Progress of Wesleyan Methodism in Leek Circuit* [Leek, 1853], pp. 43–44, 62, 83–86).
56 John Wedgwood, a distant relative of Josiah's, gave up a lucrative business to become a missionary. Prior to his conversion in 1811 he had read Paine's *Age of Reason*. The "spirit of infidelity," he later confessed, "was upon me for some time." During 1813 Wedgwood worked with Clowes in northeastern Staffordshire. He spent the next fifteen years making converts to Primitive Methodism, but not until 1829 did he allow himself to be put on the plan as a salaried preacher. Bourne had some reservations about Wedgwood. These were attributed by Wedgwood's biographer to his long adherence to free gospelism and to his habit of converting people than neglecting to form them into societies ([Thomas Bateman], *Memoir of the Life and Labours of Mr. John Wedgwood* [London, 1870], pp. 41, 51).
57 Stephen Glover, *The History of the County of Derby*, ed. Thomas Noble (Derby, 1829) 2: 101; Benjamin Gregory, *Autobiographical Recollections*, ed. J. Robinson Gregory (London, 1903), pp. 128–129. Glover noted that the Strutts were very public-spirited and concerned about the housing and general welfare of Belper's population.

58 [Clowes], *Journals*, p. 117.
59 G. Arthur Fletcher, *Records of Wesleyan Methodism in the Belper Circuit, 1760–1903* (Belper, 1903), pp. 20, 30.
60 Sampson Turner, journal entries, 3–10 October 1819, in *P.M.M.* 1 (1820): 248; Thomas Webb, journal entries, 9–23 January 1820, ibid., p. 249; Thomas Jackson, journal entries, 4 February–18 March 1821, ibid. 2 (1821): 133–134.
61 Herod, *Biographical Sketches*, pp. 309–313.
62 Bourne, in Walford, *Memoirs* 1: 408–413.

4 / The Conquest of Canaan, 1816–1819

1 Quoted in George J. Pratt, *Methodist Monographs: Headlights and Sidelights on the Movement in Derby* (Derby, 1925), p. 34.
2 Bourne, in Walford, *Memoirs* 1: 414; Bourne, *History*, p. 51.
3 Herod, *Biographical Sketches*, pp. 12–13.
4 Dow, *Life*, p. 171; Bourne, in Walford, *Memoirs* 1: 414; Samuel Smith, "Anecdotes and Facts of Primitive Methodism," *Primitive Methodist Itinerant Preacher* (1872), in Kendall, *History* 1: 221–222. In the seventeenth century "Ranter" had designated a sect of fanatical antinomians who taught the supremacy of private religious experience over all external authority.
5 Thomas Beaumont to Sidmouth, 5 June 1817, H.O. 42/166, cited in Thompson, *Making of the English Working Class*, p. 921. This latter is dated four days *before* the Pentridge rising.
6 [Bateman], *Memoir*, pp. 74–76; Bourne, *History*, p. 56; [Clowes], *Journals*, pp. 121–123; Walford, *Memoirs* 2: 11, 15, 26, 36, 38, 44; Church, *Popular Sketches*, p. 51. See also Kendall, *History* 1: 250, 265–266 and William Parkes, "The Original Methodists, Primitive Methodist Reformers," *Proceedings of the Wesley Historical Society* 35 (1965): 57–64.
7 Mary Oastler to Mary Tatham, 26 March 1816, in Beaumont, *Memoirs of Mrs. Mary Tatham*, p. 185; Sarah Kirkland Bembridge to John Barfoot, 25 May 1870, in Barfoot, "Gleanings Concerning the Late Mrs. Sarah Bembridge," *P.M.M.*, n.s. 4 (1881): 227.
8 Herod, *Biographical Sketches*, pp. 317–320; Bourne, diary entries, 12, 13 August 1816, in Walford, *Memoirs* 2: 44; Barfoot, "Gleanings," *P.M.M.*, n.s., 4 (1881): 226–227; Swift, Typescript of notes compiled from the files of Nottingham newspapers. Among the places visited by Kirkland were Ratcliffe, Cotmanhay, Codnor Park, Kirby, Lambley, Blidworth, Oxton, East Bridgford, Sutton-in-Ashfield, Mansfield, and Epperstone.
9 Thomas Bailey, *History of the County of Nottingham* (London and Nottingham, n.d.) 4: 279–283. In 1817 wheat climbed to 96s. 11d. per quarter. At that time stockingers were averaging 8s. or 9s. per week. It was said in December 1816 that the laboring poor in Nottingham were experiencing worse conditions than any in the past forty years. This situation persisted through the spring of 1817 (Thomis, *Politics and Society*, pp. 16, 20).
10 Herod, *Biographical Sketches*, pp. 287–290; Bourne, diary entry, 5 May 1817, in Walford, *Memoirs* 2: 11; John Petty, *The History of the Primitive*

Methodist Connexion from Its Origins to the Conference of 1860 (2d ed., London, 1864), p. 66; William Clowes to Hugh Bourne, 2 September 1817, in Walford, *Memoirs* 2: 19.

11 Bourne, diary entry, 23 March 1818, in Walford, *Memoirs* 2: 43; John Harrison, journal, 8 February–4 April 1818, in Herod, *Biographical Sketches*, pp. 344–351; Dow, *Life*, p. 187; Herod, *Biographical Sketches*, pp. 187–189; Walford, *Memoirs* 2: 35–38.

12 Herod, *Biographical Sketches*, pp. 343, 353, 419. The quotation is from Harrison's journal.

13 The Wesleyans in Nottinghamshire were also troubled by both disciplinary and monetary matters in 1818. In June leaders were summoned to a special meeting at which they resolved to dismiss one of their number "unless he can give good reason" for his failure to attend meetings. At the quarterly meeting in July all leaders were required to pledge that they would "use their utmost endeavours to average a penny per week and a shilling per quarter" for each class member in their charge. Any who balked, they agreed, ought to resign. Each leader was also requested to state "whether he intended to remain a decided Methodist" (John R. Raynes, *History of Wesleyan Methodism in the Mansfield Circuit, 1807–1907* [Mansfield, 1907], p. 8).

14 Bourne, *History*, pp. 56–58. In his journal Harrison likened the quarterly meeting in December 1818 to "that when Ezra commanded the foundation to be relaid" (in Herod, *Biographical Sketches*, p. 362).

15 Reprinted in Kendall, *History* 1: 279.

16 John Curtis, *A Topographical History of the County of Leicester* (Ashby-de-la-Zouch, 1831), pp. xx, 119; Herod, *Biographical Sketches*, pp. 13–15.

17 Curtis, *Topographical History*, p. 119; Kendall, *History* 1: 317–319.

18 *P.M.M.* 3 (1822): 204; [Clowes], *Journals*, p. 127; John Harrison, journal entries, May and June 1818, in Herod, *Biographical Sketches*, pp. 356–358. Understandably, some of the villagers at Wigstown objected to the reveilles sounded by Benjamin Gamage, an ex-trumpeter in the Royal Artillery, who contributed to the cause by awakening fellow society members for dawn prayer meetings (obituary of Benjamin Gamage, *P.M.M.* 14 [1833]: 63–64).

19 George Hanford to the Book Committee, 2 February 1823, in *P.M.M.* 4 (1823): 179–182; William Antliff, *A Book of Marvels; or, Incidents, Original and Selected, Illustrative of Primitive Methodism, Temperance, and Other Subjects* (London, 1873), pp. 178–179. Clowes recounted a similar experience with "ploughmen" in Yorkshire. When they asked for money, he dropped to his knees and began praying. The "buffoons decamped with the greatest precipitation" ([Clowes], *Journals*, p. 175).

20 Daniel Isaac, a Wesleyan itinerant assigned to the Leicester circuit from 1820 to 1822, complained that "this neighbourhood abounds with Baptists; and their churches, I think, are more than half-filled with runaway Methodists" (Isaac to P. Haswell, 30 June 1821, in James Everett, *The Polemic Divine; or, Memoirs of the Life, Writings, and Opinions of the Reverend Daniel Isaac* [2d ed., Manchester, 1851], p. 143).

21 Quoted in Kendall, *History* 1: 309–310. A liberal, Hall championed the lace

workers, published pamphlets on freedom of the press and the benefits of educating the lower classes, admired Bentham, defended Priestley, and held open communions in his chapel.

22 John Harrison, journal entries, 9 and 10 May 1818, in Herod, *Biographical Sketches*, p. 355. Benton habitually preached with a red silk handkerchief tied around his head. A Leicester convert claimed that sometimes Benton's appearance and manner "did more to rivet the attention of his hearers" than did the subject matter of his sermons (William Goodrich, quoted in [Bateman], *Memoir*, pp. 76–77).

23 J. A. Lainé, *Methodism in and around Leicester* (Leicester, n.d.), p. 12. Goodrich's father, a failed hosier, lived at St. Martin's workhouse from 1814 until his death in 1825. After his conversion to Primitive Methodism in 1818 he "faithfully reproved the bad conduct of many of the inmates," read and wrote poetry, copied extracts from religious tracts, and was allowed to leave whenever he needed to carry out his duties as a local preacher and class leader (obituary of William Goodrich, *P.M.M.* 8 [1827]: 120–131). By contrast, the younger Goodrich was fired from his job as a school usher when he joined the Ranters (diary of William Goodrich, in *P.M.M.* 53 [1872]: 747).

24 *P.M.M.* 1 (1819): 8, 15–16, 132–133, 151, 239–243.

25 Kendall, *History* 1: 329–332.

26 Daniel Isaac to P. Haswell, 30 June 1821, in Everett, *Polemic Divine*, p. 144.

27 Herod, *Biographical Sketches*, p. 300.

28 Robert Ducker, quoted in George Shaw, "William Braithwaite, the Apostle of North Lincolnshire," *P.M.M.*, 2d n.s. 2 (1895): 130.

29 George Crabbe, "The Village," in Louis I. Bredvold, Alan D. McKillop, Lois Whitney, eds., *Eighteenth Century Poetry and Prose* (2d ed., New York, 1956), p. 972.

30 Rutland favored Methodism because its adherents were good tenants and servants. About 1810 he had silenced the rector at Waltham, who wanted him to evict a person in whose house the Wesleyan society held its meetings (Barrett, "Extracts," p. 39; Joseph Gill, *The History of Wesleyan Methodism in Melton Mowbray and the Vicinity, 1769–1909* [Melton Mowbray, 1909], p. 181).

31 [Bateman], *Memoir*, p. 62.

32 John Harrison, journal entry, 29 March 1818, in Herod, *Biographical Sketches*, p. 347.

33 John Parrott, quoted in Herod, *Biographical Sketches*, pp. 347–350.

34 Herod, *Biographical Sketches*, pp. 293–294.

35 Petty, *History*, pp. 68–69. The sect finally gained an uneasy foothold in Newark after various persecutors suffered accidents or met untimely deaths. These were interpreted as "providential" indications that the Ranters were protected by a just but wrathful deity.

36 Francis White and John White, *Nottinghamshire: History, Directory, and Gazetteer of the County and of the Town . . . of Nottingham* (Sheffield, 1844), p. 404; Gill, *History*, pp. 102–103; Petty, *History*, p. 67; *P.M.M.* 2 (1821): 32.

37 Herod, *Biographical Sketches*, pp. 290–294, 350–351; Thomas Cocking, *The History of Wesleyan Methodism in Grantham and Its Vicinity* (London, 1836), pp. 285–286, 386; [Clowes], *Journals*, p. 295.

38 Curtis, *History*, p. 147; *P.M.M.* 9 (1828): 427 and 21 (1840): 215. This family "liberally assisted" the Primitive Methodists in Redmile and gave land for a chapel, which was erected in 1828.

39 [Clowes], *Journals*, pp. 128–134; [Bateman], *Memoir*, pp. 71–73; William Clowes to Hugh Bourne, 2 September 1817, in Walford, *Memoirs* 2: 18; Kendall, *History* 1: 262. While he was in prison Wedgwood composed a hymn that became a "battle song" of the movement. It began:

At Grantham Cross I did appear,
The constables did then draw near;
And from the cross they had me down,
But could not take away my crown.

Hailed as the "knight of Buckminster" in a Primitive Methodist poem celebrating the affair, Manners had long been sympathetic to Wesleyan Methodism. Twelve years earlier he had "fitted up" a large barn near his hall for Wesleyan worship (Barrett, "Extracts," p. 39).

40 Cocking, *History*, pp. 132, 152; Greenwood, *Memoir of George Sykes*, p. 92; E. J. Brailsford, *Richard Watson, Theologian and Missionary Advocate* (London, n.d.), p. 29; George Barratt, *Recollections of Methodism and Methodists in the City of Lincoln* (Lincoln, 1866), p. 45; Francis Hill, *Georgian Lincoln* (Cambridge, 1966), p. 296; *P.M.M.* 21 (1840): 181 and 22 (1841): 129; Kendall, *History* 1: 465.

41 Landowners punished adherents of Primitive Methodism by refusing to employ them. At least one laborer nearly starved to death because of this practice. Accounts of the extension of Ranterism into Kesteven, Holland, and southeastern Lindsey can be found in Herod, *Biographical Sketches*, p. 364, and in *P.M.M.* 2 (1821): 45–46, 57–60, 94; 3 (1822): 94; 11 (1830): 396; 18 (1837): 387, 439; 22 (1841): 129. According to a detailed study of religion and rural society in south Lindsey, Primitive Methodists had by midcentury established places of worship in forty-three locales. At the time of the religious census of 1851 most of their strength lay in open parishes with large populations. Societies in close parishes were rare, and almost never had the sect won a foothold in those with resident squires. The founding of societies, however, had been closely linked to "unpredictable individual enterprise." Among fifty-eight local preachers active between 1825 and 1875, more than half were farm laborers, and almost one-third were craftsmen. In proportion to the general population, farmers were underrepresented as local preachers (17 percent), but they were more important as "chief supporters" (29 percent). This difference was typical: "as in Wesleyan Methodism, the organizers and officials tended to come from a higher social level than the preachers" (James Obelkevich, *Religion and Rural Society: South Lindsey, 1825–1875* [Oxford, 1976], pp. 237–239).

42 Thomas Mozley, quoted in George Shaw, *The Life of John Oxtoby* (Hull and

London, 1894), p. 16. Ultimately, northern Lincolnshire generated more preachers for the Primitive Methodist Connexion than any other district in England (Kendall, *History* 1: 413).

43 Shaw, "William Braithwaite," *P.M.M.*, 2d n.s. 2 (1895): 130.

44 Stories about "Hell-fire Dick" abounded. For example, one convert claimed that Braithwaite's preaching caused his hair to stand on end and displace his hat. At the village of Appleby three men who tried to pull Braithwaite down from the market cross later obligingly fulfilled his prohecy: "Mark my words, if any one of these three men die a natural death, then God never sent me to preach here today." One fell off a church tower while drunk; another was gored by a bull; the third was drowned (ibid., pp. 129–131).

45 Thomas Cooper, *The Life of Thomas Cooper Written by Himself* (4th ed., London, 1873), pp. 37–39. Partly because the local leadership objected to his reading secular literature, Cooper soon broke with Primitive Methodism.

46 Shaw, "William Braithwaite," *P.M.M.*, 2d n.s., 2 (1895): 128–129; Kendall, *History* 1: 417; Bourne, *History*, p. 68. Scotter was the only village ever to be the site of a Primitive Methodist conference, that of 1829.

47 Typical of Harrison's experience was an unintended stop at Limber. En route to Caistor with Clowes and a female revivalist, he was detained by an expectant crowd: "So soon as we entered, the whole of the inhabitants were on a move to see what sort of creatures we were." The trio preached, held a prayer meeting, and never reached their destination (John Harrison, journal entries, 19–26 May and 10 June 1819, in Herod, *Biographical Sketches*, pp. 370–372, 375).

48 *East Halton: Methodism and the Village, 1790–1953* (Hull, n.d.), p. 13. The study of East Halton was compiled by a local history class cosponsored by the Workers' Educational Association and the Department of Adult Education of the University of Hull.

49 Edward Brown to Hugh Bourne, 11 January 1821, in *P.M.M.* 2 (1821): 41; Brown to Bourne, 27 February 1821, ibid., p. 86; Benjamin Hemstock to Bourne, 27 February 1821, ibid., p. 86; Herod, *Biographical Sketches*, p. 303. Herod was assigned to Grimsby in October 1820.

50 George Shaw, *Old Grimsby* (Grimsby and London, 1897), pp. 75, 78, 172–175, 228; George Lester, *Grimsby Methodism, 1743–1889, and the Wesleys in Lincolnshire* (London, 1890), p. 45; Joshua Hocken, *A Brief History of Wesleyan Methodism in the Grimsby Circuit* (Grimsby, 1839), pp. 63–64.

51 Thomas King, journal entries, 31 October–3 November 1819, in *P.M.M.* 2 (1821): 84; Shaw, *Old Grimsby*, p. 238; [Clowes], *Journals*, p. 356; Kendall, *History* 1: 440–441.

52 Shaw, "William Braithwaite," *P.M.M.*, 2d n.s. 2 (1895): 128; *P.M.M.* 53 (1872): 110–111; *P.M.M.* 14 (1833): 160–161.

53 *East Halton*, pp. 4, 14.

54 William White, *History, Gazetteer, and Directory of Lincolnshire and the City and Diocese of Lincoln* (2d ed., Sheffield, 1856), p. 632. This book was also used as a source of information for general statements about the number of Anglican places of worship in the county.

55 Ibid., p. 599.

56 *General Minutes of the Conferences of the Primitive Methodist Connexion* 1 (1814–1830): Minutes of 1823, pp. 2–3. Although the minutes of these conferences were consolidated into a single volume covering the meetings through 1830, the pagination in volume 1, which was published in 1836, begins anew with each yearly report (hereafter cited as *General Minutes of the Primitive Methodist Connexion*). Marshland circuit included some societies in the West Riding, but it was the product of missioning efforts carried out from Scotter.

57 [Clowes], *Journals*, pp. 146–147.

58 Thomas Thompson to Joseph Entwisle, 12 October 1814 (M.A.).

59 W. H. Thompson, *Early Chapters in Hull Methodism, 1746–1800* (London and Hull, 1895), p. 69; Robert Pilter to James Everett, 28 January 1816 (M.A.).

60 Herod, *Biographical Sketches*, p. 323; Hugh Bourne, journal entry, 12 March 1819, in Walford, *Memoirs* 2: 44.

61 Obituary of John Oxtoby, *P.M.M.* 11 (1830): 9–13; Shaw, *Life of John Oxtoby*, pp. 22–28. Bourne met Oxtoby at Hull in 1820 and "was surprised at his having attained so deep experience with so little information." His dialect was "very provincial" and his preaching anecdotal. According to Bourne, Oxtoby used language "stronger than most I ever was acquainted with" when praying with mourners (*P.M.M.* 11 [1830]: 46–48). In 1820 "Praying Johnny" became a local preacher, and in 1824 he was made an itinerant for the connexion.

62 [Clowes], *Journals*, pp. 148–152. The villages along the Humber were Brantingham, Hessle, Swanland, Elloughton, Ellerker, North Cave, and South Cave.

63 Herod, *Biographical Sketches*, p. 382.

64 Bourne, *History*, p. 65; Shaw, *Life of John Oxtoby*, pp. 26, 43; [Clowes], *Journals*, pp. 149–150, 209.

65 John Harrison, journal entries, 1–5 July 1819, in Herod, *Biographical Sketches*, pp. 376–377.

66 John Verity, journal entries, 8 November–2 December 1820, in *P.M.M.* 2 (1821): 93; Ann Armstrong, journal entries, 2–25 February 1821, ibid., p. 143.

67 [Clowes], *Journals*, pp. 166–167; Henry Woodcock, *Piety among the Peasantry, Being Sketches of Primitive Methodism on the Yorkshire Wolds* (London, 1889), pp. 18, 33, 96; Sir Tatton Sykes, quoted ibid., p. 135. Sykes gave land for the Primitive Methodist chapels at Wansford, Wetwang, and Sledmere (Kendall, *History* 2: 98).

68 Woodcock, *Piety among the Peasantry*, pp. 34, 57–62; *P.M.M.* 2 (1821): 176–177, 275–276; Nathaniel West, journal entry, 3 September 1821, in *P.M.M.* 2 (1821): 276; Kendall, *History* 2: 104–105; *P.M.M.*, n.s. 6 (1883): 85.

69 By the spring of 1822 three circuits were already established in the North Riding. Malton encompassed the area east of the Hambledon Hills and from the Vale of Pickering to the Cleveland Hills. North and west of Malton were

Guisborough and Brompton circuits. Thirsk was a missionary branch of Hull, and Ripon circuit (West Riding) was opening places in Wensleydale.

70 In 1823 the ratio of Primitive to Wesleyan Methodists in Doncaster was about one to eight. In Grimsby, by contrast, it was roughly one to two, while in Loughborough Ranters outnumbered Wesleyans. Such ratios can only be estimated, of course, because the Wesleyan and Primitive Methodist circuits were not strictly coterminous.

71 Nathaniel West, journal entries, 12–19 September 1820, in *P.M.M.* 2 (1821): 96; John Hutchinson, journal entries, 8 January–1 February 1821, ibid., pp. 237–238; Jonathan Clewer, journal entries, 1 October–20 November 1821, ibid. 3 (1822): 129–130; Kendall, *History* 2: 78–79.

72 Herod, *Biographical Sketches*, pp. 325–326; James Everett, *The Village Blacksmith; or, Piety and Usefulness Exemplified in a Memoir of the Life of Samuel Hick* (5th ed., London, 1834), pp. 153, 182; [Clowes], *Journals*, p. 175; *P.M.M.* 3 (1822): 250; William Beckwith, comp., *A Book of Remembrance, Being Records of Leeds Primitive Methodism* (London, 1910), pp. 11–12; [Clowes], *Journals*, pp. 160–161.

73 Kendall, *History* 2: 79–81.

74 [Clowes], *Journals*, pp. 155–156.

75 John Harrison, journal entry, 6 July 1819, in Herod, *Biographical Sketches*, p. 377; Barfoot, "Gleanings," *P.M.M.*, n.s. 4 (1881): 292.

76 John Lyth, *Glimpses of Early Methodism in York and the Surrounding District* (York, 1885), pp. 175–178, 236; Burdekin, *Memoir of Robert Spence*, p. 134. There were about 1,000 Wesleyans in York in 1827 and an equal number in the nearby villages.

77 Kendall, *History* 2: 58–59. Much of Kendall's account is based on the manuscript journals of Sampson Turner, the first superintendent of York circuit. In December 1821 York branch had a membership of only 341 and a cash balance of just 16s. 4d. Eighteen months later, the number of Primitive Methodists in the circuit had fallen to 301 (Account Book of the Quarterly Meeting, Hull Circuit, in W. J. Robson, ed., *Silsden Primitive Methodism: Historical Records and Reminiscences* [Silsden, 1910], p. 11).

78 George West, *Methodism in Marshland* (London, 1886), pp. 9, 54–57.

79 Typical was the situation in Ousefleet. Joanna Shankster, a servant there, was a Wesleyan until the society disintegrated about 1812. Hearing that the Ranters were in the vicinity, she invited them to Ousefleet, and the "work of God broke out among the neighbours." After "numbers" were converted, a Primitive Methodist society was formed (obituary of Joanna Shankster, *P.M.M.* 5 [1824]: 227).

80 West, *Methodism in Marshland*, pp. 46–56. West included a facsimile of the plan for the Wesleyan Snaith circuit as well as an account of the monies collected during the winter of 1817–1818. According to the latter, a number of the societies failed to contribute regularly to the connexional coffers.

81 *General Minutes of the Primitive Methodist Connexion*, Minutes of 1823, pp. 2–3. See also *P.M.M.* 11 (1830): 20, 212–215 and Kendall, *History* 1: 417.

82 Smith, *History* 2: 451–452.

83 Thomas Galland to Jabez Bunting, n.d. [ca. 1819], in Bunting, *Life* 2:163.

84 John Harrison, journal entry, 17 April 1819, in Herod, *Biographical Sketches*, p. 369; obituary of John Pallister, *P.M.M.* 44 (1843): 329–330. See also *P.M.M.* 4 (1823): 28.

85 Obituary of Hannah Hutton, *P.M.M.* 4 (1823): 155–156. The society at Keyingham added thirty members during the ensuing year. Extracts from the journals of itinerants serving in Holderness during 1820–1821 appeared in *P.M.M.* 2 (1821): 14, 93, 224.

86 Glover, *History of the County of Derby* 2: 260, 266–267; Kendall, *History* 1: 495.

87 Joseph Brook, journal entry, 29 December 1821, in *P.M.M. 4 (1823): 44; Kendall, History 1: 505; General Minutes of the Primitive Methodist Connexion*, Minutes of 1823, pp. 2–3. Bradwell's Primitive Methodists met in the home of a Wesleyan, George Morton, whose family were locally prominent landowners.

88 Quoted in Kendall, *History* 2: 76. See also [Clowes], *Journals*, p. 297.

89 In a single quarter in 1822 thirty-six itinerants were deployed in the circuit, and during the half-decade between 1822 and 1827, 139 preachers were paid for tours of duty lasting anywhere from one or two quarters to five years (Hull Circuit Account Books, June 1822–July 1827, cited in Leonard Brown, "William Clowes in the North of England," *Proceedings of the Wesley Historical Society* 37 [1970]: 169–170). There were forty itinerants working in Hull circuit in March 1821 (Shaw, *Life of John Oxtoby*, p. 43).

90 William Myles to Jabez Bunting, 5 June 1819 (M.A.). The New Connexion may also have suffered some losses to the Primitive Methodists in Hull. In 1820 one of its itinerants found the Hull circuit "in an awful state" (John Kearton to Andrew Lynn, 21 February 1820 [M.A.]). Although neither the Wesleyan nor the New Connexion Hull circuit was coterminous with that of the Primitive Methodists, all three would have included Hull and its immediate vicinity.

91 *P.M.M.* 1 (1820): 220, 225; Bourne, *History*, p. 69.

92 Thomas Bateman, journal, in Kendall, *History* 1: 512–513.

93 Bourne, *History*, pp. 58–64; Bourne, diary entries, December 1818–March 1819, in Walford, *Memoirs* 2: 45–49.

94 Bourne, *History*, p. 64; *P.M.M.* 1 (1820): 229.

95 *Methodist Magazine* 44 (1821): 294–295, 459–461; George McDermott to Charles Colwell, 31 August 1822 (M.A.); A. Tomkinson to Jonathan Crowther, 8 May 1821 (M.A.); John Davis to John Laycock, 17 March 1820 (M.A.).

96 Thomas Bateman, "Reminiscences of the Early Days of the Primitive Methodist Connexion," *P.M.M.*, n.s. 4 (1881): 85–86. Bateman was the son of a farmer and land surveyor at Chorley. His family were conscientious churchgoers, but, prior to Wedgwood's arrival Thomas also attended some Wesleyan meetings. Nineteen at the time of his conversion, Bateman became a prominent layman in the Primitive Methodist Connexion.

97 Kendall, *History* 1: 548. This backing from some of the gentry may have been a consequence of negligence in the diocese of Chester, where pluralism, absenteeism, and hunting-and-drinking clergy were then commonplace.

98 Bateman, "Early Days," *P.M.M.*, n.s. 4 (1881): 85–89.

99 Two of the newcomers were well chosen to follow in Wedgwood's wake. Thomas Webb, "from his appearance, might have been just taken from the plough," but he was "more methodical in his preaching." Bateman characterized Sampson Turner as sedate, practical, and a good organizer.

100 Bateman, "Early Days," *P.M.M.*, n.s. 4 (1881): 294–295, 468; Bourne, journal entries, October–November 1819, in Walford, *Memoirs* 2: 63–67; Kendall, *History* 1:515–516. A few of the places listed on the preaching plan for Burland branch in 1820 were in Wales or in Shropshire.

101 Bateman, "Early Days," *P.M.M.*, n.s. 4 (1881): 294, 297; Thomas Brownsword, journal entry, 18 March 1821, in *P.M.M.* 2 (1821): 187; Kendall, *History* 1: 556.

102 *General Minutes of the Primitive Methodist Connexion*, Minutes of 1823, pp. 2–3.

5 / Confronting the Philistines

1 David Stoner to John Hanwell, 9 September 1821 (M.A.).

2 Alfred Camden Pratt, *Black Country Methodism* (London, 1891), p. 156; Kendall, *History* 1: 519.

3 Jonathan Edmundson to Jonathan Crowther, 16 November 1819; Richard Waddy to Jabez Bunting, 11 October 1820; Waddy to Bunting, 31 January 1816; John Walmsley to Mr. Owen, 16 October 1816 (all M.A.).

4 The New Connexion may afterwards have been the victim of Ranter growth. In 1822, when Dudley became the circuit town, membership was falling, and by 1823 it had dropped to 319.

5 John Freeman, *Bilston Wesleyan Methodism* (Bilston, 1923), pp. 20–21; Pratt, *Black Country Methodism*, pp. 42–43, 83; Kendall, *History* 1: 519–522; *P.M.M.* 11 (1830): 362.

6 Brownsword, journal entry, 2 July 1820, in *P.P.M.* 2 (1821): 34–35; Bonsor, journal entries, 31 July, 1 August, 18 October 1820, ibid., pp. 33–34; *P.M.M.* 1 (1820): 245.

7 Bonsor submitted similarly optimistic reports during 1821 (journal entries, December 1820–June 1821, in *P.M.M.* 2 [1821]: 131–132, 188–190).

8 Obituary of Evan Thomas, *P.M.M.* 17 (1836): 416–418; obituary of Samuel Colfax, ibid. 3 (1822): 21.

9 Pratt, *Black Country Methodism*, pp. 42–45; John Walmsley to Mr. Owen, 16 October 1816 (M.A.); John Cloake to Jabez Bunting, 29 March 1820, in Ward, ed., *Early Correspondence*, p. 37. Birmingham and Dudley accounted for slightly less than three-fourths of the Wesleyan membership in 1819.

10 John Britain, journal entry, 18 June 1830, *P.M.M.* 11 (1830): 361.

11 [Clowes], *Journals*, p. 173.

12 Robert Wood to Jabez Bunting, 4 April 1818 (M.A.).

13 James Everett to James Sigston, 14 August 1820 (M.A.).

14 Gilbert, journal entries, 12–13 July 1820, in *P.M.M.* 2 (1821): 213–215.

15 An incident at Horbury in September 1820 illustrates the anti-authoritarian sentiments of the people. While Joseph Brook was preaching outdoors to an audience of 500, the local parson sent a constable to arrest him. The crowd refused to let the constable near Brook and begged the missionary to remain overnight in the village (Brook, journal entries, 12–13 September 1820, ibid., p. 120).

16 John Day, quoted in *P.M.M.* 12 (1831): 314. Day was a class leader at Flockton who joined the Primitive Methodist society in 1820.

17 Obituary of George Buckley, *P.M.M.* 17 (1836): 341–342.

18 William Taylor, journal entry, 1820, ibid. 2 (1821): 41–42; Thomas Holloday, journal entry, 1821, ibid. 3 (1822): 35.

19 Obituary of Samuel Kirk, ibid. 8 (1827): 335–336; obituary of George Taylor, ibid., pp. 222–223, 263.

20 George Chisholm to F. White, 2 November 1820, in *P.M.M.* 2 (1821): 21–22; *P.M.M.* 2 (1821): 228, 251–252; 4 (1823); 175: 40 (1859): 557.

21 John Taylor, *Reminiscences of Isaac Marsden of Doncaster* (2d ed., London, 1892), pp. 5–6. See also William Taylor, journal entry, 16 March 1821, in *P.M.M.* 2 (1821): 254.

22 Gilbert, journal entry, 5 August 1821, in *P.M.M.* 3 (1822): 34; Holloday, journal entries, 1822, ibid., pp. 34, 213.

23 Bourne, *History*, p. 71; Gilbert, journal entry, 3 June 1821, in *P.M.M.* 3 (1822): 10; Holloday, journal entries, May–June 1821, ibid., pp. 69–70, 109.

24 *P.M.M.* 1 (1820): 245; 2 (1821): 254.

25 Philip Ahier, "Lectures on Methodism in Huddersfield," pp. 45–46, Methodist Archives.

26 The Wesleyans lost 340 members from the Huddersfield and Holmfirth circuits between the summer of 1819 and that of 1820. The total in the Huddersfield New Connexion circuit fell by almost 100 during the same period, a phenomenon attributed by the conference of 1820 to economic distress (*New Connexion Minutes*, 1820, p. 35). According to the conference address, destitution "so dispirited the minds of many of our members" and "excited feelings so acute that they have withdrawn from their classes . . . and almost abandoned themselves to hopeless despondency." The Methodist New Connexion was especially strong around Halifax and Huddersfield, where the weavers were suffering from the negative effects of the putting-out system.

27 Joel Mallinson, *History of Methodism in Huddersfield, Holmfirth, and Denby Dale* (London, 1898), pp. 78–79. The Ranter camp meeting at Wolfstones coincided with a "great revival" in progress around Thong and Honley. Holloday initiated the conversion of Edward Brooke, a gentleman who later conducted cottage meetings among the weavers and prayed with workers in the mills. Brooke worshiped for a short time with the Primitive Methodists but later became a Wesleyan local preacher (John Holt Lord, *Squire Brooke:*

A Memorial of Edward Brooke of Fieldhouses, near Huddersfield [London and Leeds, 1874], pp. 10–12, 42).

28 Holloday, in *P.M.M.* 6 (1825): 261.

29 Chapman, *John Wesley & Co.*, p. 50; William Myles to John North, 5 October 1819 (M.A.); *New Connexion Minutes*, 1818, p. 37; Holloday, journal entry, 10 January 1822, in *P.M.M.* 3 (1822): 213; Thomas Preston to Joseph Agar, 30 April 1822 (M.A.); Preston to Jabez Bunting, 2 February 1821 (M.A.); Letter of John Whiteley, 28 November 1821, in *P.M.M.* 3 (1822): 100–101; Myles to Jabez Bunting, 18 August 1820, in Ward, ed., *Early Correspondence*, p. 47. The society at Sowerby Bridge met in a large auction chamber lent by John Whiteley. A constable in the village, he was pleased to note that, since the arrival of the Primitive Methodists, "there are not half the robberies committed in these parts that there were before."

30 Quoted in John Mayhall, *The Annals and History of Leeds and Other Places in the County of York from the Earliest Period to the Present Time* (Leeds, 1860), p. 687.

31 Leeds had 62,534 inhabitants in 1811 and 83,758 in 1821. The population was twenty times larger in 1841 than it had been in 1700, and between 1801 and 1841 it tripled (Frank Beckwith, "The Population of Leeds during the Industrial Revolution," *Thoresby Miscellany* 12 [1954]: 177–178). Only after the Municipal Corporations Act was passed in 1835 did Leeds acquire a borough government that would concern itself with matters like sanitation and street paving.

32 W. R. W. Stephens, *The Life and Letters of Walter Farquhar Hook* (7th ed., London, 1885), pp. 240–241. The New Connexion had 664 members in 1819. Its Leeds circuit employed three itinerants and twenty-seven local preachers to serve seventeen societies. There were more than 4,000 members in the Wesleyan societies included in the Leeds circuit in 1820.

33 Beckwith, comp., *Book of Remembrance*, pp. 10–12. Bramwell was still popular in Leeds. An audience of almost 10,000 gathered in front of Sigston's school to hear a sermon delivered on the occasion of his funeral in 1818 (Sigston, *Life* 2: 370).

34 Wray, "Methodism in Leeds," pp. 55, 73.

35 In 1816 the conference had directed all itinerants to pray regularly for the monarch and for "all constituted civil authorities." The conference address of 1820 rejoiced that, in spite of economic distress during 1819, the majority of New Connexion Methodists had not been drawn into political activities (*New Connexion Minutes*, 1816, 1819, 1820).

36 Barfoot, "Gleanings," *P.M.M.*, n.s. 4 (1881): 147.

37 Samuel Smith to George Herod, n.d., in Beckwith, comp., *Book of Remembrance*, pp. 11–13.

38 [Clowes], *Journals*, pp. 170–171.

39 Beckwith, comp., *Book of Remembrance*, pp. 38, 47; *P.M.M.* 5 (1824): 604; Coulson, quoted in *P.M.M.* 11 (1830): 266. Although Leeds circuit was small in area, it boasted almost 1,000 members and employed sixteen preachers, nine probationers, and nine exhorters. In September 1821, only four months

after it attained circuit status, the quarterly meeting designated Bradford and Dewsbury as subsidiary missions. The plan for Bradford listed twelve places, the most distant of which was Otley; Dewsbury mission had thirteen stations and extended southwest almost to Huddersfield and Halifax. Facsimiles of the 1821 plans for Leeds and its missions are printed in Beckwith, n.p. The forty members at Great Horton were "mostly poor weavers," and the society at Armley, also a weaving village, had eighty adherents in 1822.

40 William H. Yarrow, *The History of Primitive Methodism in London* (London, 1876), pp. 10–19. In 1823 Leeds abdicated responsibility for the London mission. Hull adopted it, but, when Clowes visited there in 1824, he found the cause "heavy and sluggish." His conclusion: "It is more difficult to get souls converted in London than in the provinces." History proved him right. During the next half-century a series of abortive attempts were made to establish Primitive Methodism in the metropolis. When they were not simply ignored, the missionaries were harassed (ibid., pp. 21–26).

41 David Stoner to Joseph Entwisle, 11 December 1823 (M.A.).

42 It was, however, growth in the Bradford circuit that accounted for most of this advance. Membership there climbed from 324 in 1823 to 441 in 1824. Unlike Leeds, Bradford continued to grow during the late 1820s.

43 The number is not exact because there is no separate total for Tadcaster, which was still a branch of Hull. An estimate of 230 was used, since the figures available were 246 (in 1821) and 214 (in 1837).

44 Because Halifax was not opened until 1821, the issue of timing is irrelevant there. It should be remembered that there was a somewhat less delayed Wesleyan revival around Huddersfield in 1821.

45 *P.M.M.* 1 (1820): 230–231; ibid. 13 (1832): 319; Ann Brownsword, journal entries, 15 February 1820, ibid. 1 (1820): 233, 24 June 1820, ibid. 2 (1821): 19; Thomas Webb, journal entry, 19 March 1820, ibid. 1 (1820): 234.

46 W. B. Stephens, ed., *History of Congleton* (Manchester, 1970), pp. 86, 138, 217–218.

47 J. B. Dyson, *The History of Wesleyan Methodism in the Congleton Circuit* (London, 1856), pp. 124–130; *P.M.M.*, n.s. 11 (1888): 158.

48 Robert Pilter to Maximilian Wilson, 9 June 1820 (M.A.); Mort, quoted in Lockley, *Story of Stockport*, p. 38; Christopher Atkinson, in *New Connexion Magazine* 70 (1867): 4.

49 *P.M.M.* 2 (1821): 19.

50 Ibid. 7 (1826): 490–491; Bourne, diary entries, 4–5 June 1820, 26 August 1820, in Walford, *Memoirs* 2: 93, 95.

51 For a discussion of Peterloo as a manifestation of "class war" on the part of the Manchester yeomanry , see Thompson, *Making of the English Working Class*, pp. 752–754.

52 Joseph Entwisle to Jabez Bunting, 4 October 1808 (M.A.); Bunting to George Marsden, 24 June 1815 (M.A.); John Cranshaw to James Everett, 9 September 1819 (M.A.); John Stephens to Bunting, 1 February 1821, in Ward, ed., *Early Correspondence*, pp. 61–62; John Riles to Bunting, 18 September 1923 (M.A.).

53 John Stephens, *The Mutual Relations, Claims, and Duties of the Rich and the Poor* (3d ed., Manchester, 1819), p. iii; *Letter to the Reverend John Stephens*, pp. 7–8. Stephens delivered his sermon on 12 September 1819; the fact that the printed version reached a third edition before the end of the year suggests that it enjoyed a sizable readership. Among the radicals at Bolton it was said that Stephens had "'received a cheque for £10,000 for services done to Government, signed *Sidmouth*'" (Ward, *Religion and Society*, p. 89).

54 Jackson, *Recollections*, pp. 173–176; Stephens to Bunting, 1 February 1821, in Ward, ed., *Early Correspondence*, p. 62. A white top hat was the badge of Henry Hunt, a colorful demagogue who liked to be called the "Champion of Liberty." The foremost public speaker of the reform movement, "Orator" Hunt had been billed as the central attraction at the meeting that became "Peterloo." At the time of the incident described by Jackson, wearing a white hat was a way of identifying oneself as a political radical and of advertising sympathy with the now imprisoned "St. Henry of Ilchester."

55 Stephens to Bunting, 9 February 1821, in Ward, ed., *Early Correspondence*, p. 62; *P.M.M.* 2 (1821): 19–20; Walter Carter, journal entries, 30 June–2 July, 22 July 1821, in *P.M.M.* 3 (1822): 11–12; John Verity, journal entries, 22 July, 21–22 August 1821, ibid., pp. 44–45.

56 *P.M.M.* 3 (1822): 263.

57 Waller's account of his conversion and early experiences as a Primitive Methodist local preacher were printed in *P.M.M.* 3 (1822): 259–263, 281–284. See also Kendall, *History* 2: 17–19, and Ward, *Religion and Society*, p. 125.

58 Kendall, *History* 2: 36. Within four years of Hathorn's arrival in Manchester, southeastern Lancashire had four Primitive Methodist circuits with a combined membership of almost 2,000.

6 / The Primitive Methodist Experience

1 Bourne, *History*, p. 6.

2 Barker, *Catechism*, p. 35.

3 Bourne, *History*, pp. 66–67. The Wesleyan conference included no lay delegates. Itinerants representing district meetings were free to participate, but all conference decisions were liable to veto by the Legal Hundred. Until 1814 vacancies in this body were filled solely on the basis of seniority; thereafter, the conference was allowed to fill every fourth vacancy from among those young preachers who had itinerated for a minimum of fourteen years. In the New Connexion conference the ratio of laymen to preachers was one to one.

4 Also published in pamphlet form, this article was written by Hugh Bourne, who believed it to be "the first treatise on chairmaning [sic] ever published in England" (*History*, p. 55).

5 *P.M.M.* 1 (1820): 208–213, 215.

6 Ibid., pp. 214–215, 217–219.

7 Kendall, *History* 1: 358–359; Walford, *Memoirs* 2: 92, 100–103, 112.

8 John Coulson to John Walford, 1853, in Walford, *Memoirs* 2: 127.

 9 Ibid., pp. 131–136; Bateman, "Early Days," *P.M.M.*, n.s. 5 (1882): 221–223.
10 Statistics on membership were not even recorded in 1826. Bateman stated that some traveling preachers had falsified numbers (presumably to compensate for declines in membership).
11 John Harvey, *A Lecture on the Jubilee of Primitive Methodism* (London and Leeds, 1861), p. 15. The same factors were blamed by John Petty (*History*, pp. 251–252).
12 Bateman, "Early Days," *P.M.M.*, n.s. 5 (1882): 282.
13 *General Minutes of the Primitive Methodist Connexion*, Minutes of 1830, p. 5; Kendall, *History* 1: 378. Perhaps by way of reacting to his own early career as a bit of a fop, Clowes held strong convictions about the need for Primitive Methodists to wear unadorned clothing and simple hairstyles. This belief, reflected in several of his journal entries, was based on two rationales: plainness in dress was enjoined by the gospel, and it made the Ranters readily identifiable. A mourner in Leicestershire, wrote Clowes, "got liberty" just because, by following some women who were wearing plain bonnets, he found himself led to a Primitive Methodist prayer meeting ([Clowes], *Journals*, p. 127).
14 Reproduced in Kendall, *History* 1: 380.
15 Walford, *Memoirs* 1: 337.
16 Kendall, *History* 1: 517.
17 Interview, *P.M.M.*, n.s. 4 (1881): 221.
18 Ibid. 6 (1825): 270. Keeping preaching appointments on time had to be achieved with little recourse to clocks or watches, aids to punctuality that most of the poor did not own.
19 Kendall, *History* 1: 372.
20 *P.M.M.* 1 (1820): 210–211.
21 "Personal Recollections of the Late Alderman Henry Smethurst, J.P., of Grimsby," ibid., 2d n.s. 1 (1894): 517. Evidently Smethurst was one of those Methodists who moved up the social and economic ladder just as Wesley had predicted would happen.
22 Barker, *Catechism*, p. 36.
23 *P.M.M.* 4 (1823): 118, 228–230.
24 *Buck's Theological Dictionary*, quoted in *P.M.M.* 27 (1846): 180.
25 Wesley F. Swift, "The Women Itinerant Preachers of Early Methodism," *Proceedings of the Wesley Historical Society* 29 (1953): 84.
26 Joseph Ritson, *The Romance of Primitive Methodism* (London, 1909), p. 136.
27 John Wesley to Mary Bosanquet, 18 June 1771, in Zechariah Taft, *Biographical Sketches of the Lives and Public Ministry of Various Holy Women* (2 vols., Leeds, 1825, 1828), 1: 34. Wesley had repeated this line of reasoning in letters addressed to Sarah Mallet between 1787 and 1790. These implied that he expected her to travel, but that she would not do so unaccompanied or in the absence of male counsel (ibid., pp. 85–90).
28 The full quotation from Barker, *Catechism*, p. 37, is as follows: "Females, while invited to be useful in leading classes, visiting the afflicted, teaching the young, and exhibiting lovely examples of domestic piety, are not introduced

into stations of authority and publicity." Barker itinerated for the New Connexion from 1817 until his death in 1830. His was the accepted view in the 1820s.

29 Shaw, *Bible Christians*, p. 33. According to the listing in Oliver A. Beckerlegge, *United Methodist Ministers and Their Circuits* (London, 1968), almost half of the Bible Christian itinerants in 1820 were female.

30 A woman persuaded that she had an extraordinary call to preach might address only other women, only in her home circuit or by written invitation from the head of another circuit, and only after gaining the approval of both her superintendent and the quarterly meeting (*Wesleyan Conference Minutes* 2: 187).

31 Nightingale, *Portraiture*, p. 455; Jabez Bunting to George Marsden, 18 October 1803 (M.A.); John Pawson to the Wesleyan Society at Dover, 25 October 1802 (M.A.); Zacharias Taft, *A Reply to an Article Inserted in the "Methodist Magazine" for April 1809, Entitled "Thoughts on Women's Preaching Extracted from Dr. James McKnight"* (Leeds, 1809), p. iii. Taft was married to the famous and now officially silenced revivalist Mary Barritt.

32 *P.M.M.* 5 (1824): 26, 51–53, 73, 123, 147, 169.

33 Hymns no. 28 and no. 29, in Bourne, comp., *Hymns*, n.p.; John Skevington, journal entry, 24 February 1822, *P.M.M.* 4 (1823): 46; obituary of John Shaw, *P.M.M.* 1 (1819): 144.

34 *P.M.M.* 56 (1875): 108.

35 Joseph Peart, letter, 11 January 1825, ibid. 6 (1825): 156–159. In this letter Peart described the astonishing progress of Primitive Methodism among the colliers of North Shields.

36 Walford, *Memoirs* 2: 202.

37 William Howitt, *The Rural Life of England* (3d ed. rev., 1844, reprinted in The Development of Industrial Society Series, Shannon, 1971), pp. 267–269.

38 Kendall, *History* 2: 44. Garner's remark was made during an indoor revival, but the same attitude prevailed at camp meetings. Such physical manifestations, however, became increasingly less usual. Clowes, whose "shouts of glory" had once resounded through the streets of Tunstall and "made the chapel like a cock-pit," had "since been convinced that religion does not consist in bodily movements, whether shouting, jumping, falling, or standing" ([Clowes], *Journals*, pp. 46, 74). In 1828 Bourne observed of trances: "And in revivals this thing still occasionally breaks out. It is a subject at present not well understood and which requires to be peculiarly guarded against impropriety and imposture" (journal entry, 23 October 1828, in Walford, *Memoirs* 2: 180–181).

39 Jonathan Ireland, quoted in Kendall, *History* 2: 33; Howitt, *Rural Life*, p. 568.

40 Kendall, *History* 2: 33–34.

41 Obituary of Thomas Taylor, *P.M.M.* 11 (1830): 352–353.

42 An observer reported hearing the "wild sound" of a Primitive Methodist hymn drifting over a "dim heath where they were holding their camp meetings": "It was the dialogue of a spirit questioning and answering itself in the

passage of death and the entrance into the happy land, and the chorused words of 'All is well!—All is well!' came over the shadowy waste with an unearthly effect" (Howitt, *Rural Life*, p. 568).

43 Bourne, comp., *Hymns*, n.p. This is the 1832 edition of the hymnal. The extracts quoted are from hymns that appeared in the 1809 *Camp Meeting Hymn Book*. They are numbered and were quoted from in the following sequence: nos. 17, 51, 25, 54, 26, 36, 55, 99, 24, 23, 9.

44 [Clowes], *Journals*, pp. 46, 21.

45 Walford, *Memoirs* 2: 77, 81, 142–143.

46 Bateman, "Early Days," *P.M.M.*, n.s. 4 (1881): 36.

47 Kendall, *History* 1: 372.

48 Nathaniel West, journal entry, 14 March 1824, in *P.M.M.* 6 (1825): 213.

49 Bourne, "Experience," ibid. 16 (1835): 151–152.

50 [Clowes], *Journals*, p. 81. One such anecdote told of an elderly churchman, adept at praying from a book, who failed to heed Clowes's warning that he must be "born again" or spend eternity "shut up in hell." The old man died suddenly just a week after putting Clowes off with the vague promise to hear him preach "another time." Clowes found him in a brook where he had fallen en route home from the Cheadle wake (ibid., pp. 105–106). Clowes's preaching so terrified one convert that he could neither eat nor sleep (*P.M.M.* 14 [1833]: 104–105).

51 Herod, in Beckwith, *Book of Remembrance*, pp. 26–27.

52 *P.M.M.* 18 (1837): 373.

53 Ibid. 2 (1821): 151–153.

54 Ibid., pp. 63–67.

55 Ibid. 4 (1823): 83–85, 103, 125–126.

56 All of these examples—and there were many like them—were taken from obituaries of people who joined the Primitive Methodist Connexion before 1822.

57 Obituary of Ann Wilson, *P.M.M.* 11 (1830): 212–215.

58 Ibid. 13 (1832): 228–233; ibid. 14 (1833): 379; Kendall, *History* 2: 25.

59 The content of this paragraph was based on obituaries published in the *Primitive Methodist Magazine:* 3 (1822): 42; 6 (1825): 369; 24 (1843): 329–330; 9 (1828): 105; 11 (1830): 272–274; 8 (1827): 120–124; 22 (1841): 424–426; 10 (1829): 81–89.

60 Ibid. 13 (1832): 304; 5 (1824): 71–72; 10 (1829): 281; 15 (1834): 105–107; 2 (1821): 173; 3 (1822): 55, 147; 12 (1831): 381–382.

61 The statistics cited were based on the eighty-one obituaries that were printed in volumes 1–3 of the connexional magazine, plus the nineteen most detailed ones from the fourth volume.

62 This would not have been true of the general membership, of course. These having been the first obituaries, they also gave the impression that Primitive Methodists had an unusually brief life-span; thirty of the ninety-one whose ages were stated died before they were twenty-five.

63 In some cases the occupations of fathers or husbands were used in compiling these figures.

64 Although occupational listings were made for all counties, statistics were compiled only for Leicestershire and Derbyshire.

65 *P.M.M.* 10 (1829): 192; ibid. 7 (1826): 139; ibid. 1 (1820): 26; ibid. 13 (1832): 104–105; [Clowes], *Journals*, p. 76; *P.M.M.* 10 (1829): 43–46; ibid., n.s. 4 (1881): 369.

66 *P.M.M.* 2 (1821): 8.

67 Robert Currie, *Methodism Divided: A Study in the Sociology of Ecumenicalism* (London, 1968), p. 90. Primitive Methodist membership never exceeded 1 percent of the total population aged fifteen and over. The ratio of two "hearers" to one member is based on the statistics collected on "Census Sunday" in 1851 and is often used by authors writing about nineteenth-century Methodism.

68 *P.M.M.* 5 (1824): 147.

69 Ibid. 3 (1822): 200.

70 Bourne, comp., *Hymns*, pp. viii–xii; [Clowes], *Journals*, p. 59.

71 *P.M.M.* 9 (1828): 118–121; ibid. 17 (1836): 31; ibid. 18 (1837): 391.

72 Ibid. 3 (1822): 31–33; ibid. 4 (1823): 62–63.

73 Religious females figured prominently in diary entries made by Bourne between 1807 and 1811. He greatly admired "Praying Nanny" Cutler at this time, but mentions of women as "mothers" in the societies appeared more often than references to females as revivalists. Bourne published his pamphlet, *Remarks on the Ministry of Women*, in 1808 while he was under the influence of the Quaker Methodists.

74 Kendall, *History* 1: 244. The use of boys as preachers became even more common after 1840. John Petty, the connexion's other historian, was still wearing knee breeches when he began preaching.

75 Ibid., p. 10; Bourne, journal entries, 18 June 1816, September 1816, 6 April 1818, in Walford, *Memoirs* 2: 2, 28.

76 *P.M.M.* 1 (1819–1820): 10–13, 13–14, 92–98, 147; ibid. 4 (1823): 94–95. "A Treatise on the Duty of Parents" was serialized in vol. 4.

77 It was also in 1824 that the Wesleyans began publishing *The Child's Magazine and Sunday-Scholar's Companion*. This was the forerunner of *The Kiddies' Magazine*, which later claimed the distinction of being the first periodical for children (Frank Cumbers, *The Book Room* [London, 1956], p. 63). Later in the century, as new members increasingly came from Primitive Methodist homes, the connexion also published a *Juvenile Magazine* and *Springtime: A Magazine for Our Young Men and Maidens*. The circulation figure for the *Children's Magazine* appears in Kendall, *History* 2: 12. A facsimile for the first page of the first number of "this excessively rare publication" is on p. 11.

78 Walford, *Memoirs* 2: 122.

79 *P.M.M.* 4 (1823): 182. The writer of this communication, George Hanford, claimed that "many" in the county of Leicester had benefited from reading the obituaries.

80 Bourne, journal entry, 12 January 1811, in Walford, *Memoirs* 1: 304.

81 *General Minutes of the Primitive Methodist Connexion*, Minutes of 1829,

p. 4. Regulations governing the use of tobacco began to appear in 1822. In 1823 a traveling preacher was allowed to smoke if a physician stated in writing that this was a "necessity." Six years later, itinerants were advised to deal with the problem of "wind" by smoking camomile flowers or by swallowing a spoonful of mustard seeds with a water chaser. "This is a fine remedy" that "sets aside all need of tobacco."

82 *P.M.M.* 1 (1820): 218.

83 Ibid. 14 (1833): 184.

84 Kendall, *History* 2: 472.

85 Bourne, in Kendall, *History* 1: 151. Bourne began to distrust extraordinary perceptions of the divine will long before 1828, when he counseled two young women: "(1) None to go in vision if they can avoid it. (2) Not to lay too much stress on it. (3) That faith . . . is greater than these things." These were the "general advices usually given in our Connexion" (journal entry, 23 October 1828, in Walford, *Memoirs* 2: 180–181).

86 James Wood, *An Address to the Members of the Methodist Societies on Several Interesting Subjects* (London, 1812), p. 4.

87 Bourne, journal entry, 12 July 1829, in Walford, *Memoirs* 2: 184; journal entry, 17 October 1811, ibid. 1: 340; Kendall, *History* 2: 278, 312.

88 Printed in Walford, *Memoirs* 1: 169–170.

89 *P.M.M.* 26 (1845): 559–561; ibid. 56 (1875): 108, 615; Robson, ed., *Silsden Primitive Methodism*, pp. 1–2, 5–6, 11, 55, 312–313, 345, 402, 405–407, 411–413.

90 The Bible Christians, the Methodist New Connexion, and the United Methodist Free Churches came together in 1907 to form the United Methodist Church. This body, the Wesleyan Methodist Church, and the Primitive Methodist Church amalgamated in 1932. On the subject of the latter see John C. Bowmer, "Methodist Union," *Proceedings of the Wesley Historical Society* 43 (1982): 101–110.

91 Smith, "Anecdotes and Facts," quoted in Kendall, *History* 1: 122.

92 Bourne, in Kendall, *History* 1: 138.

93 Walford, *Memoirs* 2: 103.

94 [Hugh Bourne], *The Christian Baptist: On the Mode of Baptizing, Intended as a Check to Discord Sowing* (2d ed., Bemersley, 1828). The pamphlet was reprinted in *P.M.M.* 10 (1829), where the quoted phrase appears on p. 405.

95 Bourne, journal entries, 9–10 December 1819, 17, 21 November 1819, in Walford, *Memoirs* 2: 67–70; journal entry, 28 December 1817, ibid., pp. 13, 21.

96 Bourne, journal entries, 1843, ibid., pp. 298, 301. A nineteenth-century biographer explained that Bourne "was aware of the difficulty of preserving spirituality of mind in the atmosphere of political agitation, and the danger that if politics and religion became mixed in the church and in the pulpit, the interests of religion were almost sure to be damaged" (William Antliff, *The Life of Hugh Bourne* [2d ed. rev. Colin McKechnie, London, 1892], p. 160).

97 Bourne, in Antliff, *Life*, pp. 180–181.

98 Ibid., pp. 100–101.

99 Thomas Bateman, in Kendall, *History* 1: 491.

100 In 1836 itinerants were forbidden to speak at political meetings or parliamentary elections. Membership in secret orders was also banned (*General Minutes of the Conferences of the Primitive Methodist Connexion* 2: 37).

101 H.O., 42/200, 1819, in Robert F. Wearmouth, *Methodism and the Working Class Movements of England, 1800–1850* (London, 1937), p. 169.

102 Kendall, *History* 1: 336–338. Kendall quoted from "a short MS account" written by Skevington. Skevington's break with Primitive Methodism in 1836 was connected with financial problems concerning the Loughborough chapel, for which he was the trust treasurer. He later wrote of the sect, "I still revere it." His application for readmission was denied in a note penned by Bourne (ibid., p. 339).

103 Obituary of Joseph Harrison, *P.M.M.* 51 (1870): 679–680. There is no Joseph Harrison listed as an itinerant in the relevant minutes of either the Wesleyan or the New Connexion.

104 Joseph Featherstone, quoted in *P.M.M.* 21 (1840): 330.

105 Robert Pilter to Jabez Bunting, 23 October 1819, in Ward, ed., *Early Correspondence*, 21–23. In fact, the offender was finally expelled, and many sympathizers departed in protest. For a time most went to a new Independent Methodist chapel, where the political creed was antirevolutionary, but "petition for a reform of abuses" was considered one of their "privileges as Englishmen." The Independent Methodists had financial difficulties, and in 1821 they suffered a schism. In 1822 the Ranters did "greedily gather up" many Tynesiders (Pilter to Bunting, 5 July 1820, ibid., p. 39; H. Kelly, *An Impartial History of Independent Methodism in the Counties of Durham and Northumberland* [Newcastle, 1824], pp. 10–13, 17, 22–24).

106 Herod, *Biographical Sketches*, pp. 12–13.

107 Robert Key, quoted in Ritson, *Romance of Primitive Methodism*, pp. 284–285.

108 France to Thomas Jackson, 14 November 1816 (M.A.).

109 Petty, *History*, pp. 151–152.

110 Entwisle to Miss Tooth, 9 February 1821 (M.A.); Entwisle to George Marsden, 13 February 1821 (M.A.). Conversions may also have been encouraged by two other factors: David Stoner, Entwisle's colleague in the circuit, was one of the few revival preachers still active in the Wesleyan Connexion, and the Liverpool guidelines had by then been implemented in Bradford.

111 James Myers, *A History of Primitive Methodism in Guiseley* (Guiseley, 1910), p. 19; *P.M.M.* 6 (1825): 238; Kendall, *History* 2: 43.

112 *P.M.M.* 14 (1833): 376–377. Tommy Hepburn and his lieutenants in the United Colliers had Primitive Methodist backgrounds (Robert Colls, *The Collier's Rant: Song and Culture in the Industrial Village* [London and Totowa, N.J., 1977], p. 100). The Primitive Methodist conference of 1832 suggested means of dealing with a member who "walks disorderly," but did not specify what such conduct was (*General Minutes of the Conferences of the Primitive Methodist Connexion* 2, Minutes of 1832, p. 3). Participation in a strike may or may not have fallen into this category. It is worth noting

that less than half the gains made in 1831–1832 were forfeited after the strikes failed. The "movings" in South Shields may have been prompted by evictions, since, like pubs and company stores, houses were ordinarily owned by the proprietors of the mines. Losses in these three northern circuits were atypical; circuits elsewhere grew during the cholera epidemic, and these increases were reflected in the membership totals reported in 1833.

113 *P.M.M.* 19 (1838): 352–355.
114 Woodcock, *Piety among the Peasantry*, pp. 169–170.
115 Robson, ed., *Silsden Primitive Methodism*, pp. 83–84.
116 In *Methodism and the Trade Unions* Robert Wearmouth observed that of eighty religiously inclined trade union leaders active between 1880 and 1930, forty-six were Primitive Methodists, even though the connexion claimed only one-third of the Methodist membership in Great Britain (p. 38).
117 Quoted in Walford, *Memoirs* 2: 142.
118 *P.M.M.* 20 (1839): 22, 57–61.

Conclusion

1 Currie, Gilbert, and Horsley, *Churches and Churchgoers*, pp. 140–141; Currie, *Methodism Divided*, p. 95.
2 John Harrison has suggested that, for its followers, popular millenarianism supplied a needed "new ideology to take account of the disruption or weakening of the old social order and to sanction new aspirations" (*Second Coming*, p. 219). Primitive Methodism performed the same service for a different and larger group of people.
3 The districts identified by Howitt in the late 1830s as still "primitive" were also areas where Primitive Methodism was able to gain a following (*Rural Life*, pp. 100, 108, 466).
4 A. H. John, "Farming in Wartime: 1793–1815," in E. L. Jones and G. E. Mingay, eds., *Land, Labour, and Population in the Industrial Revolution: Essays Presented to J. D. Chambers* (London, 1964), pp. 30–31, 33–34.
5 Howitt, *Rural Life*, p. 390.
6 Elie Halévy, *England in 1815*, trans. E. I. Watkin and D. A. Barker (2d ed. rev., New York, 1949), p. 41. Halévy estimated that half of the magistrates were clergymen, but cited Cobbett's claim that in rural areas two-thirds of them were. He also noted that Sidney and Beatrice Webb gave the figure of one-quarter for 1832.
7 Particularly insightful with regard to this topic are W. R. Ward's book, *Religion and Society in England, 1790–1850*, and his article, "The Tithe Question in England in the Early Nineteenth Century," *Journal of Ecclesiastical History* 16 (1965): 67–81.
8 John L. Hammond and Barbara Hammond, *The Town Labourer, 1760–1832* (new ed., London, 1928), pp. 24–27.
9 Bateman, "Early Days," *P.M.M.*, n.s. 4 (1881): 296; Kendall, *History* 2: 9.
10 Barker, *Catechism*, pp. 35–36.

11 Robert Hopkins to Jabez Bunting, 3 August 1820 (M.A.).

12 Thomas Stanley to James Everett, 23 September 1820 (M.A.).

13 Ritson, *Romance of Primitive Methodism*, p. 208.

14 Zachariah Taft to Jabez Bunting, [18] May 1822, in Ward, ed., *Early Correspondence*, p. 89.

15 Robert Johnson to Jabez Bunting, 4 December 1824, in Ward, ed., *Early Correspondence*, pp. 102–103.

16 [Clowes], *Journals*, p. 209.

17 Letter, Joseph Reynolds, 8 August 1821, in *P.M.M.* 2 (1821): 184.

18 Ritson, *Romance of Primitive Methodism*, p. 81.

19 Hatton, *Methodist Remembrances*, p. 17.

20 Jackson, *Recollections*, pp. 148–149.

21 *Strictures on the Truth and Primitive Methodism* (Hull, n.d.), p. 15.

22 Currie, Gilbert, and Horsley, *Churches and Churchgoers*, p. 216.

23 Semmel, *Methodist Revolution*, p. 169.

24 Bunting, *Life* 2: 177.

25 Barker, *Catechism*, p. 35. See also Kendall, *History* 1: 311.

26 *Methodist Magazine* 44 (1821): 461–462.

27 Bunting, *Life* 2: 193–194.

28 *Methodist Magazine* 44 (1821): 534–535.

29 Wray, "Methodism in Leeds," pp. 86, 113.

30 *Methodist Magazine* 44 (1821): 381.

31 *Wesleyan Methodist Magazine* 1 (1822): 96–98, 164–166.

32 Ibid., p. 250. This comment was made with reference to the "shutting down of [Richard] Carlile's shop," an action which the *Magazine* highly approved.

Select Bibliography

I. Contemporary and Near-Contemporary Sources

A. Manuscripts
Methodist Church Archives, John Rylands University Library of Manchester:
Barrett, Robert Newton. "Extracts from the Unpublished Journal of One of John Wesley's Ministers, *viz.*, Reverend John Barritt."
Preachers' Letters and Portraits Collection.
Unpublished Minutes of the Methodist New Connexion, 1797–1823.
Wray, Thomas. "Facts Connected with the History of Methodism in Leeds and Its Vicinity."

B. Minutes, Regulations, and Resolutions
General Minutes of the Conferences of the Primitive Methodist Connexion. Vols. 1–2 (1814–1840).
The General Rules of the Methodists of the New Connexion. Hanley, 1823.
Minutes of a Meeting Held at Nottingham in the Month of August, 1819, by the Delegates of the Society of People Called Primitive Methodists. Nottingham, 1819.
Minutes of the Conversations between Preachers and Delegates in the Methodist New Connexion. 1797–1820.
Minutes of the Methodist Conferences, from the First Held in London by the Late Reverend John Wesley, A.M. in the Year 1744. Vols. 1–5 (1744–1824).
Minutes of the Yearly Meetings of the Independent Methodists. 1813–1815.
Resolutions of a Meeting of the General Committee of the Societies of the Late Reverend John Wesley Convened for the Purpose of Taking into Consideration a Bill Brought into the House of Lords by the Right Honourable Lord Viscount Sidmouth. London, 1811.
Resolutions of the Methodist Ministers of the Manchester District, Assembled at Liverpool, May 23, 1811, on the Subject of a Bill Introduced into Parliament by the Right Honourable Lord Viscount Sidmouth, to Which Is Added an Abstract of the Debate in the House of Lords on Tuesday, May 21, 1811, When the Said Bill Was Rejected. Liverpool, 1811.
Rules of the Independent Wesleyan Society Established in Manchester, March 16, 1825. Manchester, 1825.

C. Methodist Periodicals

Arminian Magazine, Consisting of Extracts and Original Treatises on Universal Redemption. Vols. 1–20 (1778–1797).

Methodist Magazine, Being a Continuation of the Arminian Magazine. Vols. 21–44 (1798–1821).

Methodist Magazine for the Year 1819, Conducted by the Camp-Meeting Methodists Known by the Name of Ranters, Called Also Primitive Methodists. Vol. 1 (1819–1820).

Methodist Magazine, or Evangelical Repository (New Connexion). Vols. 1–18 (1798–1815).

Primitive Methodist Children's Magazine. Vol. 3 (1827).

Primitive Methodist Magazine. Vols. 2–58 (1821–1877); n.s., vols. 1–26 (1878–1903).

Tent Methodists' Magazine and Register of Events Connected with the Spread of the Gospel at Home. Vol. 1 (1823).

Wesleyan Methodist Magazine. Vol. 1 (1822).

D. Books, Articles, and Pamphlets

An Address to the Lower Class of His Parishioners on the Subject of Methodism. Ipswich, 1806.

Atmore, Charles, and Blanshard, Thomas, in Behalf of a Committee Appointed by Conference. *Letter to the Societies in the Connexion Established by the Late Reverend John Wesley.* London, 1819.

Bailey, Thomas. *History of the County of Nottingham.* Vol. 4. London and Nottingham, n.d.

Baines, Edward. *History, Directory, and Gazetteer of the County Palatine of Lancaster.* Vol. 2. Liverpool, 1825.

Barker, David. *A Catechism of the Methodist New Connexion, Shewing the Origin of That Community, with the Great Principles on Which It Is Founded.* London and Ashton-under-Lyne, 1834.

[Bateman, Thomas]. *Memoir of the Life and Labours of Mr. John Wedgwood.* London, 1870.

[Bateman, Thomas]. "Reminiscences of the Early Days of the Primitive Methodist Connexion." Serialized in *Primitive Methodist Magazine,* n.s., 3–5 (1880–1882).

[Bateman, Thomas]. "Reminiscences of Village Preaching Over Fifty Years Ago." *Primitive Methodist Magazine,* n.s., 3 (1880): 99–105.

[Beaumont, George]. *The Helmet; or, An Answer to the Eighth Resolution of the Minutes of Conference . . . 1813.* Sheffield, n.d.

Beaumont, Joseph. *Memoirs of Mrs. Mary Tatham.* London, 1838.

Belsham, Thomas. *A Letter to the Right Honourable Lord Viscount Sidmouth upon the Subject of the Bill Lately Introduced by His Lordship into the House of Peers.* London, 1811.

Bicheno, James. *The Signs of the Times; or, The Overthrow of the Papal Tyranny in France the Prelude of Destruction to Popery and Despotism, but of Peace to Mankind.* London, n.d.

Blackner, J. *History of Nottingham.* Nottingham, 1815.

[Bourne, Hugh]. *The Christian Baptist: On the Mode of Baptizing, Intended as a Check to Discord Sowing.* 2d ed. Bemersley, 1828.

Bourne, Hugh, comp. *A Collection of Hymns for Camp Meetings, Revivals, &c. for the Use of the Primitive Methodists.* Bemersley, 1832.

[Bourne, Hugh]. "Experience of a Person in Regard to Acquiring a Knowledge of the Doctrine of a Present Salvation." *Primitive Methodist Magazine* 16 (1835): 32–36, 150–152, 376–380, 457–462.

Bourne, Hugh. *History of the Origins of the Primitive Methodists, Giving an Account of Their Rise and Progress up to the Year 1823.* 2d ed. Bemersley, 1835.

Bramwell, William, ed. *The Salvation Preacher, Recommended to the Serious Perusal of Preachers and People of All Denominations.* Nottingham, 1800.

Bramwell, William. *A Short Account of the Life and Death of Ann Cutler.* New ed. Whitby, 1819.

Burdekin, Richard. *Memoir of the Life and Character of Mr. Robert Spence of York.* York and London, 1827.

A Burning and Shining Light: A Memorial of William Clowes. 2d ed. London and Hull, 1851.

Byron, James. *Thoughts on the Evil of Persecution Occasioned by the Rioting at Newent.* Gloucester, 1806.

Church, Thomas. *Popular Sketches of Primitive Methodism.* New ed. London, 1850.

[Clark, Mary Ann]. *An Account of the Religious and Literary Life of Adam Clarke.* Edited by J. B. B. Clark. Vol. 2. London, 1833.

[Clowes, William]. *The Journals of William Clowes, a Primitive Methodist Preacher; Containing Chronicles of Events Relative to His Unregenerate State, His Conversion to God, His Call to the Ministry, the Commencement and Progress of the Primitive Methodist Connexion, and to His Itinerant Labours Therein from the Year 1810 to That of 1838.* London, 1844.

Cocking, Thomas. *The History of Wesleyan Methodism in Grantham and Its Vicinity.* London, 1836.

A Collection of Hymns for the Use of the Methodist New Connexion. 9th ed. Hanley, 1821.

Cooper, Thomas. *The Life of Thomas Cooper Written by Himself.* 4th ed. London, 1873.

Crowther, Jonathan. *The Methodist Manual.* Halifax, 1810.

Crowther, Jonathan. *A Portraiture of Methodism; or, The History of the Wesleyan Methodists.* London, 1815.

Curtis, John. *A Topographical History of the County of Leicester.* Ashby-de-la-Zouch, 1831.

Douglas, James. *Methodism Condemned; or, Priestcraft Detected.* Newcastle-on-Tyne, 1814.

Dow, Lorenzo. *A Collection of Spiritual Songs Used in the Great Revival at the Camp Meetings in America.* Liverpool, 1806.

Dow, Lorenzo. *The Dealings of God, Man, and the Devil, As Exemplified in the*

Life, Experience, and Travels of Lorenzo Dow . . . Together with His Polemic and Miscellaneous Writings Complete, to Which is Added "The Vicissitudes of Life" by Peggy Dow. 2d ed. Edited by John Dowling. 2 vols. in 1. Cincinnati, 1860.

Dow, Lorenzo. *Travels and Providential Experiences, &c. of Lorenzo Dow.* Dublin, 1806.

Dugdale, Thomas. *Curiosities of Great Britain: England, and Wales Delineated, Historical, Entertaining, and Commercial.* 8 vols. N.p., n.d.

Dunn, Samuel. *Memoirs of Mr. Thomas Tatham and of Wesleyan Methodism in Nottingham.* London, 1847.

[Entwisle, W.] *Memoir of the Reverend Joseph Entwisle, Fifty-four Years a Wesleyan Minister.* Bristol, 1848.

Everett, James. *Memoirs of the Life, Character, and Ministry of William Dawson.* London, 1842.

Everett, James. *The Polemic Divine; or, Memoirs of the Life, Writings, and Opinions of the Reverend Daniel Isaac.* 2d ed. Manchester and London, 1851.

Everett, James. *The Village Blacksmith; or, Piety and Usefulness Exemplified, in a Memoir of the Life of Samuel Hick.* 5th ed. London, 1834.

Falsehood Exposed; or, Truth Vindicated, Being a Critique of Mr. Nightingale's "Portraiture of Methodism." London, 1808.

A Few Words on the Increase of Methodism Occasioned by "Hints" of a Barrister and the Observations in the "Edinburgh Review." London, 1810.

Finney, Charles Grandison. *Lectures on Revivals of Religion.* 5th ed. London, 1838.

Furness, John. *The Principles and Conduct of Methodists Vindicated.* Shrewsbury, 1811.

Glover, Stephen. *The History of the County of Derby.* Edited by Thomas Noble. Vol. 2. Derby, 1829.

Greenwood, W. *Memoir of the Life, Ministry, and Correspondence of the Late Rev. George Sykes of Rillington.* Malton, 1827.

Hall, Robert, and Grundell, John, eds. *The Life of Mr. Alexander Kilham, Methodist Preacher.* Nottingham, [1799].

Hatton, William. *Methodist Remembrances, Comprising a Contrast Between the Original and Present State of Methodism and the Methodists.* Birmingham, 1823.

[Henshaw, William]. *Copy of an Interesting Letter from Mr. William Henshaw, Methodist Preacher, Plymouth Dock, to Mr. William Bramwell, Methodist Preacher, Birstall.* London, (1814).

Herod, George. *Historical and Biographical Sketches, Forming a Compendium of the History of the Primitive Methodist Connexion up to the Year 1823.* 2d ed. London, 1851.

Hill, John. *A Vindication of the Methodists in the Societies of the Late Reverend John Wesley, from Several Accusations of the Present Day, Especially Those Contained in the "Annual Review" of Mr. Arthur Aikin.* London, 1806.

History, Topography, and Directory of the Town of Nottingham, and the Adjacent Villages. Nottingham, 1834.

Hocken, Joshua. *A Brief History of Wesleyan Methodism in the Grimsby Circuit.* Grimsby, 1839.

Howitt, William. *The Rural Life of England.* 3d ed. rev., 1844. Reprinted in The Development of Industrial Society Series. Shannon, 1971.

Huntingford, George Isaac. *A Charge Delivered to the Clergy of the Diocese of Gloucester.* London, 1807.

Jackson, Thomas. *Memoirs of the Life and Writings of the Reverend Richard Watson.* 3d ed. London, 1840.

Jowett, John. *Disaster: A Poem Occasioned by the Breaking Down of the Ranters' Preaching House at Keighley.* Bradford, 1822.

The Jubilee of the Methodist New Connexion, Being a Grateful Memorial of the Origin, Government, and History of the Denomination. London, 1848.

Kelk, Thomas. *Thoughts on the Right Management of the Best Business in the World.* London, 1811.

Kelly, H. *An Impartial History of Independent Methodism in the Counties of Durham and Northumberland.* Newcastle, 1824.

Kilham, Alexander. *An Account of the Trial of Alexander Kilham, Methodist Preacher, before the General Conference in London.* Nottingham, [1796].

Lay Preaching Defended: A Few Plain Remarks for the Consideration of the People Called Methodists, Occasioned by the Conduct of Mr. Charles Atmore, Superintendent of the London East Circuit, toward the Community Preachers. London, 1820.

Lee, Jesse. *A Short History of the Methodists in the United States of America, Beginning in 1766 and Continued till 1809.* Baltimore, 1810.

A Letter to a Country Gentleman on the Subject of Methodism, Confined Chiefly to Its Causes, Progress and Consequences in His Own Neighbourhood. Ipswich, 1805.

A Letter to the Lord Bishop of Lincoln, Respecting the "Report from the Clergy of a District in the Diocese of Lincoln" in Which Report the Increase of Methodism Is Considered As a Cause of the Declension of Religion. London, 1800.

A Letter to the Reverend John Stephens Occasioned by Some Recent Transactions and Occurrences in the Methodist Society in Manchester. Manchester, 1820.

Mawer, William. *The Examiner Examined; or, An Apology for the Methodists, Being an Answer to Mr. Neesham's Examination.* Lincoln, 1810.

Memoir of the Life and Ministry of the Reverend William Bramwell, with Extracts from His Letters, by Members of His Family. London, 1848.

Memoirs of the Reverend David Stoner, Containing Copious Extracts from His Diary and Epistolary Correspondence. 4th ed. London, 1840.

Methodism in 1821, with Recollections of Primitive Methodism. London, 1821.

Mort, James. *An Address to Persons of All Religious Denominations but Especially to the Methodists of Both Connexions.* Huddersfield, 1814.

Nightingale, Joseph. *A Portrait of Methodism, Being an Impartial View of the Rise, Progress, Doctrines, and Manners of the Wesleyan Methodists, in a Series of Letters Addressed to a Lady.* London, 1807.

Observations on the Importance of Adopting a Plan of Instruction for Those Preachers Who Are Admitted upon Trial in the Methodist Connexion. London, 1807.

Parrott, John. *A Digest of Primitive Methodism.* 3d ed. rev. and enlarged. London, 1866.

The Patriot: A Tale Illustrating the Pernicious Effects of Bad Principles on the Lower Orders of Society. London, 1821.

Pawson, John. *A Letter from the Late Mr. Pawson to the General Conference of the Preachers of Late in Connexion with the Reverend John Wesley.* London, 1806.

A Portraiture of Hypocrisy; or, A Narrative of Facts . . . Relative to the Extraordinary Conduct and Numerous Artifices of the Reverend Joseph N-t-n-g-le. London, 1812.

Reilly, William. *A Memorial of the Ministerial Life of the Late Reverend Gideon Ouseley, Irish Missionary.* London and Dublin, 1847.

Remarks upon the Notion of Extraordinary Impulses and Impressions of the Imagination Indulged by Many Professors of Religion, Contained in a Letter to a Friend. Bristol, 1800.

Report from the Clergy of a District in the Diocese of Lincoln Convened for the Purpose of Considering the State of Religion in the Several Parishes in the Said District As Well As the Best Mode of Promoting the Belief and Practice of it, and of Guarding, As Much As Possible Against the Dangers Arising to the Church and Government of This Kingdom from the Alarming Increase of Profaneness and Irreligion on the One Hand, and from the False Doctrines and Evil Designs of Fanatic and Seditious Teachers on the Other. 2d ed. London, 1800.

Rutherford, Thomas. *The Voice of the Rod: A Sermon Preached on the General Fast Day, October 19, 1803, at the Methodist Chapel, Great Queen Street, Lincolns Inn Fields.* London, 1803.

Salt, William. *A Memorial of the Wesleyan Methodist New Connexion from Its Formation in 1797 to the Present Time.* Nottingham, 1822.

A Selection of Letters, etc. upon the Late Extraordinary Revival of the Work of God, Chiefly Collected from the "Arminian Magazine." Manchester, 1800.

Sigston, James. *A Memoir of the Life and Ministry of Mr. William Bramwell.* 2 vols. 3d ed. London, 1821–1822.

Stanley, Jacob. *The "Portrait of the New Connexion Methodists" Examined and the "Exposition of the Proceedings of the Old Methodist Conference" Exposed.* Dudley, n.d.

A Statement of Facts and Observations Relative to the Late Separation from the Methodist Society in Manchester, Affectionately Addressed to the Members of That Body by Their Preachers and Leaders. Manchester, 1806.

Stephens, John. *Christian Patriotism: A Sermon Preached at Rotherham, February 28, 1810, the Day Appointed for a National Fast.* Rotherham, 1810.

Stephens, John. *The Mutual Relations, Claims, and Duties of the Rich and the Poor: A Sermon Adapted to the State of the Times.* 3d ed. Manchester, 1819.

Strictures on the "Chronicle of Primitive Methodism." London, n.d.

Strictures on the Expedience of the Addingtonian Extinguisher with Satirical Observations on the Influence of Methodism on Civilized Society in All Its Gradations. London, 1811.

Strictures on the Truth and Primitive Methodism. Hull, n.d.

Sutcliffe, Joseph. *A Review of Methodism.* York, 1805.

Taft, Mary. *Memoirs of the Life of Mrs. Mary Taft, Formerly Miss Barritt.* N.p., 1827.

Taft, Zacharias. *A Reply to an Article Inserted in the "Methodist Magazine" for April 1809, Entitled "Thoughts on Women's Preaching Extracted from Dr. James McKnight."* Leeds, 1809.

Taft, Zacharias. *Thoughts on Female Preaching.* Dover, 1803.

Taft, Zechariah. *Biographical Sketches of the Lives and Public Ministry of Various Holy Women.* Vol. 1, n.p., 1825; vol. 2, Leeds, 1828.

Thoughts on the Case of the Local Preachers in the Methodist Connexion. Bristol, 1820.

Treffry, Richard. *A Letter to the Reverend C. Val. Le Grice, Occasioned by His Sermon Entitled "Proofs of the Spirit; or, Considerations on Revivalism."* 2d ed. Penryn, 1814.

Treffry, Richard. *Memoirs of the Life, Character, and Labours of the Reverend John Smith.* London, 1832.

Treffry, Richard. *Memoirs of the Reverend Joseph Benson.* London, 1840.

Treffry, Richard. *Memoirs of the Reverend Richard Treffry, Junior.* London, 1838.

Truth and Error Contrasted in a Letter to a Young Gentleman, in Answer to His Apology for Joining the People Called Methodists. London, 1808.

Turner, George. *A Vindication of Richard Brothers's Prophecies, for the Honour of God.* Leeds, 1801.

Walford, John. *Memoirs of the Life and Labours of the Late Venerable Hugh Bourne.* Edited by William Antliff. 2 vols. London and Burslem, 1855–1856.

Walker, John Uriah. *A History of Wesleyan Methodism in Halifax and Its Vicinity.* Halifax, 1836.

Watmough, Abraham. *A History of Methodism in the Neighbourhood and City of Lincoln.* London, 1829.

West, Francis A. *Memoirs of Jonathan Saville of Halifax.* 3d ed. London, 1848.

White, Francis, and White, John. *Nottinghamshire: History, Directory, and Gazetteer of the County and of the Town . . . of Nottingham . . . to Which Is Added the History and Directory of the Port of Gainsborough.* Sheffield, 1844.

White, William. *History, Gazetteer, and Directory of Lincolnshire and the City and Diocese of Lincoln.* 2d ed.

Winchester, Elhanan. *The Three Woe Trumpets of Which the First and Second Are Already Past and the Third Is Now Begun under Which the Seven Vials of the Wrath of God Are to Be Poured Out upon the World.* London, 1800.

Wood, James. *An Address to the Members of the Methodist Societies on Several Interesting Subjects.* London, 1812.

Worsnop, Abraham. "A Historical Account of Ilkeston Branch of Nottingham Circuit." *Primitive Methodist Magazine* 15 (1834): 272–273.

II. Later Works

A. Unpublished Materials
Methodist Church Archives, John Rylands University Library of Manchester:
    Ahier, Philip. "Lectures on Methodism in Huddersfield." Manuscript, n.d.
    Cleland, I. David. "The Development of Wesleyan Methodist Principles and
        Ideas, 1791–1914." M.Phil. thesis, University of Nottingham, 1970.
    Leary, William. "Notes on Lincolnshire Methodist Circuits and Notes on
        Methodist Books Deposited at the Castle Archives at Lincoln." Type-
        script, n.d.
    Swift, Rowland C. "Notes Compiled from the Files of Nottingham News-
        papers." Typescript, n.d.
    Weller, John C. "Say to the Wind: A Study of the Revival of Religion in Not-
        tingham, 1780–1850." Abbreviated version of M.Phil. thesis, University of
        Nottingham, 1957.

B. Articles and Essays
Abrams, M. H. "English Romanticism: The Spirit of the Age." In *Romanticism
    Reconsidered*, ed. Northrop Frye, pp. 26–72. New York, 1963.
Baker, Frank. "The Bournes and the Primitive Methodist Deed Poll, Some Un-
    published Documents." *Proceedings of the Wesley Historical Society* 28
    (1952): 138–142.
Baker, Frank. "James Bourne (1781–1860) and the Bemersley Book-Room." *Pro-
    ceedings of the Wesley Historical Society* 30 (1956): 138–150.
Barfoot, John. "Gleanings Concerning the Late Mrs. Sarah Bembridge." *Primitive
    Methodist Magazine*, n.s., 4 (1881): 99–103, 161–165, 226–230, 289–293,
    355–360, 420–442.
Birchenough, Albert A. "The Mentor of William Clowes." *Primitive Methodist
    Quarterly Review* 48 (1906): 215–226.
Birchenough, Albert A. "The Quaker Methodist Friendships of Hugh Bourne."
    Primitive Methodist Quarterly Review 49 (1907): 245–258.
Bowmer, John C. "Methodist Union." *Proceedings of the Wesley Historical So-
    ciety* 43 (1982): 101–110.
Brown, Leonard. "The Origins of Primitive Methodism." *Proceedings of the Wes-
    ley Historical Society* 34 (1963–1964), 79–81, 114–125.
Brown, Leonard. "William Clowes in the North of England." *Proceedings of the
    Wesley Historical Society* 37 (1970): 169–172.
Cowie, L. W. "The Church of England since the Reformation." In *A History of
    the County of Stafford*, ed. M. W. Greenslade, 3: 44–91. The Victoria His-
    tory of the Counties of England, ed. R. B. Pugh. London, 1970.
Currie, Robert. "A Micro-Theory of Methodist Growth." *Proceedings of the
    Wesley Historical Society* 36 (1967): 65–73.
Hobsbawm, Eric J. "Methodism and the Threat of Revolution." In *Labouring
    Men: Studies in the History of Labour*, pp. 23–33. London, 1964.
Itzkin, Elissa S. "The Halévy Thesis—A Working Hypothesis? English Revival-
    ism: Antidote for Revolution and Radicalism, 1789–1815." *Church History*
    44 (1975): 47–56.

John, A. H. "Farming in Wartime, 1793–1815." In *Land, Labour, and Population in the Industrial Revolution: Essays Presented to J. D. Chambers,* ed. E. L. Jones and G. E. Mingay, pp. 28–47. London, 1964.

Kent, John. "Methodism and Revolution." *Methodist History* 12 (1974): 136–144.

Kiernan, V. "Evangelicalism and the French Revolution." *Past and Present* 1 (1952): 44–55.

Langton, Edward. "James Crawfoot, the Forest Mystic." *Proceedings of the Wesley Historical Society* 30 (1955): 12–15.

McLoughlin, William G., ed. Introduction to *Lectures on Revivals of Religion,* by Charles Grandison Finney. Cambridge, Mass., 1960.

Morris, G. M. "Primitive Methodists and the Miners' Unions." *Proceedings of the Wesley Historical Society* 37 (1969): 58.

Parkes, William. "The Original Methodists, Primitive Methodist Reformers." *Proceedings of the Wesley Historical Society* 35 (1965): 57–64.

Semmel, Bernard, ed. and trans. Introduction to *The Birth of Methodism in England,* by Elie Halévy. Chicago and London, 1971.

Shaw, George. "William Braithwaite, the Apostle of North Lincolnshire." *Primitive Methodist Magazine,* 2d n.s., 2 (1895): 127–132.

Swift, Wesley F. "The Women Itinerant Preachers of Early Methodism." *Proceedings of the Wesley Historical Society* 28 (1952): 89–94, 29 (1953): 76–83.

Ward, W. R. "The Tithe Question in England in the Early Nineteenth Century." *Journal of Ecclesiastical History* 16 (1965): 67–81.

Wilkinson, John T. "William Clowes, 1780–1851, a Centenary Tribute." *Proceedings of the Wesley Historical Society* 28 (1951): 8–12.

C. Books and Pamphlets

Ahier, Philip. *The Story of Castle Hill, Huddersfield.* Huddersfield, 1946.

Allen, Richard. *History of Methodism in Preston and Its Vicinity.* Preston, 1866.

Andrews, Stuart. *Methodism and Society.* Seminar Studies in History, ed. Patrick Richardson. London, 1970.

Antliff, William. *A Book of Marvels; or, Incidents, Original and Selected, Illustrative of Primitive Methodism, Temperance, and Other Subjects.* London, 1873.

Antliff, William. *The Life of Hugh Bourne.* 2d ed., revised by Colin McKechnie. London, 1892.

Baker, Frank. *The Story of Cleethorpes and the Contribution of Methodism through 200 Years.* Cleethorpes, 1953.

Barrett, George. *Recollections of Methodism and Methodists in the City of Lincoln.* Lincoln, 1866.

Beanland, Arthur; Morley, Herbert; Oswald, William; Topham, John; and Kemish, L., comps. *One Hundred Years of Primitive Methodism in Great Horton.* Bradford, 1924.

Beckerlegge, Oliver A. *United Methodist Ministers and Their Circuits.* London, 1968.

Beckwith, William, comp. *A Book of Remembrance, Being Records of Leeds Primitive Methodism.* London, 1910.

Brailsford, E. J. *Richard Watson, Theologian and Missionary Advocate.* London, n.d.

Brownson, W. J.; Gair, J.; Mitchell, T.; and Prosser, D. S., comps. *Heroic Men: The Death Roll of the Primitive Methodist Ministry.* London, n.d.

Bunting, Thomas Percival. *The Life of Jabez Bunting, D.D., with Notices of Contemporary Persons and Events.* Vol. 1, London, 1859; vol. 2, London, 1887.

Chapman, E. V. *John Wesley & Co. (Halifax).* Halifax, 1952.

Colls, Robert. *The Collier's Rant: Song and Culture in the Industrial Village.* London and Totowa, N.J., 1977.

Cumbers, Frank. *The Book Room.* London, 1956.

Currie, Robert. *Methodism Divided: A Study in the Sociology of Ecumenicalism.* London, 1968.

Currie, Robert; Gilbert, Alan; and Horsley, Lee. *Churches and Churchgoers: Patterns of Church Growth in the British Isles since 1700.* Oxford, 1977.

Dimond, Sydney G. *The Psychology of the Methodist Revival.* London, 1926.

Dixon, James. *Memoir of the Late Reverend William Edward Miller, Wesleyan Minister.* 2d ed. rev. London, 1866.

Dury, G. H. *The East Midlands and the Peak.* London and Edinburgh, 1963.

Dyson, J. B. *A Brief History of the Rise and Progress of Wesleyan Methodism in the Leek Circuit.* Leek, 1853.

Dyson, J. B. *The History of Wesleyan Methodism in the Congleton Circuit.* London and Leeds, 1856.

East Halton: Methodism and the Village, 1790–1953. Hull, n.d.

Evans, Seth. *Methodism in Bradwell.* New Mills, 1907.

Fellows, W. Alan, comp. *One Hundred and Fifty Years of Methodism in Arnold, 1800–1950.* New Basford, 1950.

Fletcher, G. Arthur. *Records of Wesleyan Methodism in the Belper Circuit, 1760–1903.* Belper, 1903.

Founded on the Rock: A Chronicle of Wesleyan Methodism in Berry Brow to 1897. Edinburgh, n.d.

Freeman, John. *Bilston Wesleyan Methodism.* Bilston, 1923.

Gay, John D. *The Geography of Religion in England.* London and Worcester, 1971.

Gilbert, Alan D. *Religion and Society in Industrial England: Church, Chapel, and Social Change, 1740–1914.* London and New York, 1976.

Gill, Joseph. *The History of Wesleyan Methodism in Melton Mowbray and the Vicinity, 1769–1909.* Melton Mowbray, 1909.

Greenslade, Michael W., and Stuart, D. G. *A History of Staffordshire.* Beaconsfield, 1965.

Gregory, Benjamin. *Benjamin Gregory, D.D., Autobiographical Recollections.* Ed. J. Robinson Gregory. London, 1903.

Griffin, Alan R. *Mining in the East Midlands, 1550–1947.* London, 1971.

Halévy, Elie. *A History of the English People in the Nineteenth Century.* Vol. 1, *England in 1815*, trans. E. I. Watkin and D. A. Barker; vol. 2, *The Liberal Awakening, 1815–1830*, trans. E. I. Watkin. 2d. ed. rev. New York, 1949.

Hall, Joseph. *An Alphabetical List of the Circuits in Great Britain, with the*

Names of the Ministers Stationed in Each Circuit from 1765 to 1885. London, 1897.

Hammond, John L., and Hammond, Barbara. *The Town Labourer, 1760–1832.* New ed. London, 1928.

Hammond, John L., and Hammond, Barbara. *The Village Labourer, 1760–1832.* 4th ed. London, 1927.

Harrison, John F. C. *Quest for the New Moral World: Robert Owen and the Owenites in Britain and America.* New York, 1969.

Harrison, John F. C. *The Second Coming: Popular Millenarianism, 1780–1850.* New Brunswick, N.J., 1979.

Harvey, John. *A Lecture on the Jubilee of Primitive Methodism.* London and Leeds, 1861.

Harwood, George H. *The History of Wesleyan Methodism in Nottingham and Its Vicinity.* 2d ed. rev. Nottingham, 1872.

Harwood, H. W. *History of Methodism in Midgley.* Halifax, 1933.

Hill, Francis. *Georgian Lincoln.* Cambridge, 1966.

Hobsbawm, Eric J. *Primitive Rebels: Studies in Archaic Forms of Social Movement in the 19th and 20th Centuries.* Manchester, 1959.

Hunter, Frederick. *Methodism in Stockport and District.* Stockport, n.d.

Jackson, Thomas. *Recollections of My Own Life and Times.* Ed. B. Frankland. London, 1878.

Jennings, Bernard, ed. *A History of Nidderdale.* Huddersfield, 1967.

Johnson, Charles Albert. *The Frontier Camp Meeting, Religion's Harvest Time.* Dallas, 1955.

A Jubilee Memorial of the Local Preachers' Conferences, Biographical and Historical Sketches. Nottingham, 1876.

Jutsum, H. *Jubilee Memorial of Tiviot Dale Wesleyan Chapel and Including a Brief History of Methodism in Stockport.* Stockport, 1876.

Kendall, H. B. *The Origin and History of the Primitive Methodist Church.* 2 vols. in 1. London, [ca. 1906].

Kent, John. *The Age of Disunity.* London, 1966.

Knox, Ronald A. *Enthusiasm: A Chapter in the History of Religion.* New York and Oxford, 1950.

Lainé, J. A. *Methodism in and around Leicester.* Leicester, n.d.

Le Bon, Gustave. *The Crowd: A Study of the Popular Mind.* London, 1896.

Lester, George. *Grimsby Methodism, 1743–1889, and the Wesleys in Lincolnshire.* London, 1890.

Lockley, W. H. *The Story of Stockport Circuit of the United Methodist Church.* Stockport, 1909.

Lord, John Holt. *Squire Brooke: A Memorial of Edward Brooke, of Fieldhouses, near Huddersfield.* London and Leeds, 1874.

Lyth, John. *Glimpses of Early Methodism in York and the Surrounding District.* York and London, 1885.

Mallinson, Joel. *History of Methodism in Huddersfield, Holmfirth, and Denby Dale.* London, 1898.

Martin, David. *A Sociology of English Religion.* London, 1967.

Mathews, H. F. *Methodism and the Education of the People, 1791–1851.* London, 1949.

Mayhall, John. *The Annals and History of Leeds and Other Places in the County of York from the Earliest Period to the Present Time.* Leeds, 1860.

Mounfield, Arthur. *The Quaker Methodists.* Nelson, 1924.

Myers, James. *Eventide Review of Primitive Methodism in Otley Circuit.* Leeds, 1920.

Myers, James. *A History of Primitive Methodism in Guiseley.* Guiseley, 1910.

[Naylor, William]. *The Friend of Many Years: A Memorial of Mr. Thomas Simpson of Armley near Leeds.* Wednesbury, 1864.

Obelkevich, James. *Religion and Rural Society: South Lindsey, 1825–1875.* Oxford, 1976.

O'Dea, Thomas F. *Sociology and the Study of Religion, Theory, Research, Interpretation.* New York and London, 1970.

O'Dea, Thomas F. *The Sociology of Religion.* Englewood Cliffs, N.J., 1966.

Patterson, W. M. *Northern Primitive Methodism.* London, 1909.

Peel, Frank. *Spen Valley: Past and Present.* Heckmondwike, 1893.

Petty, John. *The History of the Primitive Methodist Connexion from Its Origin to the Conference of 1860.* 2d ed. rev. and enlarged. London, 1864.

Pratt, Alfred Camden. *Black Country Methodism.* London, 1891.

Pratt, George J. *Methodist Monographs: Headlights and Sidelights on the Movement in Derby.* Derby, 1925.

Raynes, John R. *History of Wesleyan Methodism in the Mansfield Circuit, 1807–1907.* Mansfield, 1907.

Ritson, Joseph. *The Romance of Primitive Methodism.* London, 1909.

Robson, W. J., ed. *Silsden Primitive Methodism: Historical Records and Reminiscences.* Silsden, 1910.

Rothwell, Stephen. *Memorials of the Independent Methodist Chapel, Folds Road, Bolton.* Bolton, 1887.

Russell, Samuel J. *Historical Notes of Wesleyan Methodism in the Rotherham Circuit.* Rotherham, 1910.

Sandeen, Ernest R. *The Roots of Fundamentalism: British and American Millenarianism, 1800–1930.* Chicago and London, 1970.

Seed. Alexander. *Norfolk Street Wesleyan Chapel, Sheffield.* Sheffield, 1907.

Sellers, Charles Coleman. *Lorenzo Dow, the Bearer of the Word.* New York, 1928.

Semmel, Bernard. *The Methodist Revolution.* New York, 1973.

Shaw, George. *The Life of John Oxtoby.* Hull and London, 1894.

Shaw, George. *Old Grimsby.* Grimsby and London, 1897.

Shaw, Thomas. *The Bible Christians, 1815–1907.* London, 1965.

Sheahan, James Joseph. *History of the Town and Port of Kingston-upon-Hull.* 2d ed. Beverley, 1866.

Slater, George. *Chronicles of Lives and Religion in Cheshire and Elsewhere.* London, 1891.

Smith, Benjamin. *Methodism in Macclesfield.* London, 1875.

Smith, George. *History of Wesleyan Methodism.* Vol. 2, *The Middle Age.* London, 1858.

Smith, William. *History of Wesleyan Methodism in the Ilkeston Circuit, 1809 to 1909.* Long Eaton, 1909.

Soloway, Richard Allen. *Prelates and People: Ecclesiastical and Social Thought in England, 1783–1852.* London and Toronto, 1969.

Stark, Werner. *The Sociology of Religion: A Study of Christendom.* 3 vols. London, 1967.

Stephens, W. B., ed. *History of Congleton.* Manchester, 1970.

Sutton, J. F. *The Date-Book of Nottingham.* Nottingham, 1852.

Sweet, William Warren. *Religion on the American Frontier, 1783–1840.* Vol. 4, *The Methodists.* New York, 1946.

Taylor, Ernest R. *Methodism and Politics, 1791–1851.* London, 1935.

Taylor, Gordon Rattray. *The Angel-Makers: A Study in the Psychological Origins of Historical Change, 1750–1850.* London, Melbourne, and Toronto, 1958.

Taylor, John. *Reminiscences of Isaac Marsden of Doncaster.* 2d ed. London, 1892.

Thomis, Malcolm I. *Politics and Society in Nottingham, 1785–1835.* Oxford, 1969.

Thomis, Malcolm I. *Responses to Industrialization: The British Experience, 1780–1850.* Newton Abbot, Vancouver, and Hamden, Conn., 1976.

Thomis, Malcolm I., and Holt, Peter. *Threats of Revolution in Britain, 1789–1848.* Hamden, Conn., 1977.

Thompson, Edward P. *The Making of the English Working Class.* 2d ed. rev., paperback. Harmondsworth, 1968.

Thompson, W. H. *Early Chapters in Hull Methodism, 1746–1800.* London and Hull, 1895.

Thrupp, Sylvia L., ed. *Millennial Dreams in Action: Essays in Comparative Study.* The Hague, 1962.

Timmins, H. Thornhill. *Nooks and Corners of Shropshire.* London, 1899.

Vickers, James. *Independent Methodism: Origin, Constitution, Polity.* Wigan, 1910.

Wach, Joachim. *Sociology of Religion.* Chicago and London, 1967.

Ward, John. *Historical Sketches of the Rise and Progress of Methodism in Bingley.* Bingley, 1863.

Ward, W. R., ed. *The Early Correspondence of Jabez Bunting 1820–1829.* Camden 4th ser., London, 1972.

Ward, W. R. *Early Victorian Methodism: The Correspondence of Jabez Bunting 1830–1858.* Oxford, London, and New York, 1976.

Ward, W. R. *Religion and Society in England, 1790–1850.* London, 1972.

Warner, George. *A Sketch of Bramwell, with His Great Thoughts on Important Subjects.* N.p., 1863.

Warner, Wellman J. *The Wesleyan Movement in the Industrial Revolution.* London, New York, and Toronto, 1930.

Wearmouth, Robert F. *Methodism and the Trade Unions.* London, 1959.

Wearmouth, Robert F. *Methodism and the Working-Class Movements of England, 1800–1850.* London, 1937.

Weisberger, Bernard A. *They Gathered at the River: The Story of the Great Revivalists and Their Impact upon Religion in America.* Boston and Toronto, 1958.

West, George. *Methodism in Marshland.* London and Goole, 1886.

Wilkinson, John T. *Hugh Bourne, 1772–1852.* London, 1952.

Wilkinson, John T. *William Clowes, 1780–1851.* London, 1951.

Williams, Raymond. *The Country and the City.* New York, 1973.

Woodcock, Henry. *Piety among the Peasantry, Being Sketches of Primitive Methodism on the Yorkshire Wolds.* London, 1889.

Woodcock, Henry. *The Romance of Reality, Being Sketches of Homespun Heroes and Heroines and the Part They Played in the Making of Primitive Methodism.* London, n.d.

Yarrow, William H. *The History of Primitive Methodism in London.* London, 1876.

Yinger, J. Milton. *Religion, Society, and the Individual: An Introduction to the Sociology of Religion.* New York, 1967.

Yinger, J. Milton. *Sociology Looks at Religion.* New York and London, 1963.

Index

COMPOSED BY THE COMPOSING ROOM, KIMBERLY, WISCONSIN
MANUFACTURED BY EDWARDS BROTHERS, INC., ANN ARBOR, MICHIGAN
TEXT AND DISPLAY LINES ARE SET IN PALATINO

Library of Congress Cataloging in Publication Data
Werner, Julia Stewart, 1936–
The Primitive Methodist Connexion.
Bibliography: pp. 227–240
Includes index.
1. Primitive Methodist Church (Great Britain)—
History. I. Title.
BX8376.G7W47   1984   287'.442   84-40161
ISBN 0-299-09910-5